Configurations of Masculinity

Christine Di Stefano

Configurations of Masculinity

A FEMINIST PERSPECTIVE ON

MODERN POLITICAL THEORY

Cornell University Press

ITHACA AND LONDON

First published 1991 by Cornell University Press.

International Standard Book Number 0-8014-2534-4 (cloth)
International Standard Book Number 0-8014-9765-5 (paper)
Library of Congress Catalog Card Number 90-55730
Printed in the United States of America
*Librarians: Library of Congress cataloging information appears on the last page of
the book.*

For the Book Baron

Contents

Preface

THIS WORK IS poised between two distinct theoretical discourses and interpretive agendas: a canonical literature that has only recently and selectively been subjected to gender-interested analysis; and an increasingly sophisticated, multi-disciplinary feminist theory whose agenda includes the simultaneous utilization and destabilization of gender categories. Just as gender is finally making an appearance within political theory, it is being relentlessly rethought and deconstructed within feminist theory. But what some feminists now see as a monotonous opposition between male and female, men and women, masculine and feminine is a bit less monotonous to those who have been "conversing" with and about political "man." To be sure, "women" as a category have made various appearances in western political thought. But in modern, as opposed to ancient or medieval, political theory, they are nearly completely absent, subsumed within a humanist rhetoric of "man," from which, of course, they are occasionally distinguished as the subordinate exceptions. These instances of differentiation and exclusion tend to be analyzed as aberrations within modern political theory, as irrational instances of failure in the supposedly egalitarian modern humanist imagination. The reigning assumption has been that the contemporary female reader does and should locate herself against the feminized exception and with the generic modern citizen.

I mean to contest this interpretive stance by focusing more precisely on the figure of modern political man, to look for the gender-specific man in modern political theory's construction and invocation of "man." One set of available tools at hand for this search, which began for me well over a decade ago, lay with object relations theory. Whereas many feminists were using this theory to elaborate alternative accounts of women's experiences, some have used it instead to think through the gender-specific aspects of male-constructed discourses.

These two projects were, and continue to be, distinct, although by no means unrelated. The first lies at the heart of feminist theory, construed as a theory of and for women; and the category of "women" has been variously defined, contested, deconstructed, and redefined as part of this theoretical activity. The second project is less of a substantive contribution to feminist theory and more of a strategic application of feminist insight to nonfeminist contexts. It is a kind of ground-clearing or rearranging operation, designed to make space for feminist activity within discursive terrain that would otherwise be less hospitable to feminist theorizing. In this book I highlight the specifically gendered modern masculine subject in "man" as he has been invoked, insinuated, constructed, and reproduced within modern political theory.

This work employs particular constructs of gender that are insufficiently supple for feminist theory proper—that is, for the sophisticated theorization of "women" and its gendered cohort "men," for the contemporary analysis of what Teresa de Lauretis has termed "technologies of gender."[1] I do not offer any such theorization here. Rather, I develop a partial specification of the figure of modern "man" in the political theories of Thomas Hobbes, Karl Marx, and John Stuart Mill;

---

[1]Teresa de Lauretis, "The Technology of Gender," in *Technologies of Gender: Essays on Theory, Film, and Fiction* (Bloomington: Indiana University Press, 1987).

and I do so with the admittedly partial specification of a feminized "other" to which he stands opposed and therefore connected. This is not to disclaim my efforts but to situate them correctly so that they will not be misunderstood or misappropriated.

What is most obviously partial about my specification of the feminized other, the (m)other, is that it does not involve specific dimensions of race, ethnicity, class, and other factors that mark us all just as surely as gender does. Undoubtedly my decision to read for gender and not for other dimensions of social location represents a privileging of some characteristics and an occlusion of others. To this extent, my interpretive account, like any other, is complicitous with particular forms of contemporary privilege and power even as it engages others.

The texts I take up here are amenable to a variety of critical readings. I focus on a particular construction of masculinity, which I situate within a modern, Eurocentric frame of reference. My interest is in modern western conceptions of gender and in modern political theory. I make no claims on behalf of a general or all-purpose account of gender; nor does my analysis extend to the gendered dimensions of premodern or postmodern political theories.

European modernity is implicated in the emergence and consolidation of modern western science and industrial capitalism, the subdivision of civil society into various and presumably distinct spheres, and the secular-inspired decline of teleology and ontology. For feminist purposes, modernity is noteworthy for this reason: the privatization of the self in relation to ultimate questions of morality and ontology has a significant counterpart in the enlarged realm of the private sphere, which has become simultaneously privatized and feminized. As Seyla Benhabib writes: "An entire domain of human activity, namely, nurture, reproduction, love, and care, which becomes the [white] woman's lot in the course of the development of modern, bourgeois society, is excluded from moral and political considerations, and confined to the realm of 'nature.' "[2] Modern women inhabit terrain that has been defined as nonpolitical. Modern men, by contrast, have developed and pursued strategies of collective decision making designed to protect, if not enhance, their autonomy as individuals. In effect, the modern project of autonomy, of secular self-creation, is gendered. This political project, which is variously inscribed within the classic texts of modern political theory, has simultaneously been enacted within the "private" social configuration of the bourgeois nuclear family: individualized selfhood and autonomy are acquired and defined through gestures of separation from the maternal care giver.

The modern nuclear family is the empirical site of psychoanalytically inspired gender theory, which is best appropriated as a theory of modern western gender rather than as a universal or all-purpose account. In its rendering of gender, object relations theory (the version of psychoanalytic theory that I will employ) relies on a particular model of family life that is privatized in relation to the "public" world of politics and markets and patterned according to a sexual division of labor in which individual women are the primary caretakers of children.

Object relations theory cannot be used to interpret and account for the lives of actual men and women whose families do not conform to the white, bourgeois, nuclear model. But it certainly can be used to illuminate gender as a cultural ideological formation within modern western societies. During the modern era, which dates roughly from the seventeenth century, certain conceptions of gender that are still familiar to us came to dominate the social field, even if particular men and women could never fully live these conceptions. (Men and women who do not embody dominant conceptions of gender because of their location in other grids of power such as

---

[2]Seyla Benhabib, "The Generalized and the Concrete Other: The Kohlberg-Gilligan Controversy and Moral Theory," in *Women and Moral Theory*, ed. Eva Feder Kittay and Diana T. Meyers (Totowa, N.J.: Rowman and Littlefield, 1987), 160.

class and race, or because of their resistance to the prescriptive norms of gender, may yet feel the power of those conceptions acutely, if differently.) My quarrel with some contemporary suggestions that we deconstruct gender is that to do so simply ignores gender as a dualistic power grid that insists on dividing human beings into the specified categories of "men" and "women." Modern Eurocentric racism functions, I believe, in a similar way, dividing human beings into the (impossible yet potent) categories of "white" and "nonwhite."

Although I am most sympathetic to the arguments of feminist theorists such as Joan Scott, who declares that "we need a refusal of the fixed and permanent quality of the binary opposition [between male and female, men and women], a genuine historicization and deconstruction of the terms of sexual difference,"[3] we also require a reasonably developed sense of what those (arbitrary and conventional) terms of sexual difference consist of. Otherwise, how will we get past them? In this sense, then, I hope that my work will provide a basis for subsequent rereadings in modern political theory that further develop the project of feminist criticism and reconstruction of the gendered canon.

The hazards of invoking psychoanalytic theories for interpretive and explanatory projects are now well documented. In spite of their significant differences, which turn on the question of the extent to which social reality is linguistically constituted, the Anglo-American variant (object relations theory) and its French cousin (Lacanian theory) share an important liability to which this book is not immune: the definition of "women" in derivative relation to "man," whether as "lack" in the presence of the phallus or as "other" in relation to the son. This makes it extremely difficult to address the variegated relationships of women to "woman," which, as feminists of color insistently and rightly argue, have been systematically ignored within mainstream, white feminist theory. And yet, this definition of women in relation to "man" also captures a

[3]Joan Wallach Scott, "Gender: A Useful Category of Analysis," in *Gender and the Politics of History* (New York: Columbia University Press, 1988), 40–41.

significant dimension of gender politics, including what de Lauretis calls "the heterosexual contract."[4] Modern gender, it seems to me, organizes and represents the world "as if" women stood in a derivative (but also opposed) relation to "man." In this sense, gender must be approached as simultaneously "real" and "false"; that is, as a set of representations that (in conjunction and tension with other representations) creates a world of fixed, yet also unstable, meanings, relations, and identities, which simultaneously produce and do violence to specific subjects in specific ways.

The instability of gender is underplayed, in different manners, within object relations theory and French poststructural theory. Object relations theory refers to a world of actual experience in "the family," which is then implicated in cultural forms of gendered representations and practices (for example, nature as woman, sexually segregated labor markets). In this account, "experience" is treated as if it existed outside of or prior to those representations to which it gives rise, and it is rendered in simplified terms of description that fail to capture the variegated textures of early childhood and family life. Lacanian-inspired theory sees gender as constructed in language; all "experience" is symbolically mediated and dependent on the signifier-phallus. Here, the predictable construction of gendered subjects issues out of language understood as symbolic order. In the former account, the gendered subject is treated as an effect of social practices, especially of a sexual division of labor in raising children; in the latter, gendered subjectivity is treated as an effect of signification.

But for all their differences concerning the properly specified relationships among gender, social practices, and language, these theories share a remarkably close sense of the gendered codings of meaning for which they seek to account, namely, that the principle of masculinity rests on the repression of what is deemed feminine. It is this basic insight that I utilize in these readings. I have chosen to employ the object

---

[4]De Lauretis, "The Technology of Gender," 25.

relations version of this claim rather than the Lacanian, which I find too seamless to admit of much more than permanent instability within "the subject" and around the presence of the signifier-phallus. When "the subject" is treated simply as an "effect" of signification, and signification itself is constituted in relation to the always phallic signifier, "gender" takes on a dull, repetitive, and deterministic aura that lacks historical specification. Lacanian gender, however, is defined as a set of "positions" within language that may be variously adopted by males or females. This creates two problems for the theorization and destabilization of gender relations: gender is ubiquitous, and yet it bears no clear relation to males and females who become genderized as "masculine" and "feminine" subjects. If gender "positions" were in fact randomly distributed among males and females, which they are not, then gender theory would be less closely allied with the feminist project than it is. For my purposes, object relations theory provides a preferred, if still imperfect, means of understanding how specifically modern gendered representations are embedded within a world of practices, institutions, and structures that might be altered for the better.

In my version of just desserts in the afterlife, special places of reward are reserved for the unfortunate families of graduate students. William Heintzelman and Kristina Heintzelman lived and suffered with this work during its first draft, providing daily encouragement and support over several years, for which I am grateful.

At the University of Massachusetts at Amherst, William Connolly, Jean Elshtain, and Sara Lennox gave me the space and freedom with which to pursue my own insights in my own ways, even when they disagreed. I have tried to put their criticisms to work. Robert Ackermann read the entire manuscript and provided much-needed encouragement.

Over the years I have benefitted from friendship and intellectual dialogue with many colleagues, including Terry Aladjem, Lance Bennett, Patrick Dobel, Nancy Hartsock, Susan Hekman, Nancy Hirschmann, Ynestra King, Michael

McCann, and Lisa Orlando. Diana Coole, Arthur di Quattro, James Foster, John Keeler, and Jo Peters provided extensive comments on my interpretation of Hobbes.

I am grateful to the members of the National Endowment for the Humanities Summer Seminar for College Teachers titled " 'What Is Enlightenment?' ": An Eighteenth-Century Question and Its Twentieth-Century Implications," directed by James Schmidt of Boston University, in the summer of 1989, for their spirited and critical comments on portions of this work. During that summer Paola Di Stefano and James Steinberg provided a loving and fun-filled home away from home, while Noah instructed me in the delights and duties of aunthood.

The University of Washington has provided a supportive and stimulating environment for work in political theory and feminist theory. I am also grateful to my friends and colleagues at Seattle Rape Relief for the opportunity to be part of the world of feminist practice, and to Maureen Sawyer for helping me articulate my "internally persuasive" voice.

I also thank my parents, Joseph Di Stefano and Jane Dament Holbrook, who encouraged all of their five children to discover, define, and pursue a chosen life for themselves, and who contributed much toward that end. Nima Eshghi and Julie Hanson provided invaluable assistance tracing stray bibliographic sources. Joseph and Amalia Di Stefano gave me a room of my own, fabulous food, and welcome help with the bibliographic compilation. I am indebted to Diane Wolf for her steady, delightful friendship and ongoing encouragement to finish "the book." Spencer Carr was generous beyond the call of duty with his fine editorial suggestions, and I am grateful to him for his professional encouragement and advice.

I also extend long-overdue thanks to several teachers from my undergraduate years at Ithaca College: Marty Brownstein, Robert Kurlander, and Jake Ryan made me feel welcome in political science; Zillah Eisenstein introduced me to the challenge and necessity of feminist theory. Several anonymous reviewers have helped me clarify the dimensions and implications of my arguments, and Holly Bailey of Cornell University Press has been unfailingly helpful in her capacity as editor.

Chapter 2 contains material reprinted with permission from my "Masculinity as Ideology in Political Theory: Hobbesian Man Considered," in *The Women's Studies International Forum*, vol. 6 (Oxford: Pergamon Press, 1983). Part of Chapter 3 was published as "Masculine Marx," in *Feminist Interpretations and Political Theory*, ed. Carole Pateman and Mary Shanley (Cambridge: Polity Press, 1991). Chapter 4 contains material reprinted from "Rereading J. S. Mill: Interpolations from the (M)Otherworld," in *Discontented Discourses: Feminism / Textual Intervention / Psychoanalysis*, ed. Marlene Barr and Richard Feldstein (Urbana: University of Illinois Press, 1989). I am grateful to the various editors and reviewers for their helpful criticisms and encouragement. Finally, I thank Random House, Inc., for permission to reprint from Isak Dinesen, "The Old Chevalier," in *Seven Gothic Tales*, first published by Random House in 1934 and subsequently published as a Vintage Books edition in 1972, copyright © 1961, by Isak Dinesen.

CHRISTINE DI STEFANO

Seattle, Washington

Configurations of Masculinity

Feminism, Political Theory, and the Politics of Interpretation

> There was, we discovered, a circle effect—men attend to
> and treat as significant what men say and have said. The
> circle . . . extends back in time and as far as our records
> reach. What men were doing has been relevant to men,
> was written by men about men for men. . . . A tradition is
> formed, traditions form, in a discourse with the past within
> the present. . . . From this circle women have been almost
> entirely excluded. . . . They could share in this circle only
> by receiving its terms and relevances. These have been and
> still are to a large extent the terms and relevances of a
> discourse among men.
> —Dorothy Smith, "A Sociology for Women"

WESTERN POLITICAL THEORY is a historical and canonical discourse located predominantly among white European men, and produced by such men for themselves. What does this characterization of the legacy imply for the contemporary political theorist who is also a woman and a feminist? What does it suggest for her assessment of and relationship to the male-dominated canon of "great works" and "great thinkers"? Should the historic exclusion of women from the enterprise of political theory be viewed as an unfortunate but minor contingency? Or is it better treated as a constitutive feature of a theoretical legacy that must be handled with thoroughgoing critical suspicion, if it is to be handled at all?

On one view, the historic exclusion of women from political theory can be corrected by adding them to the theoretical conversation. This "add women and stir" approach is advanced in two ways: women are encouraged to join the conversation both as political theorists and as objects of theoretical scrutiny whose specific political needs and interests merit exploration and articulation.[1] The benefits of membership include a cultural literacy from which women were previously and unfairly barred: the historical legacy of great political theorists who are dealing with the enduring political questions, issues, and dilemmas that concern all human beings.

From another perspective, however, the historic exclusion of women from political theory is viewed with a deeper suspicion: the integrationist call to "add women and stir" is scrutinized with more careful attention to the extant ingredients.[2] At issue is the generic humanist assumption of the former perspective, the notion that we are all just people thinking human thoughts and struggling with the human condition, that the differences that mark us as men and women are less significant than the similarities that bind us together into a single cohort—humanity—or, a bit more specifically, citizens within contemporary western culture.

The feminist challenge to generic presumptions and assertions that treat the historical legacy of patriarchy, sexism, misogyny, and sexual segregation as unfortunate but relatively minor side effects that we have finally outgrown with the maturity of the modern age is informed by the discovery and utilization of gender as a category of theoretical analysis. Among the discourses, practices, and institutions that can no longer claim ungendered innocence we may name modern science, bureaucracies, models of moral and cognitive development, conceptions of reason in the western philosophical

[1] This position is advanced in Judith Evans, "Feminism and Political Theory," in *Feminism and Political Theory*, ed. Judith Evans et al. (London: Sage, 1986), 1–16.
[2] This position is argued by Kathleen B. Jones and Anna G. Jónasdóttir, "Introduction: Gender as an Analytic Category in Political Theory," in *The Political Interests of Gender*, ed. Kathleen B. Jones and Anna G. Jónasdóttir (London: Sage, 1988), 1–10.

tradition, and models of citizenship bequeathed by western political theory.[3] As Sandra Harding has consequently argued: "What we took to be humanly inclusive problematics, concepts, theories, objective methodologies, and transcendental truths are far less than that. Indeed, these products of thought bear the mark of their collective and individuals creators, and the creators in turn have been distinctively marked as to gender, class, race, and culture."[4]

To readers familiar with the feminist literature on gender that she describes, the motivating impulse and focus of this book will come as no surprise. As an exploration of the gendered dimensions of the political thought of three key figures in modern political theory—Thomas Hobbes, Karl Marx, and John Stuart Mill—this work is part of the contemporary feminist effort to recuperate, so as to resist and transform, previously unnoticed and unspecified gendered meanings in the canon of political theory.

The voluminous and still growing research on gender as

[3]For feminist critiques of modern western science, see Sandra Harding, *The Science Question in Feminism* (Ithaca: Cornell University Press, 1986); and Evelyn Keller, *Reflections on Gender and Science* (New Haven: Yale University Press, 1985). On the masculine bias of bureaucracy, see Kathy Ferguson, *The Feminist Case against Bureaucracy* (Philadelphia: Temple University Press, 1984). Models of moral and cognitive development are critically scrutinized for their gender biases in Mary Field Belenky et al., *Women's Ways of Knowing: The Development of Self, Voice, and Mind* (New York: Basic Books, 1986); and Carol Gilligan, *In a Different Voice: Psychological Theory and Women's Development* (Cambridge, Mass.: Harvard University Press, 1982). Conceptions of reason are explored by Genevieve Lloyd, *The Man of Reason: "Male" and "Female" in Western Philosophy* (Minneapolis: University of Minnesota Press, 1984). Critical scrutiny of notions of citizenship elaborated in western political theory is offered in Wendy Brown, *Manhood and Politics: A Feminist Reading in Political Theory* (Totowa, N.J.: Rowman and Littlefield, 1988); Jean Bethke Elshtain, *Public Man, Private Woman: Women in Social and Political Thought* (Princeton: Princeton University Press, 1981); Susan Moller Okin, *Women in Western Political Thought* (Princeton: Princeton University Press, 1979).

[4]Harding, *The Science Question in Feminism,* 15. For a related argument aimed at political theory, see Jane Flax, "Political Philosophy and the Patriarchal Unconscious: A Psychoanalytic Perspective on Epistemology and Metaphysics," in *Discovering Reality: Feminist Perspectives on Epistemology, Metaphysics, Methodology, and Philosophy of Science,* ed. Sandra Harding and Merrill B. Hintikka (Dordrecht: Reidel, 1983), 245–281.

a historical and extant phenomenon suggests that men and women are differently constituted as modern human subjects and that we inhabit, experience, and construct the social world in ways that are notably different and sometimes incommensurable;[5] that we are just beginning to see and to understand the feminine dimensions of public and private life (indeed, that *public* and *private* are themselves gendered terms);[6] and that what has passed as a humanistically impartial vocabulary of power, reason, morality, interests, autonomy, justice, history, theory, progress, and enlightenment is actually imbued with gendered masculine meanings and values.[7]

The implications of this literature for the contemporary enterprise of political theory are substantial. To the extent that this canonical literature has been written, interpreted, and formed as a tradition by masculine subjects and within gendered contexts of production and reception, we can expect that gender has left its symptomatic mark. This expectation, in turn, generates a distinctive and diverse feminist agenda within political theory that may be schematized thus: (1) to reread the texts of the tradition with a view to uncovering

[5]Nancy Chodorow, *The Reproduction of Mothering: Psychoanalysis and the Sociology of Gender* (Berkeley: University of California Press, 1978); Dorothy Dinnerstein, *The Mermaid and the Minotaur: Sexual Arrangements and Human Malaise* (New York: Harper and Row, 1976); Luce Irigaray, *This Sex Which Is Not One*, trans. Catherine Porter (Ithaca: Cornell University Press, 1985); Jean Baker Miller, *Toward a New Psychology of Women* (Boston: Beacon Press, 1976).

[6]Jessie Bernard, *The Female World* (New York: Free Press, 1981); Zillah Eisenstein, *The Radical Future of Liberal Feminism* (New York: Longman, 1981); Nancy C. M. Hartsock, *Money, Sex, and Power: Toward a Feminist Historical Materialism* (New York: Longman, 1983); Linda J. Nicholson, *Gender and History: The Limits of Social Theory in the Age of the Family* (New York: Columbia University Press, 1986); Judith H. Stiehm, ed., *Women's Views of the Political World of Men* (Dobbs Ferry, N.Y.: Transnational Publishers, 1984).

[7]Nancy Hirschmann, *Rethinking Obligation: A Feminist Method for Political Theory* (Ithaca: Cornell University Press, forthcoming); Morwenna Griffiths and Margaret Whitford, eds., *Feminist Perspectives in Philosophy* (Bloomington: Indiana University Press, 1988); Luce Irigaray, *Speculum of the Other Woman*, trans. Gillian C. Gill (Ithaca: Cornell University Press, 1985); Mary O'Brien, *The Politics of Reproduction* (Boston: Routledge and Kegan Paul, 1981); Carole Pateman and Elizabeth Gross, eds., *Feminist Challenges: Social and Political Theory* (Boston: Northeastern University Press, 1986).

previously undetected gendered meanings; (2) to turn to (usually obscure) texts written by women in the effort to incorporate different gendered meanings and possibilities into the canon; and (3) to contest the very notion of a tradition as an oppressive and patriarchal fiction and radically redefine the enterprise of political theory so that it is no longer systematically engaged with canonical works. This book adopts the first approach.

These interpretive strategies, it should be noted, are neither mutually exclusive nor necessarily related; my adoption of the first strategy should not be construed as criticism or rejection of the other two. For example, work done at the level of rereading canonical texts often generates so much hostility and cynicism toward the tradition that some theorists are prompted to agree with Mary O'Brien's exasperated hope that "perhaps we shall one day take off these corsets, not in rage but with relief that we no longer need them."[8] Other feminist critics of the tradition would take issue with O'Brien's image of the corset-text and insist that the canon of texts is well worth rereading and preserving, albeit in a qualified sense. On this view, these texts are invaluable aids in the process of understanding women's historic construction and exclusion as political subjects in western culture. As Wendy Brown argues: "From a feminist standpoint and for feminist purposes, the tradition of political theory will not tell us much about women but it will tell us a great deal about men and a socially male construction of politics and thinking, manhood and womanhood, values and desires. And these are very useful things to know."[9]

Feminist critics across the disciplines share an avowed and politicized interest in the ways in which the conventions and categories of gender are involved in the production of canoni-

[8]Mary O'Brien, "Between Critique and Community," review of *Money, Sex, and Power*, by Nancy C. M. Hartsock, *Women's Review of Books* 1 (April 1984), 11.
[9]Wendy Brown, "Where Is the Sex in Political Theory?" *Women & Politics* 7 (Spring 1987), 4.

cal literatures. This interest helps situate feminist criticism in relation to methodological debates within political theory, particularly as they bear on the question of the interpretation and understanding of texts. These debates involve three key methodological constituencies: one group is chiefly concerned with the identification and elucidation of perennial issues; another aims for the historical recovery of original authorial meanings and intentions; and the third may be characterized by its appeal to hermeneutically inspired interpretive license. Those schooled in political theory are familiar with this configuration of methods, which has been extensively reviewed and discussed over the past decade.[10]

The perennial issues group, most closely identified with the figure of Leo Strauss, is prepared to define the enterprise and subject matter of political theory within a delineated field of issues, authors, and texts. Authentic political theory goes into decline with the modern, secular, and individualist theories of Machiavelli and Hobbes; it is effectively finished with Marx. The task of the contemporary theorist is to retrieve the often obscure but originally intended meaning of "great" theorists who reflected on the "truths" of politics under circumstances that were often oppressive and decadent. The great theorist is perceived as a hero of sorts, one who preserves important political truths (sometimes in code form so as to avoid censorship) that constitute the "tradition" of political theory. The task of the contemporary political theorist, who functions as an underlaborer, is to preserve these notable quests for political truth from extinction.[11]

The historically oriented group situates political theory

[10]For helpful commentary see John G. Gunnell, *Political Theory: Tradition and Interpretation* (Cambridge, Mass.: Winthrop, 1979); and Dominick La Capra, "Rethinking Intellectual History and Reading Texts," in *Rethinking Intellectual History: Texts, Contexts, Language* (Ithaca: Cornell University Press, 1983), 23–71.
[11]See Leo Strauss, *"What Is Political Philosophy?" and Other Essays* (Glencoe, Ill.: Free Press, 1959). For another example of the perennial issues approach, see Dante Germino, *Beyond Ideology: The Revival of Political Theory* (Chicago: University of Chicago Press, 1976).

within the framework of intellectual, political, and cultural history. Its prominent practitioners include Quentin Skinner, J. G. A. Pocock, and John Dunn, many of whose works are dedicated to the excavation and recovery of textual meaning thought to be irremediably located in the specific historical context of the author's place and time. Authorial intention is privileged as the source of textual meaning, and the point of interpretation is to correctly locate a text historically so that what an author could and did mean to say are properly delimited within a specified range of linguistic possibilities. Rather than treating political theory as a set of truth claims, this approach casts it as a culturally specific form of discourse.[12]

In one important respect, feminist criticism is compatible with this historical approach insofar as the latter acknowledges an appreciation for gender as part of the specific social contexts within which texts are produced and received. But because gender often tends to operate at a tacit cultural level, feminist interpretation can be accommodated within this historical camp only if "intention" is allowed to designate unconscious or less than fully articulated meanings.

A more formidable obstruction to the inclusion of feminist criticism within the historical camp is that the feminist critic tends not to minimize her own presence and interest in the activity and outcome of interpretation. To the extent that the feminist reader openly embraces her political interests and commitments, she violates an essential methodological rule of the historical interest in discovering meaning. Feminist critics who are primarily engaged in the retrieval of meaning, and who believe in the integrity of the text and the constitutive link between authors and their literary productions, will be more likely to minimize their potentially invasive presence. They will cultivate a reasoned, scholarly, and impeccably documented method and presentation.

[12]See Quentin Skinner, "Meaning and Understanding in the History of Ideas," *History and Theory* 8 (1969), 3–53; and "Motives, Intentions and the Interpretation of Texts," *New Literary History* 3 (1972), 393–408.

Other political theorists, following the third strategy, eschew this approach in favor of a more avowedly interested and constructivist mode of rereading. Within this hermeneutic model of interpretation, textual meaning is said to emerge from (rather than to reside in) the interplay between text and reader; furthermore, it is believed that the meaning of a text may be multiple and in excess of an author's express, intended, or even unconscious meanings. The encounter between reader and text is judged to be more important than the text and its meaning in and of itself. Understanding is thought to take place in the process of relating a text to one's own situation rather than in trying to reinsert it into its original habitat. Specific hermeneutic interpretations may be more or less sensitive to the original historical context of texts; they may be more or less respectful of the author and text as entities independent of the reader. Yet, the (now questionable) recuperation of original meaning is no longer sufficient as an indicator of understanding; and the prejudices of the reader-interpreter-critic are treated as aspects of, rather than impediments to, the interpretive process and the achievement of understanding.[13]

Feminist readers of political theory are most often affiliated with the historical and performative branches of interpretation. Like other practitioners of these methods, they are likely to part company with those political theorists who invoke "the" tradition of political theory and read this tradition for its illumination of perennial political issues. Indeed, feminist theory problematizes the very notion of a perennial issue of any kind, since the cogency of this term relies on its implied relation to some feature or features of a "human" condition. But it is precisely this idea of a "human" condition that femi-

[13]Hans-Georg Gadamer, *Truth and Method* (New York: Crossroad, 1975); David Couzens Hoy, *The Critical Circle: Literature, History, and Philosophical Hermeneutics* (Berkeley: University of California Press, 1982); Paul Ricoeur, *Hermeneutics and the Human Sciences: Essays on Language, Action, and Interpretation*, ed. and trans. with introduction by John B. Thompson (Cambridge: Cambridge University Press, 1981).

nism has unmasked as a probably partial and gendered fiction.[14]

Feminist readers are also potential allies of those who would activate interpretation and increase the role of the reader-critic to an even greater extent than the hermeneutic mode—with its promise of an eventually shared horizon of meaning between author and reader, past and present—allows. For while hermeneutics preserves a focus on the intertextual field of texts and historically specific audiences, postmodern strategies of interpretation tend to employ the text as a mere pretext for intervention and invention. Here, the activity of criticism takes precedence over that of interpretation. In effect, authors and texts lose any claim to integrity. Critical interpretation becomes a whirl of free-form associative play unabashedly motivated by the interests and concerns of the reader. The hermeneutic "conversation" has been replaced by a less respectful and more playful form of interaction between critic and text. The hermeneutic problematization of pure and disinterested interpretation is replaced by frank, if not gleeful, acknowledgment of the impossibility of interpretation. And so the text is massaged, or deconstructed, or otherwise manipulated to meet the avowed and explicit interests of the critic, who now dominates the scene of interpretation without apology. Rereading has become rewriting.[15]

Feminist readers of political theory, myself included, have been less daring than their literary cousins. It may be that the interpretive license exercised by postmodern critics is evoca-

<hr/>

[14]For elaborations of this point, see Jane Flax, "Postmodernism and Gender Relations in Feminist Theory," *Signs: Journal of Women in Culture and Society* 12 (Summer 1987), 621–643; Harding, *The Science Question in Feminism;* Nancy Fraser and Linda Nicholson, "Social Criticism without Philosophy: An Encounter between Feminism and Postmodernism," in *Feminism/Postmodernism,* ed. Linda J. Nicholson (New York: Routledge, 1990), 19–38.

[15]See Jonathan Arac, ed., *Postmodernism and Politics* (Minneapolis: University of Minnesota Press, 1986); Jonathan Culler, *On Deconstruction: Theory and Criticism after Structuralism* (Ithaca: Cornell University Press, 1982); Andreas Huyssen, "Mapping the Postmodern," in Nicholson, *Feminism/Postmodernism,* 234–277; Michel Foucault, "What Is an Author?" in *The Foucault Reader,* ed. Paul Rabinow (New York: Pantheon, 1984), 101–120.

tive of Straussian textualism, whose intellectual elitism and politically conservative overtones are less than appealing to many feminists. Or perhaps we are held back from these methods because we tend to believe that our canonical texts are informed by a political realm of structures, practices, and meanings that are not exhausted by their literary representations.

Feminist literary criticism, which selectively spans the methodological terrain and positions just sketched, provides a rich and useful set of resources for those interested in the project of reassessing canonical political theory. Of special relevance to the interpretations I develop here is the notion of *rereading*, which refers to the process of reassessing texts (canonical as well as "minor" works) in the light of new questions and deliberately specified, often politicized, perspectives. Rereading eschews the notion of disinterested, objective, or innocent readings, promoting instead a deliberately interest-based relationship with and interpretation of texts. Specifically *feminist* rereadings take gender, as it "informs and complicates both the writing and the reading of texts,"[16] as their avowed point of departure. The dream of *the* correct interpretation, along with its cohort assumption, that of *the* text, is willingly surrendered to an alternative conception of textual meaning that is plural, multivocal and multivalent, possibly internally contradictory or self-contestatory, and necessarily generated out of an interpretive process that simultaneously resists, reflects on, and recreates "the text." On this hermeneutically inspired view, meaning is not simply or primarily inherent in texts but is produced by readers who are always (whether or not they are willing to admit it) using particular interpretive strategies. Hence, every reading of a text is also a rewriting, but one that does not aim for permanent or definitive status as the final interpretive word. This willingness to surrender interpretive

---

[16]Elizabeth Abel, "Introduction," in Abel, ed., *Writing and Sexual Difference* (Chicago: University of Chicago Press, 1982), 1. See also Elizabeth A. Flynn and Patrocinio Schweickhart, eds., *Gender and Reading: Essays on Readers, Texts, and Contexts* (Baltimore: Johns Hopkins University Press, 1986).

authority yields a freer-flowing interpretive license, one less bound by questions of provable authorial intent or by the search for a unifying interpretive narrative that provides a more comprehensive interpretation of the text under consideration. Granting from the start that "all interpretive strategies are partial and incomplete," a feminist literary critic such as Annette Kolodny can argue that "different literary critics necessarily report different gleanings or discover different meanings, meanings which reflect not so much the *text qua text* but *the text as shaped by* the particular questions or analyses applied to it."[17] For feminist critics, such questions and analyses derive from a guiding intuition, namely, "that gender is a crucial determinant in the production, circulation and consumption of literary discourses."[18]

This guiding intuition is elaborated into a working hypothesis in Chapter 1, where I explore the initial plausibility of a demonstrable connection between modern masculine gender and the political theories of Hobbes, Marx, and John Stuart Mill. In Chapters 2, 3, and 4, each treating an individual theorist, I show how rereadings guided by this intuition generate new and timely insights. I conclude with some thoughts on contemporary feminist political theory in the light of my rereadings, and I situate these with respect to current debates in feminist theory concerning the status of gender as a category of analysis. My aim is to develop an argument that is simultaneously plausible and provocative, such that readers will be motivated to pursue further "gender-sensitive" readings in political theory.[19]

My choice of Hobbes, Marx, and Mill was motivated in part by the desire to scrutinize a set of theorists who carry

---

[17]Annette Kolodny, "Turning the Lens on 'The Panther Captivity': A Feminist Exercise in Practical Criticism," in Abel, *Writing and Sexual Difference*, 159.

[18]K. K. Ruthven, *Feminist Literary Studies: An Introduction* (Cambridge: Cambridge University Press, 1984), 9.

[19]The term "gender sensitive" comes from Tamsin Lorraine, *Gender, Identity, and the Production of Meaning* (Boulder, Colo.: Westview Press, 1990).

diversified forms of contemporary influence and appeal. Although Hobbes and Mill may be characterized as "liberal" political theorists, each speaks with a very different voice and on behalf of different political problems and agendas. Many regard Hobbes as the political theorist par excellence of liberal market society, and I agree. Mill articulated principles of individualism, liberty, and tolerance that are a part of our contemporary political culture. Furthermore, he was a feminist. Marx, of course, is typically invoked as a significant critic of liberalism and its market economy. Under Marx's scrutiny, the liberal "individual" takes on some peculiar dimensions that are less discernible within the horizon of liberal theory. What all three share as modern political theorists is a commitment to the notion that political arrangements are conventional and subject to human decision as well as error; that the evaluation of such arrangements must be made with reference to human desires and abilities rather than to divine plan or cosmological schemas.

I make no claim to have come up with the perfect representative sample of all modern political theorists. Such a sample, if invoked, would be nothing other than an artifact of the interpreter's scheme. Besides, no particular group of theorists could be said to capture the full terrain of modern political thinking. Finally, I am less interested in making general claims about modern political theory as a whole than in using each theorist as a particular window onto the conceptual gendered landscape of modern political theory.

For all of their significant—and much elaborated upon— differences from one another, Hobbes, Marx, and Mill share a number of assumptions, commitments, and aspirations concerning the realm of politics and the enterprise of political theory. Each lays claim to a humanistic, generic terrain that is belied by the substance and action of his theory. Hobbes invokes the figure of "Mankind" out of which the political ruler must "read" himself. Marx counterposes his "real, active men" to the pathetic, frozen subject of liberal political economy. While Mill acknowledges cognitive perspectivism within the rubric of "opinion," he dreams of a world united by rational discussion and redeemable truth claims, a social world that rests in the truthful center of previous "oscillations." What is interesting here is not simply that each failed to deliver on his claims. The impulse to such generalization, to a united and nondifferentiated human "we" that is the audience for and object of the theory, is also noteworthy and less benign than we might initially appreciate. For these generalizations in the name of "mankind," of "real men," are implicated in related mirror images of "difference." That is, they require an "other" from which to stand apart and against. This "other" of modern political theory is often a feminized mirror image that bears a striking resemblance to the figure of the mother in psychoanalytic discourse.

In this study I will often refer to the psychoanalytic figure of the mother as (m)other. This term connotes several important themes which the reader is encouraged to keep in mind in subsequent chapters. To begin with, this maternal figure is not a physically present empirical character, although she is very much implicated in the modern nuclear family form. Rather, she is a fantasized imago. As a fantasy, she embodies conflicting, dichotomized, and ambivalent desires: she is a split object. But furthermore, her very existence as a discrete object in the mind's eye is predicated on the cognitive experience of separation between ego and mother (and within the developing "self") which initially constituted an undifferentiated unity. More specifically yet, as I will detail in Chapter 1, the figure of the (m)other is centrally implicated in the construction and acquisition of modern masculine identity. She has a "privileged" position vis-à-vis modern masculine gender identity as the original and repressed ground of that identity, as the "other" against which he derives the substance and location of his counteridentity. As such, I will argue that the figure of the (m)other inhabits a subtext in the discourse of modern political theory.

I should like to make it clear that the figure of the (m)other is not prediscursive, even if she comes to symbolize that primordial memory or fantasy. She does not stand outside of or as the ground of language and representation. She is not somehow more "real" or "basic" than the articulations of modern "femininity" and "masculinity," which derive from and in relation to her.

The (m)other revealed by psychoanalytic theory and the modern masculine imagination is a complex representational figure, simultaneously "real" and fantasized. Those who treat her in a more simplified fashion are vulnerable to two distinct errors—naturalism on the one hand and idealism on the other. The naturalistic fallacy results in biological pseudoexplanations for women's mothering, along with an underdeveloped historical appreciation for the wide varieties of maternal practice and experience. The idealist fallacy, by contrast, treats the mother as nothing but the fantasized representational projections of her offspring. The "real" mother, we should recall, is that woman who most probably gave birth to us and cared for us during our early, vulnerable, and formative years. She provided the original ground of our difficult strivings for, and resistance to, identity. The fantasized mother is the mother of huge proportions—terrifying in her power and wrath, overwhelmingly seductive in her promise of a recaptured "oceanic" environment. She is the nurturant ground of life itself and the "other" against which modern individuated selves must assert their autonomy, a struggle that assumes extrafamilial and masculine connotations. Understood in these terms, the representational missing (m)other is a complicated figure and must be handled with care.

A focus on the (m)other in these terms and for critical reinterpretive efforts must be distinguished from several potential assumptions and claims with distinctive antifeminist implications: that mothering is unproblematic for women and should not be critically exposed as an often limiting and imposed "choice"; that most women ought to be, or will continue to be, maternal caregivers; that mothers are more privileged (in terms of critical or emancipatory cognitive perception) than women who are not mothers, whether by choice or circumstance; that mothering exhausts the full range of "womanly" practices to which feminism needs to pay attention in its critical and reconstructive efforts; and, finally, that mothers cause and/or are responsible for masculine identity and behavior.

The sentimentalized and reified image of the natural, nurturant, perfect mother is the effect of historically particular sociostructural arrangements, including the public-private distinction, the privatized and feminized nuclear family within which women are responsible for the care and nurture of children, and the sexual division of labor within the family and between the family and the official economy. Object relations theory, on which this account of the (m)other relies, is best situated and utilized as a theoretical account of the psychological components of these historically specific arrangements.

In the face of such potential misunderstandings, why invoke maternal figures at all? E. Ann Kaplan's position is similar to my own:

> Motherhood thus becomes one place from which to begin to reformulate our position as women, just because men have not dealt with it theoretically or in the social realm. . . . Motherhood has been repressed on all levels except that of hypostatization, romanticization, and idealization. Yet women have been struggling with lives as mothers—silently, quietly, often in agony, often in bliss, but always on the periphery of a society that tries to make us all, men and women, forget our mothers.[20]

A focus on the maternal subtext in modern political theory, then, is aimed at this collective forgetfulness. Rereading is, among other things, a strategy of remembering.

[20]E. Ann Kaplan, "Is the Gaze Male?" in *Powers of Desire: The Politics of Sexuality*, ed. Ann Snitow, Christine Stansell, and Sharon Thompson (New York: Monthly Review Press, 1983), 322.

On the undertheorized particulars of maternal practices and thinking, see Sara Ruddick, *Maternal Thinking: Toward a Politics of Peace* (Boston: Beacon Press, 1989).

I am most sympathetic to the concerns that have been raised by feminists concerning the invocation of maternal practices. History gives us important instances of the use and abuse of maternal metaphors and images to keep women in their place. But I am also struck by the virulence with which attempts to think through undertheorized maternal practices are attacked by some feminists. This suggests (to me at least) that we have not yet come to terms with a figure who is still overinvested with powerful affect.

Each of the three theorists, I have suggested, would appear to be aiming for human comprehensiveness in his work. Such comprehensiveness, in fact, is invoked as a criterion for the truth and adequacy of self-consciously "modern" theory. Hobbes believes that his account of human nature can be cross-checked and verified by all who take the time to reflect honestly on their motivations, desires, passions, and behaviors. Mill criticizes his utilitarian predecessors for having a limited view of their human subjects, and he suggests that we must be open to the partial and hidden views of differently situated individuals. He invokes, among other things, wealth, age, and sex in making his argument. Marx believes that he has finally founded a comprehensive social theory by treating class as a significant constituent of knowledge, interests, and power. His insight into the necessary connections between social relations and intellectual "wealth" is simultaneously compelling and ironic, given his failure to appreciate the ways in which the men and women of his time were differentially embedded in social relations. Yet, none of these theorists seems to be aware of his socially elaborated sexual identity (what is now referred to as gender) as a possible constituent of his thought. Thus, they have all failed to fulfill one of their own criteria for theory. But this is not simply because women are effectively written out of these accounts. At a more profound level, the "forgotten self" of these political theories is the modern masculine self.

If we approach these theorists with a view to articulating the forgotten masculine self inhabiting their various works, we may identify three distinct versions of modern masculinity: heroic masculinity, productive masculinity, and disciplinary masculinity. Heroic masculinity as elaborated by Hobbes invokes specifically premodern connotations of manhood as the ontological ground of a generic human condition to which the Leviathan stands as a modern solution. Marx theorizes a masculinity conceived in terms of the production of self and world. Whereas Hobbes's political theory aims for the domestication of a masculinity conceived in heroic terms, Marx attempts to prepare the ground for a world in which productive masculinity would have full sway. Productive masculinity is the virile, repressed, and exploited substance of a capitalism that will finally be released under communism. Mill elaborates an account of masculinity as achievement through self-discipline. Like Hobbes's, Mill's masculinity is a beleaguered achievement, perpetually susceptible to hostile, encroaching, and often "feminized" threats. But if Mill's masculinity is less dramatically heroic than Hobbes's, it is also the product of an internalized and more thoroughgoing disciplining of inner nature. The absolute, externally imposed and coercive rule of Leviathan has been replaced by the rule-legislating, self-disciplined, and civilized self.

Each of these theorists exemplifies the complicated and vexing problem of difference. On the one hand, each may be faulted for having taken sexual difference for granted. That is, each theorist replicates features of his social environment and intellectual inheritance that are built on particular and now contestable presumptions of meaningful sexual difference. On the other hand, each fails to appreciate the ways in which such difference puts pressure on his assumptions and formulations concerning "human" requirements and possibilities.

How might the problem of difference be used as a critical means of contemporary engagement with each of these theorists? The first part of my reply is: with extreme caution. From the contemporary feminist vantage point, *difference* is a term loaded with multiple dangers, the most obvious being that it plays into and out of the very reified notions of sexual difference that feminists contest. A related problem is brought into play when difference is treated as fact rather than as representation, as something that must be brought into the world of discourse from which it has been excluded, for this ignores the discursive production of "difference."[21]

But the problem with "difference" is not only this. Shoshana Felman identifies another: "Defined by man, the conventional polarity of masculine and feminine names woman as a *meta-*

---

[21]For an excellent treatment of these issues, see Lloyd, *The Man of Reason*.

phor of man. . . . The rhetorical hierarchization of the very opposition between the sexes is then such that woman's *difference* is suppressed, being totally subsumed by the reference of the feminine to masculine identity."[22] Felman suggests that "difference" occludes an appreciation of another "difference." It is this other difference that I want to invoke, the difference of the (m)other written off by the Hobbesian mushroom metaphor of self-sprung social actors rather than the difference of the wife who makes a brief, visible appearance in *Leviathan* as part of the husband's property.

Teresa de Lauretis's image of the "space-off" is most helpful in this regard. In exploring the feminist effort to elaborate a situated and critical view from "elsewhere," which stands in marked and simultaneous opposition to the generic Cartesian "view from nowhere" and the particularistic deconstructive "dream of everywhere," de Lauretis writes:

> That "elsewhere" is not some mythic distant past or some utopian future history: it is the elsewhere of discourse here and now, the blind spots, or the space-off, of its representations. . . . Spaces in the margins of hegemonic discourses, social spaces carved in the interstices of institutions and in the chinks and cracks of the power-knowledge apparati.[23]

The space of this "elsewhere," argues de Lauretis, should not be idealistically cast as the innocent border space between representation and its "outside" but rather as the space implied by representation. She invokes the cinematic notion of

---

[22]Shoshana Felman, "Rereading Femininity," *Yale French Studies* 62 (1981), 25. For additional discussions of the theoretical status of "difference" in feminist theory, as this applies to the differences between women and men and to the differences among women, see Hester Eisenstein and Alice Jardine, eds., *The Future of Difference* (Boston: G. K. Hall, 1980).

[23]Teresa de Lauretis, "The Technology of Gender," in de Lauretis, *Technologies of Gender: Essays on Theory, Film, and Fiction* (Bloomington: Indiana University Press, 1987), 25. The phrases "view from nowhere" and "dream of everywhere" come from Susan Bordo, "Feminism, Postmodernism, and Gender-Skepticism," in Nicholson, *Feminism/Postmodernism*, 133–156.

the space-off to convey her point. The space-off is the space not visible in but inferable from the film frame; this space includes the camera and the spectator as well as the cinematic image itself.

Let me suggest that the figure of the (m)other in modern political theory is best situated within the space of the space-off. She is "there" but rarely on screen. What it takes to see her inferential presence is some predisposition toward her shadowy presence. And once she is detected, aspects of the theory fall into new patterns of resonance, alignment, and instructive tension.

The space of the space-off provides one vantage point for rereading political theory in the name of a difference that is neither purely imported from an elsewhere nor simply subordinate to and derivative of the view of the visible, specular frame. This would be a qualified difference that invokes the presence of a different, "other" subject, one that stands in collusion with but also opposition to the visible, enframed, masculine subject of modern political theory. As I shall argue in Chapter 1, the aspect of collusion lies in the pre-Oedipal and fateful linkage between (m)other and son. The aspect of opposition resides in the adult denial of this linkage. Hence, the (m)other of the space-off functions as a representational support for the gendered masculine subject of modern political theory, but also as a recurring threat to his construction of self and world.

The absence of the (m)other in modern political theory is richly orchestrated; it can take a variety of forms. It is based on a forcible expulsion that is subsequently denied, that is, "forgotten." Such forgetfulness is maintained in the layers of discourse and argument within which she is wrapped and handed from theorist to reader and back again. The forgetfulness is so successful that no surprise or recognition is registered when she reappears—in a Hobbesian sovereign who is self-generating through time, in a capitalism that reproduces itself with inexorable deliberateness, in a sadistic and vindictive nature that would like to make us suffer and eat us up. The explusion and denial of the (m)other is handily captured in Hobbes's proposal that we imagine ourselves "like mushrooms." It is presupposed in Mill's conception of a discrete, abstract, and self-disciplined individual who is entitled to be left alone on the basis of a public-private distinction that he freely traverses. It is even enacted, as we shall see, within his feminism. It is embodied in Marx's vision of human beings as essentially self-creating producers.

If each of these characterizations of humanity and social life shares in a profound denial of the (m)other, each is also threatened, in different ways, by the prospect of her reappearance on the scene. In the case of Hobbes, she threatens to turn the mushroom metaphor into an absurd and even humorous construct. We hear her laughing in the shadows of his state of nature. For Mill, the return of the (m)other threatens to clutter the liberal individual's carefully manicured identity; to impede his liberty to be left alone in the absence of his effects on others. She poses a fundamental challenge to the nature-culture distinction so dear to Mill by straddling it; as "nature," she stands in perpetual and dangerous opposition to "culture." In Marx's case, she provokes a rethinking of the basic categories of labor, production, and history. She is unmoved by the communist ideal because she cannot abide a neat and inverted distinction between freedom and necessity. Small wonder that she has been seen as politically conservative, if not reactionary, by Marxist scholars.[24]

The (m)other is crucially implicated in vivid theoretical portraits of nature, as I shall show specifically in the case of Marx and Mill. The mutually implicated fates of women and nature in the modern west are secured by means of symbolic dichotomies and associations that link women to nature through the maternal function and set masculinized Reason in opposition to a feminized nature. Mill's paranoid account of just such a vile, vindictive, and feminized nature set in opposition to civilization inflects his subsequent portrayal of the "individ-

[24]For a related argument, see Joan Wallach Scott, "Women in *The Making of the English Working Class*," in *Gender and the Politics of History* (New York: Columbia University Press, 1988), 68–90.

ual," who is only apparently genderless. Marx's portrayal of naturalized necessity as the objectified ground of man's creative impulses and labors also requires the banishment of the (m)other, for it masculinizes the category of labor. This is most evident in his version of an architectlike labor that writes out reproductive maternal labor and women's labors of caring. Antipathy toward nature, virulent in Mill, ambivalently cast by Marx, is further implicated in misogynistic attitudes toward women.

Masculine-specific, antimaternal cognitive commitments have a noticeable effect on the political theorist's portrayal of "human nature." In the case of Hobbes and Mill, an atomistic conception of the individual prevails. This liberal individual inhabits a terrain populated by self-sprung persons whose discrete identities are autogenerated and self-contained. Inviolable egos such as these embody the modern masculine fantasy of secular omnipotence and self-sufficiency. The enactment of this fantasy, however, carries a price, as Elizabeth Berg notes, for the absolute denial of the (m)other "cuts man adrift in an endless search for the origin that he has effaced in his desire to be self-generating."[25] In Marx, this fantasy results in a vision of what Charles Taylor has termed "situationless freedom."[26] For Mill, it requires a struggle against a forever threatening nature insinuating itself from within and without civilized order. And in Hobbes, it inspires the model of a civil order governed by a self-generating but ontologically ungrounded political authority.

Whereas Hobbes's and Mill's subjects are defined essentially in terms of preconstituted individual desires, which are cautiously advanced and protected through negotiations with other individuals, Marx invokes a social conception of the modern subject. His subject is not constituted prior to history and society; rather, he is a complex ensemble of his history and social relations, as are his desires and needs. Neverthe-

[25]Elizabeth Berg, "The Third Woman," *Diacritics* 12 (Summer 1982), 18.
[26]Charles Taylor, *Hegel* (Cambridge: Cambridge University Press, 1975), 557.

less, Marx's version of the subject shares with Hobbes's and Mill's the modern dream of self-creation. Like theirs, his fantasy subject is housed within a framework that cannot abide the complexities of social and carnal vulnerability. This orientation lies at the heart of his voluntarist conception of labor; it is given full sway in his vision of communism.

Effaced maternal origins have resonant connections with the modern, plastic conception of human nature that we find significantly developed in Marx and Mill. (Hobbes's earlier gesture toward this modern intuition was to underdescribe human nature as far as he could, to build his theory on a minimalist set of incontestable claims about the human condition.) Whereas Marx developed the "man makes himself" version of this conception (along with its mirror image of economic determinism), Mill embraced self-discipline (with its own behavioral mirror image of social influences) as the significant determinant of human action, motivation, and potential. Each version promotes an ontological emptiness that makes it particularly difficult to address the question of human needs. This is, of course, a characteristic dilemma of modern political theory, one that is by no means necessarily resolvable by alternative theories, feminist or otherwise. But we have yet to appreciate its gendered connotations.

I also want to explore gender-specific aspects of epistemology. Mill's methodological individualism is a forthright instance of a masculine epistemological orientation, for it recapitulates, in nearly classic form, a social scene inhabited by a stereotypical modern masculine subject, one with clearly demarcated ego boundaries who engages in tidy transactional relations with other similarly constructed subjects. The reconstruction of social phenomena as the products of simplified and predictable processes of cause and effect is methodologically attainable within an environment populated by "individual men." Hobbes's geometry-inspired political science was an earlier version of this methodological impulse, enhanced and simplified by his nominalism. Marx's dialectical method, of course, is quite different. It is aimed at understanding a complex system of relations which also constitute the "objects" within it. This is quite different from a methodological approach to preconstituted objects who only subsequently engage in social relations. Nevertheless, Marxian dialectics imbibes distinctively masculine preoccupations and presuppositions.

Like Hobbes, Marx is a conflict theorist, although the language each uses to describe social antagonism is quite different. Within Hobbes's scheme, conflict is a necessary by-product of social relations: human beings bump up against one another in competitive movement toward objects of desire. For Marx, by contrast, conflict inheres in social reality itself. The dialectical constitution of human beings and social reality presupposes contradictions, whether latent or manifest. Masculinity is exhibited in Marx's account through the dichotomous rendition of class relations that he presents. The self-other opposition of Hobbes's state of nature, in which every ego is the Self, and all others are the Other, is transposed in Marx's account into one grand self-other conflict, proletariat on the one side, bourgeoisie on the other. Marx suggested, of course, that the bourgeois ideologues had it backwards—that is, that their privileged and generic identity was historically illusory and dependent on an exploited laboring class. His alternative account, however, recapitulates the dichotomous contrast and anticipates its eventual resolution as a one-sided unconditional victory. Ironically, Marx's futuristic vision of communism fails to accommodate the very dialectical interplay that is so compelling in his account of history and of social life within modern industrial capitalism. Between the historical transcendence of class, politics, and necessity, he has left exceedingly little for the dialectic to get its hands on. This is reminiscent, as we shall discover, of Hobbes.

Marx and Hobbes share a distinctive impulse that is rooted in their ultraconflictual accounts of social relations. Each projects a future and desirable social order that is remarkably conflict-free. We can understand these utopian theoretical projections, in part as responses to anxiety in the face of incessant conflict, whether it takes the form of a perpetual state of war or class struggle. The shape of this conflict carries gendered connotations. Marx and Hobbes had the courage to face up to the conflicts of their times and of their theoretical imaginations, but they also needed an exit. The unreal cast of their solutions, however, suggests that the original formulations of the problem were skewed.

Each theorist, as I shall argue in greater detail, is evocative of Freud's description of the boy who finds it self-evident that "a genital like his own is to be attributed to everyone he knows."[27] This "phallic prerogative" serves, in the case of Hobbes, to write women out of his account of the state of nature and civil society. In the case of Mill, it assimilates liberated women to liberal man. In Marx, it results in a failure to theorize labor adequately, along with a theoretical replication of a sexual division of labor that will not acknowledge "women's work" even as it legislates it. To the extent that Marx's materialist theory fails to engage with the gendered arena of necessity in human affairs and relations, it fails dismally both as an account of extant social reality and as a proposal for revolutionary change. But the problem here is not simply women's absence as gendered subjects. For this absence is orchestrated by the silent presumption that modern masculinity is the norm. To bring women into political theory, then, requires that we "bring men back in."[28]

The theoretical construction and elaboration of social problems and their solutions by Hobbes, Marx, and Mill is implicated in an anthropological foundation that is detectably masculine. Each theorist works with a "cherished conception of the self,"[29] which imbibes aspects of modern masculine identity. While these aspects are elaborated in significantly differ-

---

[27]Sigmund Freud, *Three Essays on the Theory of Sexuality*, vol. 7 of *The Standard Edition of the Complete Works of Sigmund Freud*, trans. and ed. James Strachey (London: Hogarth, 1975), 195.

[28]David Morgan, "Men, Masculinity, and the Process of Sociological Enquiry," in *Doing Feminist Research*, ed. Helen Roberts (London: Routledge and Kegan Paul, 1981), 94.

[29]William Connolly, "Personal Identity and Political Interpretation," paper delivered to the Rutgers Conference on Public Language and Political Education, New Brunswick, New Jersey, April 1978.

ent ways and within different theoretical schemas, we may also understand them as elements of a shared frame of reference. As I will propose, this modern masculinist frame of reference may be treated broadly as an ideology. The point of such an analysis is not to lump the three theorists together into an undifferentiated collection of "masculine thinkers." Such a move erases more than it reveals. But it is plausible to suggest that the concept of modern masculine ideology enables us to understand them as distinct thinkers partaking in and contributing to a discursive subtratum—that is, a kind of preconscious conversation with its own bounded, if permeable, horizon.[30] In effect, we can appreciate the uniqueness of each theorist in the new light that is cast by the suggestion that they also share a set of similar concerns that may be termed masculinist.

I will not attempt to anticipate potential objections to my rereadings of Hobbes, Marx, and Mill, for that would take us too far afield. But there is one issue that I would like to take up briefly here; it involves the charge of political and social nonrelevance. The audience to which this set of comments is directed is situated within the contemporary ranks of feminist critics who ask: "Why should we want to get in on the historical 'conversation' about political life that has been monopolized by European males for the past two millennia? Why should we continue to lavish attention on Eurocentric, male-stream traditions?" Among feminist literary critics this discussion involves the distinction between androcriticism, or critical efforts directed toward the literary canon of primarily male-authored works, and gynocriticism, which takes as its object texts by women that have traditionally been ignored or deval-

---

[30] I use the psychoanalytic term *preconscious* here deliberately. It should not be confused with *unconscious*. The former denotes a thought or wish that is temporarily lost to conscious memory but may be elicited with some prodding. The latter denotes a thought or wish that is actively kept from a consciousness to which it will most likely never be revealed.

ued as "lesser" works.[31] An important issue here is the extent to which the inherited canon is strengthened rather than destabilized as a result of androcriticism. The ongoing public debate about "cultural literacy," the general education curriculum, and the declining readership for the "great books" of western civilization is also implicated in this discussion.[32] Unfortunately, the defense of "tradition," of great literary works that partake of and reflect on "our" particular mode of civilized life, has become publicly identified with a conservative and self-righteous group of white males who evince little critical interest in the political history and exclusionary tactics of tradition building or in those works and peoples who have been systematically excluded and silenced and are now making a bid for cultural recognition. Terms such as *tradition, canon, seminal,* and *great* are being contested, and rightly so.

Why, then, should women want to get in on the conversation?[33] The answer to this question depends, in good measure, on our sense of relationship to the past, to "culture," to inherited modes of discourse and cultural self-understandings. But this sense of relationship (more or less alienating for particular women and men) need not dictate a singular prescribed course of action. Feminism has benefitted as much from those who have worked to articulate new grounds of sensibility and memory as from those who have sought to rework the old ground. With this in mind, I would like to proffer support for

[31]For a discussion of androcriticism and gynocriticism, see Elaine Showalter, "Feminist Criticism in the Wilderness," *Critical Inquiry* 8 (1981), 179–205.

[32]See Allan Bloom, *The Closing of the American Mind* (New York: Simon and Schuster, 1987). For a very different view, see Rick Simonson and Scott Walker, eds., *Multicultural Literacy* (St. Paul: Graywolf Press, 1988). For criticism of Bloom, see Kathleen B. Jones, "Le Mal Des Fleurs: A Feminist Response to *The Closing of the American Mind,*" *Women & Politics* 9 (1989), 1–22.

[33]The term *conversation* is obviously a misnomer insofar as it perpetuates a purely benign view of the constitution of traditions. It may also support the mistaken notion that political theorists since Plato have read the work of their precursors and are actually conversing with them. On this point, see Gunnell, *Political Theory.* I return to some of these issues in my conclusion, particularly as they involve pedagogical dimensions of the canonical literature, the definition of "the conversation," in political theory.

the position that some feminists should be involved in this alienating conversation, at least some of the time.

Freedom from cultural and political hegemony cannot proceed without some reference to the discourses we have inherited and within which we have taken shape as historically specific beings. Our freedom from (interpretations of) the past depends in part on our freedom—and willingness—to reinterpret the past so as to reconstitute the horizon of the present.[34] The cross-grained activity of rereading is one (but only one) strategy within the multifaceted feminist effort to develop critical and "womanly" modes of thinking, writing, reading, reflection, and political practice which are self-consciously rooted in and also suspicious of feminine experiences.

As an interpretive strategy, the feminist rereading of male texts seeks to "return the masculine to its own language"[35] as a means of "discovering" other voices that have been simultaneously constituted by and excluded from dominant discursive systems. (This does not mean, however, that a text simply reduces to its gendered specificity. Nor do I claim to have found all voices of the "other" in the political theories I reread here. The specific other in which I am interested is the modern feminized other.) The activity of returning the masculine to its previously unspecified site may in turn help us resist the prevailing cultural tendency to "deny the existence of the other . . . or to make any existing other into the self."[36] This tendency runs roughshod not simply over women as an otherwise (and impossibly) underdifferentiated category of persons in the contemporary west, but also on a host of peoples and cultures, as well as on variously oppressed and silenced constituencies here at home, men and women who are caught

[34]See Wayne C. Booth, "Freedom of Interpretation: Bakhtin and the Challenge of Feminist Criticism," in W. J. T. Mitchell, ed., *The Politics of Interpretation* (Chicago: University of Chicago Press, 1983), 51–82.

[35]Luce Irigaray, "The Power of Discourse and the Subordination of the Feminine," in *This Sex Which Is Not One*, 80.

[36]Carolyn Whitbeck, "A Different Reality: Feminist Ontology," in *Beyond Domination: New Perspectives on Women and Philosophy*, ed. Carol C. Gould (Totowa, N.J.: Rowman and Allanheld, 1983), 66.

and defined within the multiple power axes of class, race, ethnicity, and sexual or affectional preference, to name some of the prominent ones. Political theory, as we are coming to appreciate, is suffused with the muffled voices of such "others." To the extent that a vigorous feminist invocation of "difference" in the name of the "other"—an "other" that is simultaneously constructed by and excluded from the classical heritage of western political theory—is promoted, feminist interpretation offers a critical rethinking of the political theory legacy and a contribution to the contemporary task of reconstituting political inquiry and practice.

This rereading, then, is no mere exercise in textual criticism for its own sake. What follows is a feminist hermeneutic of sorts, but a critical hermeneutic of avowed suspicion rather than of attempted empathy. I approach the texts of Hobbes, Marx, and Mill with a view to interpreting them in a way that implicates my inescapable and acknowledged social location as a woman, and my political identity as a feminist, along with what the texts themselves have to say to me in this partial specification of location as a reader. This is a conversation— sometimes playful and teasing, often deadly serious—with the brothers and fathers of a discursive tradition to which I am deeply and irreversibly attached, yet uncomfortably so. As such, it is deliberately and unavoidably situated within the complicated interstices of identity and difference, familiarity and strangeness.

One of the foremost obstacles confronting the feminist dissident in political theory is the criticism that her work, if it exceeds the prescribed strategies of immanent criticism, is illegitimate because it raises concerns and issues that could not possibly have been available to the theorists she is reassessing. This methodological appeal is a powerful one, for it cautions against the violation of the political theorist and his work as culturally and historically embedded entities. And feminists are (or should be) sensitive to issues such as these, for they call on the capacities for empathy, respect, and imaginative projection that women are all too well versed in even as we have suffered from the failure of reciprocal exchange of such capacities from many men and—all too often—from women of power and privilege. Yet, to imagine that we can ever fully enter a distant and different time or place contains a touch of abstract, disembodied arrogance: "For we bring ourselves wherever we go; we cannot ever deliberately forget the voices that have become 'internally persuasive.' "[37] We cannot, as Wayne Booth and Hans-Georg Gadamer perceptively insist, deny or dodge the life that we have *with* various works.

The classics of political theory offer a (but by no means the only) conduit to the heart of the political imagination in the contemporary west. Readers are entitled and sometimes constrained to search for and to identify peculiarities, failures, and shortcomings of that imagination, particularly when these nourish ideas and sensibilities that carry significant import for the political fates of human beings.

[37]Booth, "Freedom of Interpretation," 77.

CHAPTER ONE

Modern Masculinity

> The existence of two sexes does not to begin with arouse
> any difficulties or doubts in children. It is self-evident to a
> male child that a genital like his own is to be attributed to
> everyone he knows, and he cannot make its absence tally
> with his picture of these other people.
> —Sigmund Freud, *Three Essays on the Theory of Sexuality*

PSYCHOANALYTIC THEORY sometimes exemplifies the selfsame
gendered symptoms it claims to analyze. This helps to explain
its ambivalent fascination and usefulness for feminists. On
the one hand, orthodox psychoanalytic theory cannot be
trusted for its rendering of feminine experience and desire; on
the other, it tells us quite a bit about the modern construction
of masculinity. Freud's account of the problem of "difference"
is an apt example. It is elaborated from the vantage point of
the male child, and it centers on the presence or absence of
the phallus. "These other people" are, of course, those without the prized male genital. But why should anatomical difference arouse difficulty and doubt in the first place? What makes
the acknowledgment of difference so difficult? How is it that
this particular difference is privileged out of the mass of potential others? And how might such a construction of difference
and its attendant "difficulty" be related to the specifics of
modern masculinity?

The male child who "cannot make its absence [that of the
phallus] tally with his picture of these other people" reminds

us of the canonical political theorist who either ignores women, belabors their differences from men so as to justify differential treatment, or attempts to turn them into little men. Each of these maneuvers is initiated from a common starting point: the androcentric assumption of the male-as-norm. Psychoanalytic theory suggests—perhaps unwittingly—that this assumption is not merely the cultural prerogative of a political master class; it is also embedded within the specific dynamics and elements of modern masculine identity.

Contemporary gender theory further explores the question of sexual difference as it was initiated by Freud and his immediate followers and as it has been rearticulated by feminist theorists and researchers. *Gender* refers to representations of sexual difference and identity which are in fact constructively imposed on human subjects. In most cultures, gender is patterned in dualistic and hierarchical modes that promote male privilege and female subordination. Nevertheless, the actual contents of gendered representations carry enormous cross-cultural variability. Hence, gender is simultaneously a ubiquitous feature of culture even as it has no fixed transcultural or transhistorical meanings.[1] In short, it is best understood as a complex convention.

Modern western culture is and has been profoundly gendered. Humanistic pretensions of the Enlightenment and the liberal legacy notwithstanding, modern western peoples inhabit a politicized cultural universe elaborately carved out and apportioned in terms of presumedly meaningful sexual differences. The key terms of the modern vocabulary of gender, which is currently in a process of radical assessment, contestation, and social transformation, are *femininity* and *masculinity*.[2]

---

[1]These general claims are culled from the contemporary anthropological literature on gender, which is reviewed in Christine Ward Gailey, "Evolutionary Perspectives on Gender Hierarchy," in *Analyzing Gender: A Handbook of Social Science Research*, ed. Beth B. Hess and Myra Marx Ferree (Newbury Park, Calif.: Sage, 1987), 32–67.

[2]For discussions concerning the contemporary status of gender differences in feminist theory and politics, see Seyla Benhabib and Drucilla Cornell, eds.,

The Object Relations Account of Modern Masculinity

There have been many revisions and criticisms of Freud's original theory of gender symbolics and acquisition.[3] Nevertheless, or precisely because of the attention that he continues to receive, Freud must be credited with developing several important insights. In *Three Essays on the Theory of Sexuality*, Freud suggested that gender differences are neither innate nor naturally distributed among male and female children. His insistence that "masculinity" and "femininity" are nonoriginary forms of identity imposed on children is a critical hallmark of the theory, and one of the reasons why many feminists find psychoanalytic theory helpful in spite of its notorious sexism.[4] Freud's theory unwittingly problematized femininity by showing how the girl must transfer her sexual attachment from her mother to her father. But the theory reinscribed femininity by accounting for the lesbian within a heterosexual framework of interpretation. Her "masculinity"

Feminism as Critique (Minneapolis: University of Minnesota Press, 1987); Judith Butler, *Gender Trouble: Feminism and the Subversion of Identity* (New York: Routledge, 1990); Sandra Harding, "The Instability of the Analytical Categories of Feminist Theory," *Signs: Journal of Women in Culture and Society* 11 (1986), 645–664; Hester Eisenstein and Alice Jardine, eds., *The Future of Difference* (Boston: G. K. Hall, 1980); Jane Flax, *Thinking Fragments: Psychoanalysis, Feminism, and Postmodernism in the Contemporary West* (Berkeley: University of California Press, 1990); Linda J. Nicholson, ed., *Feminism/Postmodernism* (New York: Routledge, 1990).

[3]Freud's account may be found in his *Three Essays on the Theory of Sexuality*, vol. 7 of *The Standard Edition of the Complete Works of Sigmund Freud*, trans. and ed. James Strachey (London: Hogarth Press, 1975), 125–245; and "Femininity," *New Introductory Lectures*, in vol. 22 of the *Standard Edition*, 112–135. See also Freud's 1931 essay on "Female Sexuality," in vol. 21 of the *Standard Edition*, 225–243, for the provocative questions he raises concerning the daughter's pre-Oedipal relationship to her mother.

[4]For a feminist defense of Freud, see Juliet Mitchell, *Psychoanalysis and Feminism: Freud, Reich, Laing, and Women* (New York: Random House, 1975), and "Introduction I," in *Feminine Sexuality: Jacques Lacan and the École Freudienne*, ed. J. Mitchell and J. Rose, trans. Jacqueline Rose (New York: W. W. Norton, 1982). For a brilliant series of immanent criticisms of Freud, see Luce Irigaray, *Speculum of the Other Woman*, trans. Gillian C. Gill (Ithaca: Cornell University Press, 1985), 13–129.

represented a turning-away from identification with the mother and a desire to be like the father. As subsequent commentators such as Adrienne Rich and Luce Irigaray point out, this simply misses the logic of Freud's own account, which suggests that within the structure of the modern nuclear family, a girl's primary eroticism will be experienced in relation to the mother rather than the father.[5] Freud was also less perceptive of the difficulties in the boy's case. Part of the reason for this is that he uses the vocabulary of masculinity to denote the infantile, pre-Oedipal sexuality of all children. Hence, masculinity becomes naturalized.

Freud showed how heterosexual prescriptions and gendered norms make different, and by no means complementary, demands on males and females, who are supposed to become masculine men and feminine women. Further, he demonstrated how precarious and unstable "normal" gendered outcomes tend to be. While boys must give up the mother as a love object and learn to identify with the father so that as adults they can have another mother-lover of their own, girls must give up the mother as love object and substitute the father as a libidinal object, yet still identify with the mother as future mothers themselves. As Freud pointed out, there is nothing "natural" about this particular set of prescriptions, and, more significantly, there are multiple opportunities for "deviant" outcomes.

Freud located the high drama of gender identity acquisition and consolidation in the Oedipal phase, and he privileged the role of the father in this civilizing process. This is the point at which boys are threatened with castration by the father if they do not give up the mother as a sexual love object; girls, by contrast, are forced to recognize their effective castration and presumably turn away from the mother in anger and disappointment. In this account, femininity is accepted as a fait

[5]Irigaray, *Speculum of the Other Woman*, 13–129; Adrienne Rich, "Compulsory Heterosexuality and Lesbian Existence," in *Powers of Desire: The Politics of Sexuality*, ed. Ann. Snitow, Christine Stansell, and Sharon Thompson (New York: Monthly Review Press, 1983), 177–205.

accompli, while masculinity is achieved as a mode of renunciation and self-discipline in the face of danger.

Object relations theory resituates the psychoanalytic narrative of modern gender acquisition in earlier, pre-Oedipal experiences and pays closer attention to the figure of the mother. Where Freud believed that the formation of gender identity coincided with the phallic phase, more recent studies indicate that gender awareness exists before the second year. In fact, it seems that gender identity—the awareness of being male or female and the sense that there is something significant and meaningful about the designation itself—coexists with the early awareness of being a separate and unique individual. This, of course, has more to do with the cultural salience and significance of gender (which parents transmit to their children) than with any intrinsic significance in the sexually differentiated body of the child.

In broad outline, object relations theory suggests that identity formation for males and females develops according to gender scripts which are first imposed and enacted during the early months and years of life.[6] The central characters of this pre-Oedipal narrative are two: mother (or female caretaker) and child. According to object relations theory, the net effect of female caretaking in the modern nuclear family is that the mother figure comes to be heavily invested with the ambiva-

[6]The following texts provide the clinical and theoretical substance for this discussion of early identity formation: Jessica Benjamin, *The Bonds of Love: Psychoanalysis, Feminism, and the Problem of Domination* (New York: Pantheon, 1988); Nancy Chodorow, *The Reproduction of Mothering: Psychoanalysis and the Sociology of Gender* (Berkeley: University of California Press, 1978); Dorothy Dinnerstein, *The Mermaid and the Minotaur: Sexual Arrangements and Human Malaise* (New York: Harper and Row, 1976); Melanie Klein, *"Love, Guilt, and Reparation" and Other Works, 1921–1945* (New York: Dell, 1974), and *The Psychoanalysis of Children* (New York: Dell, 1975); Margaret Mahler, Fred Pine, and Anni Bergman, *The Psychological Birth of the Human Infant: Symbiosis and Individuation* (New York: Basic Books, 1973); D. W. Winnicott, *Playing and Reality* (New York: Basic Books, 1971), and *Maturational Processes and the Facilitating Environment* (New York: International Universities Press, 1965). For a discussion of object relations theory, see Jay R. Greenberg and Stephen A. Mitchell, *Object Relations in Psychoanalytic Theory* (Cambridge, Mass.: Harvard University Press, 1983).

lent feelings of her charges. As Isaac Balbus describes this process:

> She is at once the being with whom the child is initially indistinguishably identified and the one who enforces the (never more than partial) dissolution of this identification. Thus it is the mother who becomes the recipient of the unconscious hostility that accumulates in children of both sexes as the result of this inescapably painful separation. The mother who is loved is also necessarily the mother who is hated.[7]

In societies such as ours, in which nearly all "mothers" are female and in which most females face likely destinies as mothers, the initial ambivalence toward the mother is subsequently transferred to women and other feminized entities and categories.[8]

The literature on pre-Oedipal experience argues that a salient aspect of the process of gender identity formation for children of both sexes, albeit with different implications, is the attainment of separation from the original and highly charged mother-child unity. This primordial experience of unity is the complicated and ambivalent ground of viable identity as we know it.

In the first month of life, the infant inhabits a foggy and undifferentiated world with no awareness of the mother as a separate person. Receiving care under the delusion of its self-nourishing omnipotence, it does not yet perceive that the satisfaction of its needs depends on an outside source. This awareness begins in the second month; "mother" (meaning whoever is the primary care giver) is gradually added to what the infant now perceives as a dualistic but still self-contained universe. Margaret Mahler described this state from the imag-

---

[7]Isaac Balbus, "Disciplining Women: Michel Foucault and the Power of Feminist Discourse," in Benhabib and Cornell, *Feminism as Critique*, 112.

[8]This ambivalence is extensively charted in Chodorow, *The Reproduction of Mothering;* and Dinnerstein, *The Mermaid and the Minotaur.*

ined infant's point of view as a symbiotic union of mother and child.

As the bodily sensory apparatus develops, the infant becomes more attuned to outside stimuli and begins to realize a definite demarcation of its body from the rest of the (emerging) object world. This marks the beginning of the end of that nirvanalike "oceanic feeling" described by Freud as the repressed memory of and desire for wholeness, often reenacted in religious yearnings and beliefs.[9]

As the mother's face gradually takes shape in the infant's growing repertoire of perceived objects, the child comes closer to recognizing that something outside itself is satisfying its needs. With the emergence of a specific preferential response to the mother—often seen in smiling patterns—observers infer that the infant is experiencing the rudiments of identity formation. The "mirroring" exchange between mother and infant, in which the mother imitates the facial and bodily gestures and sounds of her child, and thus presents an image of the child to itself, is an important social feature of this stage.[10]

The mirror process offers an early clue to the complexities of an identity formation forged out of relations of mutual reciprocity rather than simple differentiation of the infant from the primary care giver.[11] According to this account, identity is not the teleological unfolding of incipient selfhood; rather, it is constructed through processes of introjection and projection.

---

[9]Freud, *The Future of an Illusion*, in vol. 21 of the *Standard Edition*, 5–56.

[10]I refer to the mother as "she" only because this is the overwhelming empirical reality of parenthood in modern western societies; that is, most mothers are women, most fathers are men, and most single parents are women. The terms *mother* and *father* do not simply denote the biological sex of the parent, however; they also connote qualitatively different forms of parental behavior. Biological males could be, but in our society usually are not, "mothers." How and why this is the case has been a motivating question for gender theory, which aims to understand being a parent as a convention, a social role, rather than as a biologically inspired or dictated function.

[11]For an eloquent elaboration of the conceptual importance of substituting a model of reciprocal interaction for that of simple differentiation, see Benjamin, *The Bonds of Love*, 11–50.

Identification of one's self as a self seems to depend in significant measure on the mother–care giver's imitation of the infant
for it literally to behold, as well as on the infant's growing
ability to identify with and eventually introject the images of
itself that are offered by the mother and other significant
actors in its environment. These early, charged, and complex
dynamics of intersubjective interaction and reciprocity lay the
foundations for future social relations, especially those that
require empathy, the ability to identify with the imagined
position and feelings of another person.

Through play with the mother-caretaker, the child is helped
to move from primitive identification with whatever presents
itself within its field of perception to selective identification,
motivated by the desire to be *like* a particular object among
many available others. These selective identifications with
various "objects" in the infant's surroundings help to promote
a compromise between the (increasingly) contradictory desires for fusion and for independence. Selective identifications
(with everything from blankets and stuffed animals to particular persons) promote a sense of at least temporary fusion as
they bear witness to an expanding repertoire of object choices,
some of which, or aspects of which, will be introjected and
thus shape the developing self. This process is part of the
creation of a particular and bounded sense of self as a subject-
object in a world among other subject-objects.

D. W. Winnicott's work on the role of aggression in the
differentiation process highlights the delicate structuring of
mother-child interactions as it aids in the psychoanalysis of
adult-sanctioned and culturally sanctioned forms of violence.[12] The child's search for self-other boundaries involves
fantasies and activities of destruction that, perhaps counterin-
tuitively to our way of thinking, confirm the independent
existence of the mother–care giver. This primordial attempt at
mastery is greeted with relief on the part of the child when it

---

[12]For a sustained and provocative discussion of these themes, see Jessica
Benjamin, "The Bonds of Love: Rational Violence and Erotic Domination,"
Feminist Studies 6 (Spring 1980), 144–174.

fails to "destroy" the mother. Early aggressive fantasies and actions result in a beneficial and welcome collision with the resistance of the mother, for her independent presence portends the independent existence of the self. If the mother fails to provide a tangible sense of resistance, if she fails to "survive" the child's "attacks," a void is established that threatens boundlessness in the absence of touchstones for differentiation. Frustration in the face of an overly yielding or rigid mother may promote rage and heightened violence on the part of the child in its quest for evidence and assurances of its (modified) effect on the mother. The child is desperately searching for confirmation of its physical efficacy in the world; this requires a world that will stand firm over time, a world that, in Jessica Benjamin's terminology, is a "holding" rather than simply constraining or yielding environment.[13]

One potential response to the "failure" of the mother to provide a sense of firm yet flexible boundaries against which the differentiation drive can be simultaneously checked and acknowledged is for the child to provide its own substitute boundaries.[14] This involves a process known as "false differentiation," whereby an idealized and untested version of the mother becomes introjected. This now objectified (m)other, against which the self must differentiate, promotes a brittle and dualistic ego organization that bears the imprint of insufficient interaction with the primary other. The danger of merger becomes all the more seductive and terrifying (and it is seductive and terrifying enough) because it has not been successfully attempted by the child and resisted by the object of attack. A logical defense against this untested fear is an objectification and instrumentalization of the dangerous-because-unknown other. Such a dynamic exaggerates the al-

---

[13]Benjamin, The Bonds of Love, 120–121.

[14]"Failure" has far more to do with the structure and outcome of the interaction than with the responsibility or fault of the maternal caretaker. After all, I am talking about young children's fantasies here, which may be more or less open to correct interpretation and empathetic reception. Adults' abilities to decode the fantasies of children may also have something to do with their own childhood experiences, in which fantasies are played out or repressed.

ready troubling dialectic between recognition and differentiation; between the desire to differentiate from an objectified other whom we may also wish to recognize and identify with as a subject. The needs for recognition and differentiation press for satisfaction in counterproductive ways that structurally undermine the possibility for their joint fulfillment. A logical outcome of this complex emotional configuration is a relentless and repetitive search for recognition (which can come only from another subject in its own right) that proceeds by way of domination (forcing another subject to conform to one's will and thus objectifying it as the mute mirror image of one's desire).

This noted ambivalence surrounding the conflicting desires for fusion and independence is situated at the core of the miracle, or near impossibility, of thoroughly successful (in clinical terms) identity formation. For many, particularly those who have been reared within emotionally charged and privatized nuclear families that offer few opportunities for interaction with other caretakers, this primal ambivalence experienced in relation to a female mother is never fully resolved or incorporated into consciousness. Instead, it simmers restlessly in the unconscious, an easy target of reevocation in adult life.

This ambivalence is also played out in a number of familiar philosophical and political dramas, particularly as these involve relations between self and others, individual and community, liberty for oneself and obligation to others. These are, of course, some of the quintessential problems of modern liberal political theory. We also find this ambivalence in Simone de Beauvoir's assessment of the dichotomous and unstable symbolics of the feminized other, as well as in her adoption of the existential categories of immanence and transcendence.[15] As Benjamin points out, we also find it at "play" in the practice and imagery of sadomasochistic eroticism, which invokes the violation of the boundaries of the feminized other as confirmation of the mastery of the masculin-

[15]Simone de Beauvoir, *The Second Sex*, trans. and ed. H. M. Parshley (New York: Random House, 1974).

ized self.[16] How and why this infantile experience becomes culturally elaborated within socially prevalent advertisements for "normal" modern heterosexual relations whereby men tend to assume the stance of autonomy, mastery, and differentiation while women are consigned to the ranks of mute servility and objectified availability is a key issue for contemporary feminist theory.

Even with the best of all possible mothering, the anxiety of separation is unavoidable.[17] It seems to peak during the second year of life, identified as the next-to-last stage of separation and individuation. As the child gradually realizes that it pursues independence at the cost of magical omnipotence and fusion with the mother, an alternating strategy is employed whereby the child flits from the impatient desire for independence to the passionate yearning for refusion. Periodically the mother is rejected as a suffocating presence, only to be clung to in desperation at some later moment. The observed activity of clinging to and pushing away the mother is the behavioral evidence for this flux of contradictory emotions and desires. The mother–care giver may walk a fine line between solicitous behavior that the child will interpret as intrusive and a letting go that puts traumatic and resented distance between the child and its supporting world.

This is the point at which the father's role becomes crucial as a new source of support against reengulfment into maternal union. Around the eighteenth month, the child's father becomes significant as a facilitator of its separation from the mother. The modern nuclear family "romance" has now added a new player to the script, and the emotional dynamics

---

[16]Benjamin, "The Bonds of Love." It should be noted that these masculine and feminine positions may be variously occupied by males and females. Gendered symbolics and positions, it should be remembered, are constructive representations rather than mirror derivatives of "malehood" and "femalehood." The "problem" of gender "deviance" testifies to the truth of this insight, even as it relies on a notion of normal as natural.

[17]"Best" should also be understood in terms of individually underdetermined structural outcomes rather than in terms of the intentions, skills, or dedication of particular parents.

become increasingly triangulated. Bearing none, or at any rate less, of the affiliation to the messy and primordial attachments, fears, and desires experienced by the infant and young child in relation to the mother, the father is a relatively safe and stable figure who embodies the seductive appeal of an external social reality (the masculine public world of commerce, politics, and culture) that is less maternally influenced, if at all.[18] Hanna Pitkin provides a very useful summation of the primordial gendered imagery that infuses the early pre-Oedipal experience of the child vis-à-vis each parent:

> Women thus have to do with: the danger of dissolution of the self, of losing boundaries between self and others, self and world; the pre- or nonverbal, nonconceptual, nonrational; overwhelming affect and the danger of being so overwhelmed; the body and its pleasures and needs, particularly those of nurturance, eating and being eaten; helpless dependence and omnipotent domination, relationships of almost total inequality. . . .
>
> Men . . . are perceived as less engulfing, better defined, more rational and controlled, more like persons and less like magical forces. Relations with men are less bound to sheer survival.[19]

In the best of all possible parent-child relations within the modern nuclear family setting, the child will eventually learn to negotiate between the poles of ambivalence surrounding separation from the mother figure. The child will be able to maintain a mental image of the mother as a primary love object and as an individual subject in her own right, increasingly distinct from the child's mental representation of himself or

[18]We need to keep in mind that this account presupposes a sexual division of labor in the household whereby the mother assumes primary responsibility for the care of young children and the father has primary responsibility as the breadwinner in the official outside economy.

[19]Hanna Pitkin, *Fortune Is a Woman: Gender and Politics in the Thought of Niccolò Machiavelli* (Berkeley: University of California Press, 1984), 191.

herself. If the attachment to the mother as a separate object can be developed and then preserved, a coherent sense of identity and reasonably well developed capacities for social interaction are likely to result. If this attachment to the mother takes, instead, the form of an identification that blurs or exaggerates the boundaries between child and mother, identity formation will be disturbed in some ways. The ego may be too fragile, overly susceptible to environmental upsets and influences; it may become either too fluid or overly rigid.[20] Finally, the ability to unify the "good" and "bad" aspects of the maternal imago into one whole representation is important if the child's self-image, at least partially constituted by what the child is introjecting from the outside mother-world, is to develop "holistically." In other words, split maternal images may contribute to split self-images and to a host of complicated projective and introjective activities that keep the self divided and unable to function in the social world.[21]

[20]In my review of this account of human development, several caveats should be borne in mind. The first is that "human development" should be understood to be historically and culturally situated. I do not believe that an all-purpose norm of human or moral development is either possible or desirable. The second caveat is that ascriptions such as "good" or "good enough" parenting, "healthy" or "functioning" egos, should be thought of as qualitative and culturally situated tendencies rather than as fixed pronouncements. The third caveat concerns the question of maternal responsibility for children's development. A correct reading of object relations theory does not show individual mothers to be routinely responsible for the psychological and/or social pathologies of their offspring. Rather, the structurally "loaded" position of the mother makes her the target of potent affect; and the ideal-typical structure of the modern nuclear family, along with the genderized public-private distinction in society at large, contributes very little to the mediated reworking of this affect. In essence, fathers are let off the hook. On this issue, see Nancy Chodorow and Susan Contratto, "The Myth of the Perfect Mother," in Nancy J. Chodorow, *Feminism and Psychoanalytic Theory* (New Haven: Yale University Press, 1989), 79–96; and Janet Liebman Jacobs, "Reassessing Mother Blame in Incest," *Signs: Journal of Women in Culture and Society* 15 (Spring 1990), 500–514.

[21]See Robert Stoller, *Splitting: A Case of Female Masculinity* (New York: Delta, 1973), for a powerful and disturbing clinical description of the effects on an adult patient of an internalized mother figure who is split. Melanie Klein's description of the earliest split maternal image (good breast/bad breast) and of the ways in which this image enters into wider-ranging and seemingly

While this account of modern nuclear family dynamics has been used to blame mothers for the unhappiness and social maladjustments of their children, many of whom never seem to learn how to grow up, an alternative reading of this material suggests that the modern nuclear family form is structurally implicated in "pathological" outcomes. Too much affect is circulating in an overly circumscribed space with too few players. Perhaps if children were reared in less privatized settings and with a larger available stock of caretakers, including men as well as women, they would find different challenges and opportunities in the separation-individuation dynamic. Perhaps such children would be less inclined to construct the gender symbolics described by Pitkin because they would be encouraged to explore and mediate their ambivalent desires, as well as to project them onto other players. In other words, under different circumstances female mothers would no longer bear the full brunt of children's ambivalence.

Object relations theory, as outlined in this chapter, offers a significant and relevant revision of orthodox psychoanalytic theory for those interested in questions of gender identity formation; namely, a shift in focus from the child's relationship with his or her father during the Oedipal phase to the prior relationship with the mother during the pre-Oedipal phase. In the words of Melanie Klein: "The baby's first object of love and hate—his mother—is both desired and hated with all the intensity and strength that is characteristic of the early urges of the baby."[22] It is against and within the frame of this primal emotional backdrop that the subsequent struggles of

---

remote areas, including our attitudes toward nature, is instructive. See her essay "Love, Guilt, and Reparation," in *"Love, Guilt, and Reparation" and Other Works*, esp. 333–343. Thanks to the work of Dinnerstein in *The Mermaid and the Minotaur*, which builds on many of Klein's insights, the now obvious connections between split maternal images and de Beauvoir's analysis of the cultural depiction of woman in the west have been spelled out in rich detail. We should also bear in mind, however, that a divided self may be a more interesting, creative self, and that the rhetoric of unified and coherent subjectivity is belied by the psychoanalytic account of intrapsychically constituted identity.

[22]Klein, "Love, Guilt, and Reparation," 306.

separation and individuation take place. Overlaid on this dimension of ambivalence is the more specific struggle involving gender identity. That these early struggles and ambivalent desires are first experienced in relation to a *female* mother is now acknowledged to be the empirical ground for crucial differences between the identity formation processes of boys and girls in modern nuclear families.

Aspects of separation and individuation take on special and different significance for boys and girls in relation to a care giver and love object who is, in nearly all cases, female. Coppélia Kahn summarizes the difference, explicated most extensively by Chodorow and Dinnerstein, in this way:

> For though she follows the same sequence of symbiotic union, separation and individuation, identification, and object love as the boy, [the girl's] femininity arises in relation to a person of the *same* sex, while [the boy's] masculinity arises in relation to a person of the *opposite* sex. Her femininity is reinforced by her original symbiotic union with her mother and by the identification with her that must precede identity, while masculinity is threatened by the same union and the same identification. While the boy's sense of *self* begins in union with the feminine, his sense of *masculinity* arises against it. [23]

The boy is faced with the awesome task of breaking his identification with the mother (disidentifying) and setting up a counteridentification with the father. [24] A double lesson of this experience is that masculine identity is bound up with the experience of disjuncture and conflict and that it contains an ascetic dimension. A logical outcome of the socially required and enforced repudiation of identification with the maternal subject-object, particularly in cultures that promote a strict

[23]Coppélia Kahn, *Man's Estate: Masculine Identity in Shakespeare* (Berkeley: University of California Press, 1981), 10.
[24]Ralph R. Greenson, "Dis-Identifying from the Mother: Its Special Importance for the Boy," *International Journal of Psychoanalysis* 49 (1968), 370–74.

differentiation between genders and gendered social functions (for example, a sexual division of labor; a gendered division between the spheres of public and private activity), is the "mummification" of a split maternal imago, one that simultaneously promises the primal ecstasy of need satisfaction as it threatens annihilation of the independent self. The Oedipal drama plays out and helps to preserve this association between women and danger.[25] Many of these themes are, of course, recapitulated in the high drama of modern romantic imagery.

The basic ambivalence of children toward the mother, then, is heightened for boys because of the culturally prescribed need to define masculinity in contrast to maternally identified femininity. Issues of self and gender are more closely intermingled in the separation-individuation process for the boy than for the girl, whose struggle for selfhood is not so tied up with a dramatic version of achieved gender identity, for it is secured in relation to a mother-caregiver who is "like" her daughter. As Chodorow argues, the girl's struggle is more likely to be over individualized selfhood and independence, and this takes place during adolescence. If this more protracted period of identification with the mother spells unique identity problems for the girl seeking to disengage from the mother as an individual, at least the struggle for independent selfhood is overlaid on a relatively secure sense of gender identity.[26]

In spite of the high drama of the Oedipus complex articulated by Freud, it would seem that he underestimated other

[25]On the ubiquitous cultural theme of dangerous women, see: H. R. Hayes, *The Dangerous Sex: The Myth of Feminine Evil* (New York: G. P. Putnam's Sons, 1964); Wolfgang Lederer, *The Fear of Women* (New York: Harcourt Brace Jovanovich, 1968); Klaus Theweleit, *Male Fantasies*, vol. 1, *Women, Floods, Bodies, History*, trans. Stephen Conway, with Erica Carter and Chris Turner (Minneapolis: University of Minnesota Press, 1987).

[26]On the daughter's quest for identity, see Chodorow, *The Reproduction of Mothering*, 111–140; and Jane Flax, "Mother-Daughter Relationships: Psychodynamics, Politics, and Philosophy," in Eisenstein and Jardine, *The Future of Difference*, 20–40.

dramatic dimensions of the boy's struggle to attain a specifically masculine identity. A salient feature of the object relations account of modern masculine development is the negative articulation of masculine selfhood vis-à-vis the preposited maternal-feminine presence. The rudimentary building blocks of the boy's struggle to understand what it is that makes him a boy, a masculine subject and agent in a gender-differentiated and gender-organized world, consist of negative counterfactuals garnered through comparison with the mother: as a boy, I am that which is not-mother, not-female, not-feminine. Within privatized family settings, where the father is not likely to be continuously available as a positive source of substantive information on masculinity, proceeding by way of negative comparison is a sensible strategy. An additional effect of the absent-father phenomenon is that early dependence on a maternal figure in the household may require an even more vigorous and aggressive response on the part of the boy who is struggling to achieve a masculine identity. His society may lend him a helping hand by providing elaborate and rigorous rituals with which to mark his entrance into manhood.[27]

We should also keep in mind that in modern western societies, there are strong sanctions against effeminate behavior on the part of boys. This is consistent, I believe, with the suggestion that modern masculinity resembles a reaction formation rather than an originary model of selfhood. As such, it is unstable and vulnerable, particularly to the "polluting" influence of feminine elements. Rigid enforcement of masculine norms of behavior suggests a powerful horror at the pros-

---

[27]The missing-father syndrome is not exclusively associated with the modern nuclear family. Its multicultural variants have been statistically correlated with sexually inegalitarian societies. This would seem to lend some support to the object relations argument, although the correlation, which also includes the element of female-identified child rearing, does not provide conclusive proof of causal links between missing fathers and female child nurture on the one hand and sexual inegalitarianism on the other. See Peggy Reeves Sanday, *Female Power and Male Dominance: On the Origins of Male Dominance* (Cambridge: Cambridge University Press, 1981), 239–247; Eli Sagan, *Cannibalism: Human Aggression and Cultural Form* (New York: Harper and Row, 1974).

pect of mixing or confusing cherished and vulnerable categories.[28] This prospect exists as a threat precisely because it is
already presupposed and embedded in the structure of the
modern nuclear family.

The literature reviewed here suggests, then, that there are
significant links between masculinity as an achieved and precarious identity on the one hand, and a negatively conceived
femininity represented by the objectified mother, the
(m)other, on the other. The horror of identification with the
feminine, the strictness with which masculinity is defined and
established in opposition to femininity, suggests an intimate
pairing of rigidity and vulnerability in modern constructions
of masculinity. Because the defining bounds of masculinity
are so strictly set, they are all the more susceptible to invasion.
This insight provides an alternative perspective on classically
conceived masculine ego "strength," which until recently was
compared favorably in the psychological literature on sex differences to women's notorious ego boundary "problems" and
cognitive "field dependence."[29] Indeed, a related aspect of
such strength may be a brittle rigidity, the diminished ability
to accommodate a shifting and unpredictable environment
inhabited by independent fellow creatures and an enigmatic
nature.

Nancy Chodorow sums up her reconstruction of the origins

[28]In *Man-Made Language* (London: Routledge and Kegan Paul, 1980), Dale
Spender observes a relevant semantic rule in the English language: masculine
terms that have become gradually feminized in their connotations through
time are never subsequently reintroduced as terms of masculine denotation,
except when used in a derogatory fashion. Conversely, masculine terms used
to describe women are complimentary, whereas the obverse is not the case.

[29]See Jean Baker Miller, *Toward a New Psychology of Women* (Boston: Beacon
Press, 1976) for the argument that "field dependent" women are more attuned
to the social nuances of their environment than men, and that they have
noteworthy capacities to sustain multiple and complex social ties to other
persons. For a much earlier elaboration of a similar intuition, see Margaret
Fuller, *Woman in the Nineteenth Century*, intro. Bernard Rosenthal (New York:
W. W. Norton, 1971), 103: "You will often see men of high intellect absolutely
stupid in regard to the atmospheric changes, the fine invisible links which
connect the forms of life around them, while common women . . . will seize
and delineate these with unerring discrimination."

and ramifications of masculinity in a manner that bears directly on many of these themes:

> The division of labor in child rearing results in an objectification of women—a treating of women as others, or objects, rather than subjects, or selves—that extends to our culture as a whole. Infantile development of the self is explored in opposition to the mother, as primary caretaker, who becomes the other. Because boys are of opposite gender from their mothers, they especially feel a need to differentiate and yet find differentiation problematic. The boy comes to define his self more in opposition than through a sense of his wholeness or continuity. He becomes the self and experiences his mother as the other. The process also extends to his trying to dominate the other in order to ensure his sense of self. Such domination begins with mother as the object, extends to women, and is then generalized to include the experience of all others as objects rather than subjects. This stance in which people are treated and experienced as things, becomes basic to male Western culture. Thus the "fetishism of commodities," the rigid self-other distinctions of capitalism or of bureaucratic mass societies all have genetic and psychological roots in the structure of parenting and of male development, not just the requirements of production.[30]

Several of these themes are further reiterated in the familiar symbolic configuration of feminized nature/naturalized woman.

As Dorothy Dinnerstein and others have argued, the categories of "women" and "nature" share genealogical terrain.[31]

[30]Nancy Chodorow, "On *The Reproduction of Mothering:* A Methodological Debate," *Signs: Journal of Women in Culture and Society* 6 (Spring 1981), 502–503.

[31]Dinnerstein, *The Mermaid and the Minotaur.* See Susan Griffin, *Woman and Nature: The Roaring Inside Her* (New York: Harper and Row, 1978), for a remarkable poetic articulation of this genealogy. Also see Ynestra King, "Healing the Wounds: Feminism, Ecology, and Nature/Culture Dualism," in *Gender/Body/Knowledge: Feminist Reconstructions of Being and Knowing,* ed. Alison M. Jaggar and Susan R. Bordo (New Brunswick, N.J.: Rutgers University Press, 1989), 115–141.

If nature in the modern west has retained some of "her" premodern feminine connotations, these have been resituated within a field of sensibility that objectified nature, that made "her" the passive, mute matter of man's interests and designs. Nevertheless, "she" is made responsible when things go wrong, particularly when they cannot be controlled. The object relations literature suggests that the quasi-human status of women in the modern west is related to our infantile immersion in a mother-world where the mother is also the first representative of nature. It is the combination of two factors— the various traumas associated with that inevitably disappointing and increasingly threatening immersion, and our attempts to escape that immersion with the help of the father—which help to frame and to produce the woman-nature alliance.

Modern accounts of human nature stress the voluntaristic and self-defining capacities of men, who are bound by few natural and sex-specific limits. Yet, these conceptions of "human" nature end up penalizing women for their sex-specific, nature-bound activities, particularly as these involve reproduction. As Theodor Adorno and Max Horkheimer have perceptively argued: "Where the mastery of nature is the true goal, biological inferiority remains a glaring stigma, the weakness imprinted by nature as a key stimulus to aggression."[32] Political theories in which "the individual is constituted abstractly without ever getting born,"[33] populated by what Clifford Geertz has termed "bloodless universals,"[34] bear the cognitive fruit of the wish to deny natural and maternal origins. Reevoking infantile omnipotence, that primal sense of self-sufficiency which we have all lost and only partially regained, second nature conceptions go on to express the adult and detectably modern masculine desire for a self-generation and a

[32]Max Horkheimer and T. W. Adorno, *Dialectic of Enlightenment* (New York: Seabury Press, 1972), 248.

[33]Mary O'Brien, *The Politics of Reproduction* (Boston: Routledge and Kegan Paul, 1981), 62.

[34]Clifford Geertz, "The Impact of the Concept of Culture on the Concept of Man," in *The Interpretation of Cultures* (New York: Basic Books, 1973), 43.

species generation that can be self-consciously willed, created, and controlled. Not insignificantly, the body, that physical locus of dependence on the (m)other, is eliminated from these versions of achieved selfhood.

Because the familial terms of feminized immersion and masculinized escape are gendered, because the father steps in as rescuer, we are thereby enabled to maintain certain primitive emotions and gendered associations. Given the gendered structure and symbolism of modern western societies, which is by no means localized in the family alone, we may permanently sidestep an adult confrontation or mediation with a primordial (m)other whose human subjectivity is difficult and confusing to acknowledge. To the extent that the primordial (m)other is equated with nature, feelings directed at each are likely to be similar. Unconscious feelings about the mother (and, by extension, all women) and nature are likely to center around the dual strands of unresolved desire and horror. Women, like nature, pose a terrifying threat to independence, self-reliance, and autonomy. And this feminized threat, experienced by children of both sexes (and therefore often internalized by girls, thus complicating their subsequent adult sense of entitlement to independence and autonomy), is amplified for the boy child, given the gendered specification of masculinity as that which is not-mother.

The (perhaps universal) need for a "quasi-human source of richness and target of greedy rage"[35] becomes localized in feminine embodiments: Mother Nature, who is bountiful and stingy, benign and punishing; women's fetishized bodies, which promise so much that they will inevitably disappoint and so enrage; and standard bifurcated images of "good" and "bad" women. To the extent that this symbolism is permitted to maintain an apparently self-sufficient existence within such familiar couplets as male-female, culture-nature, reason-passion, mind-body, it becomes simultaneously more threatening and less amenable to dialectical query and mediation. The

[35]Dinnerstein, *The Mermaid and the Minotaur*, 101.

sexual division of labor in the household and the economy at large, along with the genderized symbolism of modern western culture, encourages us to maintain what Dinnerstein describes as "the murderous infantilism of our relation to nature" and women: "Our over-personification of nature is inseparable from our under-personification of women."[36]

Within this symbolic frame of meaning, maternal and natural reengulfment become the constitutive threats to autonomy, masculinity, and "civilization" itself. And the dangers of reengulfment are further compounded by the strict boundedness of masculinity and civilization thus conceived:

> The cultural definition of masculine as what can never appear feminine, and of autonomy as what can never be relaxed, conspire to reinforce the child's earliest associations of female with the pleasures and dangers of merging, and male with both the comfort and the loneliness of separateness. The boy's internal anxiety about both self and gender is here echoed by the cultural anxiety; together they can lead to postures of exaggerated autonomy and masculinity which can—indeed which may be designed to—defend against that anxiety and the longing which generates it.[37]

When we juxtapose the account of modern masculinity-in-development to particular sexual-social arrangements of adult life, the lifelong tasks associated with maintaining and protecting a masculine self loom as overwhelmingly demanding. The boy who had to disengage from the mother as his original ground of identity and love object, who has spent his adolescence bonding with other boys, must as an adult reunite with a woman. While Freud rightly pointed out how the girl's problematic shift from mother to father as love object spelled unique difficulties for her future relationships with men, he was less perceptive about the difficulties in the boy's case.

[36]Ibid., 109, 108.
[37]Evelyn Keller, "Gender and Science," *Psychoanalysis and Contemporary Thought* 1 (1978), 426.

As Dinnerstein points out, the man-to-woman relationship is more likely to rekindle unconscious memories of satisfaction and terror than the woman-to-man relationship. Not only does the heterosexual man enjoy direct access to the body of a woman, thereby invoking earlier memories of his relation to the maternal body, but his previous (and, in part, introjected) relation to that body became the negative ground of his struggle to achieve masculinity.[38] In other words, the man's emotional and sexual experience of a woman in the heterosexual relationship is likely to reignite memories of the pleasures, dangers, and struggles associated with his prior quest for masculine identity.

The object relations account suggests that mothers, as historical empirical subjects and as fantasized objects, occupy "privileged" positions within central arenas of modern western experience. This "privilege" functions simultaneously as a prop for and as a threat to modern masculinity. The denial of this maternal privilege becomes, in turn, a constitutive feature of distinctly patterned ways of interpreting and acting in the modern world which may be designated "masculine." Finally, as I shall detail in later chapters, maternal privilege is not only denied but is also reappropriated. The modern masculine enterprise of achieved and vulnerable autonomous selfhood is implicated in the denial and appropriation of the (m)other's power.

In this all too cursory review of the object relations literature on modern gender identity, I have traced out some of the distinguishing features of modern masculinity which, I shall subsequently argue, find their way into modern political thought. These features are induced and dynamically reproduced by specific sociopolitical circumstances and arrangements, particularly as these involve an entrenched sexual divi-

---

[38]For a thoughtful and provocative account of heterosexual sexuality, which explores the more playful and plastic vicissitudes of a sexuality that is less constrained by strictly gendered presumptions, see Joan Cocks, *The Oppositional Imagination: Feminism, Critique, and Political Theory* (London: Routledge, 1989), 150–173.

sion of labor and a specifically nuclear family form. Hence, those women who as daughters experienced a more protracted period of identification with the mother figure are also more likely to *want* to be mothers, to identify closely with their babies, to experience a curious confounding of bodily and ego boundaries in their relations with their children.[39] Yet men, who were themselves reared by female mothers and who have identities that are more strictly differentiated, are less likely to become involved in the regular, daily, intimate care of young children.[40] Finally, modern industrial and postindustrial economies provide another set of incentives for this arrangement: labor markets are sexually segregated; women's work (much of it now in the service industries) is remunerated on a lesser scale of value than men's; and affordable high-quality child-care services are still, for the most part, a pipe dream. In short, economic structures and societal priorities conspire with the modern psychology of gender to keep women responsible for mothering.

The central linchpin, then, of contemporary object relations arguments that seek to account for (and, in the case of feminists, to overcome) gender-based differences in psychology and social roles is the differences whereby boys and girls separate from the mother as these are induced by the structure of the modern nuclear family and by the relationship of this family form to modern economic arrangements.

---

[39]See Chodorow, *The Reproduction of Mothering;* and Rich, *Of Woman Born: Motherhood as Experience and Institution* (New York: W. W. Norton, 1976). For a moving literary account of the confounding of these boundaries for a black mother and her daughter under conditions of American slavery and its aftermath, see Toni Morrison, *Beloved* (New York: New American Library, 1988).

[40]This argument is not meant to deny that many genuinely nurturant fathers are active and involved parents. Despite their increasing numbers, however, they continue to be the exceptions that prove, rather than undermine, the prevalent rule. Nor should this be construed as a denial of paternal love. The important point concerns the qualitative differences between the psychological orientations to and forms of child rearing engaged in by mothers and fathers. See Benjamin, *The Bonds of Love,* 96–123; Diane Ehrensaft, "When Men and Women Mother," *Socialist Review* 49 (January–February 1980), 37–73.

To summarize, whereas the dynamics of mother-daughter separation tend toward a "failure" to differentiate completely, modern masculine identity is secured by means of an overemphasis on ego boundaries. Difference and separation from a female (m)other characterize the boy's quest for self within a familial and outlying social setting that is organized in segregated and hierarchical gendered terms. A concomitant aspect of this process is that the (m)other poses a significant threat to a masculinity acquired in rigid opposition to her. The modern masculine process of individuation and identity formation, understood in these "ideal type" terms, is susceptible to a process of "false differentiation" whereby the maternal other is strictly and unrealistically objectified in split versions rather than vitally engaged and at least partially accommodated in a more mediated and nuanced manner. False differentiation is potentially capable of becoming the ground of neurotic outlooks and activities. It can lead to a sense of unreality and lack of connection to the surrounding object world, which must be held at a safe, manageable, and nonintrusive arm's length. For some it qualifies as a world view that

> emphasizes difference over sameness, boundaries over fluidity. It conceives of polarity and opposition, rather than mutuality and interdependence, as the vehicles of growth. That is, it does not tolerate the simultaneous experience of contradictory impulses: ambivalence. Finally, this world view does not grant the other person the status of another subject, but only that of an object. By extension, this object status is granted to the entire world, which, from early on, was infused with the mother's presence. In these psychic tendencies, the basic elements of Western rationality take shape: analysis or differentiation; duality or polarity; and objectivity.[41]

This "male stance of over-differentiation, of splitting off and denying the tendencies towards sameness, merging, and re-

[41]Benjamin, "The Bonds of Love," 148–149.

ciprocal responsiveness,"[42] is characterized by a dualistically patterned posture (me/not-me) in relation to the world of nature, feminized others, and "fellow" human beings. Modern masculine differentiation partakes of a fundamental alienation and dualism, estrangement and uncertainty. Modern masculine identity also enforces a conspiracy of silence and overcompensation in relation to this powerlessness. Hence the relation of modern masculinity to psychologies of conquest.[43]

Modern Masculinity as Ideology

The literature on modern gender formation suggests that there are ways in which modern masculine experience yields certain cognitive proclivities, tendencies that structure perception such that the social world is interpreted, and hence engaged, contested, and reproduced, within the horizon of those perceptual commitments. Such perceptual tendencies may be thought of as constituting a world view, organized around the specifiable concerns of the modern masculine subject. This primacy should be evident not only in those substantive and easily identified arenas of masculine privilege and power, including what is now identified and explored as the sexism of western political and social theory, but also at the deeper and more obscure level of overall perceptual and cognitive orientation. There is good reason to suppose that a specifiably masculine cognitive orientation inhabits the terrain of modern political theory and enjoys a wide-ranging, if obscure and implicit, influence which has been underinterpreted to date.

To suggest that gender is an unavoidable dimension of modern experience and thought is not to say that it determines personality or intellectual creations in some simplistic or linear

---

[42]Ibid., 150.
[43]See Peter Schwenger, *Phallic Critiques: Masculinity and Twentieth-Century Literature* (London: Routledge and Kegan Paul, 1984); and Theweleit, *Male Fantasies.*

fashion. Yet, those who take gender, among other factors, seriously as a significant feature of being in the world find it difficult to proceed as if political theorists were just "people" thinking "human" thoughts; as if the hegemonic relationship of white European males to the canonical tradition of modern political theory were relatively inconsequential for the contemporary reassessment of that tradition.

Thinking and knowledge issue from a complex process of reflection on experience. While the cognitive mediation of experience may adopt any of a variety of postures in relation to experience (which is itself always and already interpreted), from acquiescence to resistance, such mediation must inevitably be colored by the substance and ground of its engagement. The same must be said for the varieties of accommodation to and revolt against the (often impossible and incoherent) prescriptions of modern gender. For this reason, I propose to situate masculinity within the analytic frame of ideology.

In treating masculinity as a form of ideology, I take Marxism and the sociology of knowledge as my initial points of departure. Within this epistemological tradition, specifiable cultural, historical, and social factors are acknowledged to operate as significant elements of knowledge.[44] As Jane Flax has argued: "Knowledge is the product of human beings, for whom knowing is only one form of activity. The history and life situation of the knower cannot be completely different in kind from the form and content of the knowledge that this subject produces."[45]

One can, I believe, employ a qualified notion of ideology without resorting to the claim that ideology is necessarily false or crudely epiphenomenal. That is, one can retain an appreciation for Marx and Engels' insistence on the "material" constituents of knowledge without counterposing ideology to nonideological knowledge. On this view, all knowledge is

[44]Karl Mannheim, *Ideology and Utopia* (New York: Harcourt, Brace and World, 1936); Karl Marx and Frederick Engels, *The German Ideology*, ed. C. J. Arthur (New York: International Publishers, 1970).
[45]Flax, "Mother-Daughter Relationships," 21.

ideological; and the charge of ideology does not necessarily render knowledge problematic. This would be the case only for those who embrace the dream of nonideological knowledge (as Marx himself did.) Ideology, in short, is not necessarily a dirty word, although it certainly does convey the judgment that knowledge and power are in alliance with each other. My quarrel with modern masculine ideology is that it disallows other cognitive elaborations of the social world and that it is based on an unacknowledged fear of women which results in the attempt to dominate them. In other words, modern masculinity is implicated in misogyny. This is very different from a simplistic labeling of masculine ideology as "false." Nor does this claim require the counterposing of a nonideological feminist alternative as the ground for such a critique of ideology. I have no reservations about characterizing feminist inquiry as ideological in the sense that it is another instantiation of the ubiquitous power-knowledge relation.[46]

Another hazard is that the term may seduce the reader into assuming that the social world is actually marked in some way by a specifiable distinction between "material" and "ideological" components. Once this distinction is accepted, it is easier to argue that ideology is a secondary effect or reflection of more basic material conditions. The problem here is that this runs roughshod over the "always aready" interpreted material circumstances. There is no such thing as "pure" experience

[46]My remarks here are obviously aimed at Foucault's provocative discussion of ideology. See Michel Foucault, "Truth and Power," in *Power/Knowledge: Selected Interviews and Other Writings, 1972–1977,* ed. Colin Gordon (New York: Pantheon, 1980), 109–133.

Ideology is a theoretically unfashionable concept, particularly for those who are persuaded by the postmodern critique of depth models of explanation and interpretation, wherein "reality" or "truth" is thought to reside in the privileged space beneath or behind surface "appearances." The term is also overloaded with a plethora of meanings. I have decided to utilize a qualified version of the term in my analysis because of its heuristic rhetorical force, particularly as this evokes the notion of knowledge that is illicitly generalized and complicitous with the interests of politically dominant groups. Those who are uncomfortable with the term might try substituting "power-knowledge configuration."

which precedes its representation or which can serve as the ground for ideological critique. But neither, I would add, is there representation without material.

As it is being invoked here, "modern masculine ideology" is understood to reflect, produce, and partially constitute social relations (necessarily including interpretations of those social relations) between and among men, women, humanity, and nature. It is simultaneously real and false; that is, it is "real" in that sense that it produces a world in its own image, and it is "false" in the sense that it does violence to that world and to its gendered subject-effects.

In characterizing modern masculinity as an ideology, I have in mind three related notions. My first debt is to the notion of ideology as world view. To this is added a central aspect borrowed from the notion of "standpoint." Finally, I invoke the image of "deep structure" as a descriptive aid. From the idea of standpoint I wish to invoke the claim that material life structures understanding. Standpoints are vantage points established and secured on the basis of life conditions, particularly as these involve laboring activities broadly construed. They have significant epistemological and ontological consequences; that is, sensibilities about the nature of knowledge and the nature of social reality cohere with laboring practices and their environments.[47]

From the notion of ideology as world view, two important and contestable claims are implied: (1) European males and their male cultural descendants in the New World (from approximately 1600 on) qualify as an identifiable cohort of human subjects characterized by (2) a bundle of beliefs, attitudes, and goals that have some coherence and a characteristic structure. This bundle need not be exhaustive or inclusive of all beliefs ever held by this group. It is, rather, a significant and

---

[47]See Nancy C. M. Hartsock, *Money, Sex, and Power: Toward a Feminist Historical Materialism* (New York: Longman, 1983), esp. chap. 6; and Dorothy Smith, "A Sociology for Women," in *The Prism of Sex: Essays in the Sociology of Knowledge*, ed. Julia A. Sherman and Evelyn Torton Beck (Madison: University of Wisconsin Press, 1979), 135–187.

identifiable subset of all such beliefs. Ideology in the sense of world view has the following properties, as outlined by Raymond Geuss:

(a) the elements in the subset are widely shared among the agents in the group
(b) the elements . . . are systematically interconnected
(c) they are "central to the agents' conceptual scheme" in Quine's sense
(d) the elements in the subset have a wide and deep influence on the agents' behavior or on some particularly important or central sphere of action [and]
(e) the beliefs in the subset are "central" in that they deal with central issues of human life . . . or central metaphysical issues.[48]

In this study the enterprise of political theory will be taken as a central sphere of action.

The claim that modern masculinity operates at the level of deep structure suggests that masculine ideology comprises interrelated elements that do not necessarily manifest themselves at the explicit surface of theoretical discourse. That is, while these elements may exert a significant influence on the thought of a political theorist, we may have to seek them out between the lines, in the more obscure works of a theorist's oeuvre, and/or in theoretical arguments and rhetorical strategies that are often thought to be less than central to the political theorist's main or significant contributions to political thinking.[49]

---

[48]Raymond Geuss, *The Idea of a Critical Theory: Habermas and the Frankfurt School* (Cambridge: Cambridge University Press, 1981), 10; quote from W. V. O. Quine, *From a Logical Point of View.*

[49]Jane Flax's notion of the "patriarchal unconscious" of political theory invokes a similar depth image. See Flax, "Political Philosophy and the Patriarchal Unconscious: A Psychoanalytic Perspective on Epistemology and Metaphysics," in *Discovering Reality: Feminist Perspectives on Epistemology, Metaphysics, Methodology, and Philosophy of Science,* ed. Sandra Harding and Merrill B. Hintikka (Dordrecht: D. Reidel, 1983), 245–281.

The elements of a world view were said to be widely shared, systematically interconnected, central to the agents' conceptual scheme, to have a wide and deep influence, and to be central in that they deal with central issues of human life. We are already in a position to appreciate the ways in which the elements of modern masculine ideology are or might be systematically interconnected. Heading the list is a combative brand of dualistic thinking, a persistent and systematic amplification of the primal self-other oppositional dynamic and the creation of dichotomously structured polarities with which to describe and evaluate the events, objects, and processes of the natural and social worlds. The need for singular identity and certainty with respect to one's own identity and that of other "objects" in the environment, a concomitant of which is panic in the face of threats to such unambiguous certainty, would be another perceptual tendency. The explicit or implicit denial of relatedness—to "fellow" human beings, to women, and to nature—would be tied in with an extreme version of modern masculine identity. We may also anticipate a repudiation of natural contingency, including those limits imposed by the body and the natural surroundings. In connection with this, we may expect to find examples of an identification of contingency with the feminine. We may also expect to find the (m)other lurking in the shadows of this discourse, as an invisible and unacknowledged, but inferential and significant, presence. Because of the tendencies toward a radical individualism built into the masculine differentiation process, we are likely to find versions of a solitary subject immersed in a hostile and dangerous world. Autonomy is likely to figure as a significant theme and ideal. Recapitulating the earlier experience of identity through opposition and negation, we may expect to find versions of knowledge acquired through opposition, tension, and conflict; an antagonistic and distanced relation between the subject and object of knowledge. Finally, we can expect to encounter attitudes of fear, denigration, and hostility toward whatever is identified as female or feminine, along with its idealization and glorification. Both sets of seemingly incompatible attitudes recapitulate the effects of false differentiation from, of unsuccessful rapprochement with, the maternal subject-object.

In effect, the presumption of and search for modern masculine ideology in political theory texts is bound up with the interpretive quest for a maternal subtext that, in the words of Coppélia Kahn, exhibits "the imprint of mothering on the male psyche, the psychological presence of the mother in men whether or not mothers are represented in the texts they write."[50]

Hobbes and Modern Gender: Calling the Question

This interpretive scheme is vulnerable to the objection that it runs roughshod over history; that is, that "modern masculinity" is invoked in overly seamless terms or that contemporary constructions of gender are being retroactively imposed. Of the three political theorists studied here, Hobbes (1588–1679) is the one most problematically situated vis-à-vis the object relations scheme. Whereas Marx and Mill are located within the historical frame of bourgeois nuclear family relations epitomized by Freud and object relations theory, Hobbes stands in the midst of a significant watershed in European family history. On the one hand, he was reared in a historical period whose family form and relations have been described by Lawrence Stone in terms that are simultaneously chilling and reminiscent of Hobbes's own state of nature:

What is being postulated for the sixteenth and early seventeenth centuries is a society in which a majority of the individuals who composed it found it very difficult to establish close emotional ties to any person. Children were often neglected, brutally treated, and even killed; many adults treated each other with suspicion and hostility; affect was

[50]Coppélia Kahn, "Excavating 'Those Dim Minoan Regions': Maternal Subtexts in Patriarchal Literature," *Diacritics: A Review of Contemporary Criticism* 12 (Summer 1982), 36.

low, and hard to find. . . . The lack of a unique mother figure in the first two years of life, the constant loss of close relatives, siblings, parents, nurses and friends through premature death, the physical imprisonment of the infant in tight swaddling-clothes in early months, and the deliberate breaking of the child's will all contributed to a 'psychic numbing' which created many adults whose primary responses to others were at best a calculating indifference and at worst a mixture of suspicion and hostility, tyranny and submission, alienation and rage. . . .

So far as the surviving evidence goes, England between 1500 and 1660 was relatively cold, suspicious, and violence-prone.[51]

Yet Stone detects a trend in the sixteenth and seventeenth centuries toward significant changes in the structure of English middle-class and upper-class family life: "Under pressure from the state and from Protestant moral theology, it shifted from a predominantly open structure to a more restrictedly nuclear one. The functions of this nuclear family were more and more confined to the nurture and socialization of the infant and young child, and the economic, emotional and sexual satisfaction of the husband and wife."[52] According to

[51]Lawrence Stone, *The Family, Sex, and Marriage in England, 1500–1800*, abridged ed. (New York: Harper and Row, 1979), 80. These historical differences are important, although Stone may have exaggerated them; but they should not be used to obscure extant and disturbing similarities between early modern and contemporary families. I am referring, of course, to spouse and child abuse. Stone has come under criticism for projecting contemporary standards of care and nurture onto the early modern English family and portraying its members as mean, pathological, and damaged. On this issue and for an alternative account of relations between mothers and sons which relies on structural, as opposed to psychological, dimensions of households, see Barbara J. Harris, "Property, Power, and Personal Relations: Elite Mothers and Sons in Yorkist and Early Tudor England," *Signs: Journal of Women in Culture and Society* 15 (Spring 1990), 606–632. For another account of early modern English family life, see Peter Laslett, *The World We Have Lost: England before the Industrial Age* (New York: Charles Scribner's Sons, 1965).

[52]Stone, *The Family, Sex, and Marriage in England*, 145.

Stone, the period 1660–1800 witnessed major changes in child-rearing practices among the gentry and upper bourgeoisie. It is during this time that "the mother" emerges to become a significant presence for children in a family undergoing privatization.

So the confusing facts concerning family structure and childhood during Hobbes's time would seem to be these. On the one hand, "up to the age of seven, the children were mostly left in the care of women, primarily their mother, nurse, and governess."[53] But on the other, a discernible ideology of modern bourgeois motherhood did not yet exist. As Miranda Chaytor and Jane Lewis argue, although women bore and raised children,

> mothering was not the prerogative of married women in a society where high adult mortality and frequent remarriage meant that many children were raised in the households of neighbors and kin: babies were cared for by their grandmothers, father's new wife, her widowed aunt, an older stepsister, a cousin or maid servant, as often as by their natural mothers. Seventeenth-century women valued their reputation for chastity, health and hard work, their integrity as housewives and traders; the qualities today associated with "mothering"—tenderness, self-sacrifice, caring—seem significantly absent as a source of honour and shame.[54]

Furthermore, the social system of child exchange (between families with too many mouths to feed and those that needed more labor; between upper-class families and child tenders and schools) militated against the intimacy and corresponding tensions of parent-child interaction that would become prevalent during subsequent centuries.

This historical information suggests one of two possible

[53]Ibid., 120.
[54]Miranda Chaytor and Jane Lewis, introduction to Alice Clark, *The Working Life of Women in the Seventeenth Century* (1919; rpt., London: Routledge and Kegan Paul, 1982), xxiv.

implications for the invocation of modern masculinity as an ideology during Hobbes's time. First, the fact that children were reared by *females* within an admittedly less intense psychosexual family environment is sufficient to make plausible the case for a masculine identity forged in opposition to the maternal-female.[55] And second, the "pre-Oedipal" environment here is insufficiently affect-laden to justify the retrospective application of modern masculine gender identity in the same sense in which it might be applicable to Marx and Mill.

Minimally, however, we can say this much about Hobbes's situation. He was embedded within a culture in the midst of social changes that yielded modern family life and whose gendered imagery is more like than unlike our own. To this extent we are entitled to question his work as modern and masculinist. As I concede in the next chapter, we cannot be sure that the thesis of modern masculine ideology adequately captures the actual ground of Hobbes's own frame of thought. What is plausible, however, is that his theory is open to such a gendered reading in the minds of subsequent readers. And this study, it should be remembered, is intended more as an interpretation from the contemporary feminist vantage point than as a historical reconstruction and recuperation of specific authorial intentions.

Let us now turn to the political theories of Hobbes, Marx, and Mill. I will explore the possibility that these claims and intimations concerning modern masculine ideology can be

[55]For studies of Descartes, Shakespeare, Francis Bacon, and Machiavelli which persuasively invoke object relations theory in spite of the fact that these men and their peers could not possibly have had experience of the modern nuclear family, see Susan Bordo, *The Flight to Objectivity: Essays on Cartesianism and Culture* (Albany: State University of New York Press, 1987); Kahn, *Man's Estate;* Evelyn Fox Keller, *Reflections on Gender and Science* (New Haven: Yale University Press, 1985); Pitkin, *Fortune Is a Woman.* These men were, however, reared by females; they lived during periods of significant social upheaval and change which yielded modern western culture; and they helped to inaugurate distinctively modern notions of knowledge, science, selfhood, and politics. Hobbes, I believe, also falls into this category of early modern notables.

substantiated, and, more important, that they promote plausible, useful, and even compelling rereadings which contribute to our contemporary understanding and assessment of modern political thinking. If these rereadings succeed, modern political theory qualifies less tentatively as a gendered discourse and, as such, is further amenable to feminist inquiry, scrutiny, and criticism.

CHAPTER TWO

Hobbesian (Hu)Man

He that is to govern a whole Nation, must read in himself,
not this, or that particular man; but Mankind: which though
it be hard to do, harder than to learn any Language or
Science; yet, when I shall have set down my own reading
orderly, and perspicuously, the pains left another, will be
onely to consider, if he also find not the same in himself. For
this kind of Doctrine, admitteth no other Demonstration.

—Thomas Hobbes, introduction to *Leviathan*

IN HIS MASTERWORK, *Leviathan*, Hobbes sought to provide a
comprehensive theory of civil society for a radically changing
era. During the late sixteenth and seventeenth centuries, early
modernity took shape in the midst of massive cultural and
political flux and realignment. Hobbes must be counted
among those who articulated and contributed to the specifically "modern" imposition of new form and meaning onto an
unstable, dangerous, and enigmatic world.

Modern political theory may be characterized by its radical
conventionalization of human practices, social norms, and
power-mediated relations; such practices, norms, and relations are understood to be rooted in specifically human desires, needs, and decisions, rather than in some suprahuman
mode of cosmological order or divine authority. "In modernity," as William Connolly writes,

> the insistence upon taking charge of the world comes into
> its own. Nature becomes a set of laws susceptible to human

knowledge, a deposit of resources for potential use or a set of vistas for aesthetic appreciation. While each of these orientations jostles with the others for priority, they all tend to place nature at the disposal of humanity. Human and non-human nature become material to work on. The world loses its earlier property as a text upon which the will of God is inscribed and through which humans can come to a more profound understanding of their proper place in the order of things.[1]

The task of the modern political theorist, then, is to elucidate the question of right (in the double sense of "correct" and "just") political order with reference to a world that has shrunk in ontological significance but expanded in terms of its possibilities for secular human design and manipulation. With specifically modern theorizing, and in significant contrast to contemporary postmodern concerns, human nature is thought to provide a dependable, secular ontological ground for theoretical efforts aimed at understanding and enhancing the human condition. Hobbes's account of human nature is, of course, one of the dramatic highlights of his political theory.

Why do we continue to read Hobbes today? What, aside from considerations of purely historical interest, makes him an important political thinker for our time, someone worth conversing with and against? Hobbes scholars have adduced a number of resonant connections between Hobbes's concerns and his political solutions to those concerns and the contemporary political condition. In a controversial and influential work, C. B. MacPherson has argued that Hobbes provides the first and freshest portrait of bourgeois, property-holding man. MacPherson has also suggested that we are drawn to Hobbes because his state of nature lurks in the horrifying scenario of nuclear holocaust and its sociopolitical aftermath for whoever

[1]William E. Connolly, *Political Theory and Modernity* (Oxford: Basil Blackwell, 1988), 2.

might survive.[2] Others see his principles actively at work in contemporary American politics, which preserves and perpetuates Hobbesian notions of ruthless individualism, transactional relations between individuals and among interest groups, a civil authority whose sole function is that of policeman, and a view of politics as conflict management between competing and private interests.[3] For some, Hobbes is a crucial connecting link between the more traditionally inspired political thought of the Renaissance and that of modern liberalism.[4] For others, notably the Straussian interpreters of Hobbes, he is credited with the disastrous inauguration of specifically modernist conceptions of political order and authority which have ever since steadily eroded our capacity for rigorous and ethical political theorizing. On this view, Hobbes is blamed, in the company of Machiavelli on one historical side and Nietzsche on the other, for the modern relativization of value and its decadent cohort, political pragmatism.[5] During the past decade, Hobbes has been invoked and scrutinized by new postmodern interrogators of modernity, by public-choice theorists, and by feminists who are exploring the curious and ambivalent fate of women within modern liberal theory and politics.[6]

[2]C.B. MacPherson, *The Political Theory of Possessive Individualism: Hobbes to Locke* (London: Oxford University Press, 1962); "Introduction" to Thomas Hobbes, *Leviathan*, ed. C. B. MacPherson (London: Penguin Books, 1968), 9–63.

[3]Frank Coleman, *Hobbes and America: Exploring the Constitutional Roots* (Toronto: University of Toronto Press, 1977).

[4]Albert O. Hirschman, *The Passions and the Interests: Political Arguments for Capitalism before Its Triumph* (Princeton: Princeton University Press, 1977); Norman Jacobson, *Pride and Solace: The Functions and Limits of Political Theory* (Berkeley: University of California Press, 1978), 51–92.

[5]Lawrence Berns, "Thomas Hobbes," in *History of Political Philosophy*, 3rd ed., ed. Leo Strauss and Joseph Cropsey (Chicago: University of Chicago Press, 1987), 396–429; Joseph Cropsey, "Hobbes and the Transition to Modernity," in *Ancients and Moderns: Essays on the Tradition of Political Philosophy in Honor of Leo Strauss*, ed. Joseph Cropsey (New York: Basic Books, 1964), 213–303; Leo Strauss, *The Political Philosophy of Hobbes: Its Basis and Its Genesis*, trans. Elsa M. Sinclair (Oxford: Clarendon Press, 1936; rpt., Chicago: University of Chicago Press, 1984).

[6]Connolly, *Political Theory and Modernity*, 16–40; Gregory S. Kavka, *Hobbesian Moral and Political Theory* (Princeton: Princeton University Press, 1986); Carole Pateman, *The Sexual Contract* (Stanford: Stanford University Press, 1988).

Hobbes is best known for his notorious yet compelling description of a state of nature in which life is grimly portrayed
as a war of all against all, where insecurity and fear are the
primary constants. His theoretical effort was to deduce a comprehensive theory of legitimate, uncontested, and stable civil
authority from a set of simple, supposedly incontrovertible,
and often dismal facts about human nature and the human
condition. In doing so he rejected both divine-right and major-
ity-rule theories of legitimate political authority, arguing instead for a secular, consent-based authority that would also
be capable of withstanding the vagaries of competing private
interests. The legitimacy of this authority was grounded by
Hobbes in the hypothetical consent of rational individuals in
the state of nature. These individuals would consent to a
common political authority on the basis of a rational calcula-
tion about the satisfaction of their desires for life and security
within two alternative social settings: (1) an anarchic state of
nature in which all individuals are "free" to pursue and protect any and all objects of their desires, and similarly "free"
to lose whatever they have acquired or attained at the hands
of other individuals; and (2) a civil order ruled by a central-
ized political authority to which all would be equally subject
and within which each individual would be "free" in a more
limited but also guaranteed sense. This initial basis of legitimate political authority could not, however, be renegotiated,
except by default, that is, during periods of upheaval and dissension in which civil society reverts to a state of nature.
Hence, Hobbes's political authority is fully sovereign and
self-reproducing over time. With very few exceptions, the
original contract ceding self-rule to a political ruler is nonne-
gotiable. As Hobbes presents it, the choice is clear to all
"right-thinking" minds.

   The contemporary fascination with Hobbes derives in part
from this juxtaposition of "liberal" and "traditional" arguments concerning legitimacy. On the one hand, legitimacy is
secured on the basis of individual consent. On the other hand,
Hobbes defines this consent in extremely narrow terms. For
those concerned with the authoritarian political tendencies of
postindustrial liberal societies, Hobbes offers the promise of

insight into how and why liberal politics has failed to measure up to its democratic promise.

I want to advance another frame of intersection between Hobbes's political theory and contemporary politics: that is, Hobbes's thought reflects and advances a distinctively modern masculinist orientation to the realm of social life. This reading of Hobbes by no means supersedes or replaces all others. Rather, it is offered as another interpretive angle on the work of a theorist who defies canonical packaging along limited and mutually exclusive axes of interpretation.

Placing Women as Readers and as Social Actors

Was Hobbes writing for and about humankind or men? While his theory seems to be addressed to humanity in general, and while Leviathan was rhetorically composed to reach a popular literate audience,[7] it is clear that Hobbes was writing for an adult male audience and from a male viewpoint. Literacy rates for Englishwomen of the mid-seventeenth century were quite low, and Hobbes had little reason to imagine that the women of his time would study and discuss his theoretical offering, much less be in a political position to implement it.[8]

---

[7]According to David Johnston, Leviathan "was a book of philosophy, but it was intended for a large, public audience and aimed to shape popular opinion directly, rather than through intermediaries alone. . . . It was perhaps the first work in the history of political philosophy to be designed entirely with this aim in mind." The Rhetoric of Leviathan (Princeton: Princeton University Press, 1986), 89.

[8]For information on the lives and status of Englishwomen during the sixteenth and seventeenth centuries, see Alice Clark, The Working Life of Women in the Seventeenth Century (1919; rpt., London: Routledge and Kegan Paul, 1982); Antonia Fraser, The Weaker Vessel (New York: Random House, 1984); Katherine Usher Henderson and Barbara F. McManus, eds., Half Humankind: Contexts and Texts of the Controversy about Women in England, 1540–1640 (Urbana: University of Illinois Press, 1985); Mary Prior, ed., Women in English Society, 1500–1800 (London: Methuen, 1985); Louise Tilly and Joan Scott, Women, Work, and Family (New York: Holt, Rinehart and Winston, 1978), 9–60.

Henderson and McManus argue that between 1580 and 1640, writing literacy among women in London stood at 10 percent; by the 1690s, it stood at 48 percent. Reading literacy rates may have been a bit higher. Leviathan was first published in England in 1651.

The occasional female ruler of English experience and memory is best understood as an exception to the rule of women's exclusion from political affairs and to the accepted patriarchal prerogatives of power. These prerogatives were debated and eventually recast (but not abolished) in modern form during the famous Locke-Filmer debate.[9] The political situation of women during this period is aptly summarized by Antonia Fraser:

> Under the common law of England at the accession of King James I, no female had any rights at all (if some were allowed by custom). As an unmarried woman her rights were swallowed up in her father's, and she was his to dispose of in marriage and at will. Once she was married her property become absolutely that of her husband. What of those who did not marry? Common law met that problem blandly by not recognizing it.[10]

According to Fraser, "where the status of the so-called weaker vessel was concerned, the seventeenth century saw very little improvement in real terms."[11] In reviewing the status of women in English society during the seventeenth century, we should also bear in mind that the persecution of witches and an active literary "debate" about women were in effect as well. The pamphlet wars of Renaissance England promoted a widespread popularization of still familiar antifeminine claims, highlighting and denouncing the dangerous sexual temptress, the dominating shrew, and the vain spendthrift.[12] If women during this period finally began to write in their

---

[9]For reviews and discussions of this debate, see Teresa Brennan and Carole Pateman, " 'Mere Auxiliaries to the Commonwealth': Women and the Origins of Liberalism," *Political Studies* 27 (1979), 183–200; Gordon Schochet, *Patriarchalism and Political Thought* (New York: Basic Books, 1975); Linda J. Nicholson, *Gender and History: The Limits of Social Theory in the Age of the Family* (New York: Columbia University Press, 1986).

[10]Fraser, *The Weaker Vessel*, 5.

[11]Ibid., 464.

[12]See Henderson and McManus, *Half Humankind*, 3–130.

own defense, they were constrained by the existing terms of the attack to advance counterimages of "good women" who were chaste, holy, and nurturing. The terms of this "debate" are another vital legacy of the culture that spawned liberal political theory.

Hobbes seems to have been neither perturbed by nor curious about the systematic civil inequality of women. As he observed in *Leviathan* without further comment: "For the most part Common-Wealths have been erected by the Fathers, not by the Mothers of families."[13] Several aspects of Hobbes's own theory make this silence noteworthy. For example, his deliberate underdescription of the sovereign ruler leaves the question of the sexual identity of that ruler quite open. Logically there is nothing in Hobbes's theory of legitimate sovereign authority to preclude a female's occupying the sovereign seat of authority. But this should not be taken as evidence of any particular pathbreaking generosity toward women as citizens or as rulers. Rather, Hobbes was attempting to sever the issue of legitimate authority and obedience due that authority from the personal or particular characteristics of the sovereign.

Hobbes did break ranks with the more avowedly patriarchal theorists in his description of the radical equality between all persons in the state of nature, where personal differences in wit and strength are canceled out by the simpler and more devastating ability of anyone to eliminate an opponent through calculated violence.[14] He may also be credited for his acknowledgement that the original form of parental authority was undoubtedly maternal before it was paternal: "In the state of nature it cannot be known who is the *father*, but by the testimony of the *mother*; the child therefore is his whose the

---

[13]Thomas Hobbes, *Leviathan*, ed. with intro. by C. B. MacPherson (London: Pelican, 1968), 253. All subsequent references to *Leviathan* will be to this edition.

[14]Ibid., 251–57; Hobbes, *The Citizen*, 221–220. All references to *On Man* and *The Citizen* are from Thomas Hobbes, *Man and Citizen*, ed. and intro. Bernard Gert (Gloucester, Mass.: Peter Smith, 1978).

mother will have it, and therefore her's. Wherefore original dominion over *children* belongs to the *mother:* and among men no less than other creatures, the birth follows the belly."[15] In contrast to contract theorists such as Locke and Rousseau, Hobbes smuggles many fewer patriarchal presuppositions into his state of nature. Nevertheless, this portrayal of mother-right and radical equality among adults quickly gives way to more familiar presumptions about sexual difference and the political consequences of such difference.

For example, in his discussion in *On Man* of the problem of the succession of sovereign authority, Hobbes writes: "Among children the males carry the pre-eminence; in the beginning perhaps, because for the most part, . . . they are fitter for the administration of greater matters, but specially of wars."[16] What makes them fitter and how males got to be fitter are questions Hobbes never addresses. These are questions we are entitled to ask, however, for they lie within the established radical equality in the state of nature, which he explicitly attributes to relations between males and females:

And thus in the state of nature, every woman that bears children, becomes both a *mother* and a *lord*. But what some say, that in this case the *father*, by reason of the pre-eminence of sex, and not the *mother* becomes *lord*, signifies nothing. For both reason shows the contrary; because the inequality of their natural forces is not so great, that the man could get the dominion over the woman without war.[17]

The theoretical slide into specifically male-centered presumptions about social relations, presumptions that effect a virtual elision of women as power brokers, is made manifest in Hobbes's definition of family: "A *father* with his sons and servants, grown into a civil person by virtue of his paternal

[15]Hobbes, *The Citizen*, 213.
[16]Ibid., 219.
[17]Ibid., 213.

jurisdiction, is called a *family*."[18] Female servants notwithstanding, where have the daughters and wives gone? Hobbes's definition, which pivots on the figure of the father, simultaneously requires and effaces the presence of mothers within the family. Women, together with children, do get some notice in *On Man* and again in *Leviathan* for their unique propensity for crying, which Hobbes attributes to the fact that they "have the least hope in themselves and the most in friends."[19] Presumably, women and children cry in order to elicit sympathy and aid for themselves. They are joined by cattle in *Leviathan* as those possessions that men in the state of nature stand to lose in their inevitable skirmishes with other men:

> So that in the nature of man, we find three principal causes of quarrell. First, Competition; secondly, Diffidence; thirdly, Glory.
> The first, maketh men invade for Gain; the second, for Safety; and the third, for Reputation. The first use Violence, to make themselves Masters of other mens persons, wives, children, and cattell; the second, to defend them. . . .[20]

This excerpt reveals the actual meaning embedded within an arguably generic use of "men" in Hobbes's theory, as it illustrates the curious fate of females who have somehow passed from specified equality and original mother-right to a very different status as wives. It leaves little doubt that Hobbes's "man" is not only a property holder, as C. B. MacPherson has argued, but also male and gendered. This assessment is confirmed in a number of other examples, including the following account of homosocial (between men) and heterosexual (man-to-woman) love: "The love, whereby man loves man, is understood in two ways; and good will appertains to both. But it is called one kind of love when we wish

---

[18] Ibid., 217.
[19] Hobbes, *On Man*, 59; see also Hobbes, *Leviathan*, 125–126.
[20] Hobbes, *Leviathan*, 185.

ourselves well, and another when we wish well to others. Therefore a male neighbor is usually loved one way, a female another; for in loving the former, we seek his good, in loving the latter, our own."[21]

These examples are instructive for what they suggest about Hobbes's implicit exemption of women from the life ways and standards of a civil order built on the foundation of a secular state of nature. In Hobbes's theory, females occupy a kind of nether zone, a category of persons who may be loosely located under the rubric of humanity and human nature, invoked when their specificity merits comment or is useful to Hobbes's theoretical attempts to recast the foundations of legitimate authority,[22] but who are also excluded, tacitly and explicitly, from the core substance of the theoretical argument concerning "man."

The criterion of humanist generalization is invoked by Hobbes as an attribute of his own method: "Whosoever looketh into himself, and considereth what he doth, when he does *think, opine, reason, hope, fear,* &c. and upon what grounds; he shall thereby read and know, what are the thoughts and Passions of all other men, upon the like occasions."[23] Would Hobbes have women look into themselves as a test and confirmation of his theory of human nature? It is likely that Hobbes did not have women in mind here. This is consistent with the overall ethos of the age, and it is manifest in Hobbes's failure to carry out the implications of his occasional remarks on women's status in the state of nature. To-

[21]Hobbes, *On Man,* 60.
[22]For example, Hobbes's articulation of original mother-right is bound up with his criticism of specifically patriarchal conceptions of legitimate authority, such as the notion that children owe obedience to the father because he has "created" them. Hobbes's alternative account is that children "consent" to parental authority in a contractlike form of exchange. Hobbes is then able to preserve a qualified symmetry between familial and political modes of authority while undoing the premodern patriarchal connection between them. This symmetry is qualified along the lines of a family's ability to defend itself against other marauding families. The family able to do so is a commonwealth unto itself.
[23]Hobbes, *Leviathan,* 82.

day, however, in keeping with the spirit of Hobbes's maxim that we "read mankind in ourselves," such a task is an important part of the effort to come to critical terms with the Hobbesian vision of a civil order built on the foundation of "human" passions and requirements.

Passionate Man

The quest for the man in Hobbes's account of "man" must begin with the passions. It is all too tempting to portray Hobbes as a Grand Inquisitor intent on repressing the dangerous and unruly passions of men in the interests of a secure civil peace.[24] Hobbes himself often contributes to this view, as, for example, when he writes that the "Passions unguided, are for the most part meere Madnesse."[25] Yielding to such temptation, however, generates an overly facile and misleading account. For Hobbes is a dedicated student of the passions. Furthermore, within Hobbes's account some of the passions constitute a tangible foundation for human reason and are the point of origin for attempts by men in the state of nature to secure peace. The passion for life and a reason motivated in large part by an instinctual and lusty curiosity about the world of causes and effects converge in the state of nature to produce that enlightened self-interest through which men come to appreciate the dictates of right reason and to understand the civil requirements for a lasting peace and felicitous life. If nature has made man unfit for society, it has also provided the means for man to create an artificial representation and enforcement of the naturally situated dictates of right reason, which are presumably available to all rational minds. For though the "perturbations of mind"— that is, emotions such as fear, anger, and greed—impede

---

[24]For an example of an interpretation that tends in this direction, see Jacobson, *Pride and Solace.*

[25]Hobbes, *Leviathan,* 142.

the acquisition of knowledge, "there is no man who is not sometimes in a quiet [state of] mind."[26]

Curiosity, defined by Hobbes as a "Lust of the mind," which "exceedeth the short vehemence of any carnall Pleasure,"[27] is, along with reason, what distinguishes men from animals. We would also do well to consider Hobbes's own self-attributed passion for lustily conceived intellectual activity, which he describes in vivid and sensuous terms: "How great a pleasure it is to the mind of man to be ravished in the vigorous and perpetual embraces of the most beautiful world."[28] If he calls for a harnessing of the passions in civil society, such an arrangement is designed to guarantee some security for a portion of their satisfaction against the certitude of their nonsatisfaction in a state of nature characterized by the perpetual possibility of war. He has no blueprint for the elimination of the passions in civil society, although he does argue for their artificial control: "Laws were not invented to take away, but to direct men's actions; even as nature ordained the banks, not to stay, but to guide the course of the stream."[29] It is precisely because he takes the passions so seriously that his prescriptions for civil society seem so stringent. Yet, his controls are purely external; there is little hint in his work of a desire to tamper with the passions themselves, to attempt a reconstruction of the human subject. If Hobbes's ideal society leaves no room for destabilizing public discourse and social revolt on matters of conscience, at least he has the good grace to leave conscience and the realm of desire alone. Bentham,

---

[26]Hobbes, The Citizen, 148.

[27]Hobbes, Leviathan, 124.

[28]"Author's Epistle," from Thomas Hobbes, English Works, vol. 1, cited in Miriam Reik, The Golden Lands of Thomas Hobbes (Detroit: Wayne State University Press, 1977), 80. This sexual imagery, of course, is also of a piece with the Baconian sexualization of nature and the male scientific intellect on the model of heterosexual seduction. For a related discussion of Bacon, see Evelyn Keller, Reflections on Gender and Science (New Haven: Yale University Press, 1985), 33–42.

[29]Hobbes, The Citizen, 268. Compare this with John Stuart Mill's suggestion that certain instincts should be "extirpated" through "disuse," which is examined in Chapter 4.

the Panopticon, and the interfering clinical gaze were not far behind;[30] but such modernist dreams of manipulation and control designed to bridge (that is, "humanize") the gap between human nature and social order were not on Hobbes's agenda.

Hobbes's work, then, offers an invitation to consider the passions in their full scope. It is on this terrain that we must initially search for hints of an identifiably modern masculine outlook. Because the passions are the building blocks of his method, contributing to his extensive and related treatments of human nature, social relations, the state of nature, civil authority, and political obligation, they provide the logical starting point for an inquiry into his conception of politics. The question that we bring to Hobbes is this: Is modern masculinity inscribed within his account of the passions?

Man is portrayed by Hobbes as a kind of desiring machine. The relevant point is not so much whether Hobbes believed that this portrayal was literally true. Rather, it is that for Hobbes, the language pertaining to the movement of a desiring machine was the only way to apprehend human nature scientifically.[31] By "scientific" inquiry, Hobbes meant the systematic, deductive elaboration of relationships between causes and their effects or consequences. His attempt to develop a scientific method is made manifest in his painstaking step-by-step reconstruction of man, which begins with the smallest and presumably least-contested bits of usable information, which are then logically combined into more complex formulas. These bits of data name the elementary motions of a body toward or away from various other objects. He begins his catalogue of the simple passions with "appetite," or desire, and "aversion," which denote movement toward or away

[30]See Michel Foucault, *Discipline and Punish: The Birth of the Modern Prison,* trans. Alan Sheridan (New York: Random House, 1979).

[31]On this point, see Michael Oakeshott, "Introduction" to his edition of Thomas Hobbes, *Leviathan* (Oxford: Basil Blackwell, n.d.), and "The Moral Life in the Writings of Thomas Hobbes," in his *Rationalism in Politics* (London: Methuen, 1962), 248–300.

from other moving objects that are perceived to cause pleasure or pain. His subsequent definition and cataloguing of those passions that constituted the linguistic fare of his time is built on the simple foundation of aversive or appetitive motion. "Love" is but another name for desire when the desired object is present, approachable, and attainable. "Contempt" is "nothing else but an immobility . . . of the Heart, in resisting the action of certain things."[32] Finally, the more complex passions and their behavioral manifestations such as courage, ambition, jealousy, and admiration involve such things as the perceived likelihood of attainment of the desired object, the specific objects that are loved or hated, and the simpler passions in various combinations. Weeping and laughter, for example, are both "sudden motions" prompted by "sudden dejection" and "sudden glory," respectively, in the face of unexpected pleasure or pain.[33]

Hobbes's approach to the passions is a scrupulously analytic one in which he attempts to give his avowed nominalist method full play. He seeks to provide a rigorous means of defining standard terms of everyday language such that his subsequent discussion of human nature, social relations, and civil society, along with the anticipated objections of critics, will not be muddled by imprecise thinking and confusing rhetoric. For "the Light of humane minds is Perspicuous Words, but by exact definitions first snuffed, and purged from ambiguity."[34] What is especially striking about Hobbes's catalogue of the passions is his attempt to simplify radically, and thus to master cognitively, the various yearnings and torments of the heart and mind by rendering them in a vocabulary of mechanical motion.

While Hobbes's subsequent account of human nature is undoubtedly pessimistic, it is important to bear in mind that his catalogue of the passions contains an itemization of many we would label "good" in the sense of being conducive to

[32]Hobbes, *Leviathan*, 120.
[33]Ibid., 125–126.
[34]Ibid., 116.

happiness and sociability. Hobbes's individual is surely an egoist; but he is not necessarily antisocial. Courage, benevolence, magnanimity, good will, and kindness find their way into the catalogue of the passions that Hobbes lays out in *Leviathan*.[35] While life in the state of nature may be "solitary, poore, nasty, brutish, and short,"[36] human beings are by no means invariably nasty. Unfortunately, nasty behavior sets the pace for everyone else, who must anticipate and preempt it by means of countervailing behavior.

Those who would refute Hobbes by pointing out various features of human behavior or sensibility that are conducive to peaceful social relations are taking the wrong tack, for these are never enough to override the fundamental anarchy of social interaction. Hobbes's point is not that human beings are especially evil or deliberately antisocial. It is rather that we inevitably get in one another's way. As appetitive machines that engage incessantly in the pursuit of pleasure and avoidance of pain, we cannot help "bumping" into and thereby impeding the "motion" of others. Totally impeded motion is what we commonly refer to as death. For Hobbes, the social world is a crowded and therefore dangerous and inhospitable arena of striving machines in motion: "So that in the first place, I put for a generall inclination of all mankind, a perpetuall and restlesse desire of Power after power, that ceaseth onely in Death."[37]

For my purposes, the noteworthy aspect of Hobbes's chronicle of the passions is not that it paints an ugly portrait of human nature but rather that it presents a view of desire,

---

[35]It is interesting that Hobbes chose to eliminate "compassion" from the *Leviathan* version of the human passions. He provides a rather extensive definition in *On Man* which is worth citing: "To grieve because of another's evil, that is, to feel another's pain and to suffer with him, that is, to imagine that another's evil could happen to oneself, is called compassion." Hobbes, *On Man*, 61. It is doubtful that Hobbes forgot to include this in *Leviathan*, given the close overlap between the two sections in each work. Obviously he had his reasons for keeping it out. Perhaps he feared it would undercut the political message he was trying to get across in *Leviathan*.
[36]Hobbes, *Leviathan*, 186.
[37]Ibid., 161.

motivation, and identity that is strictly *self*-originating and self-driven. The Hobbesian self is clearly and unambiguously delineated. Objects of desire derive from and exist for the individual will. Commonality of desire—for example, the universal fear and avoidance of death—figures only as a sum total of individual desires bound in externally oriented allegiance toward a shared common object. What is markedly absent here, as many Hobbes critics have noted—without, however, seeing the gendered contours of this gap—is the notion of types of desire constituted socially or intersubjectively. Objects of desire for Hobbes can refer only to individual—never to collectively or intersubjectively constituted—yearnings. Those who might invoke persuasion, as a counterexample to Hobbes's ultraindividualized conception of desire, must contend with the Hobbesian retort that persuasion, after all, is nothing but the "displacement" of one will by another.

In the Hobbesian world, desire is a private and individual affair, some of whose outward effects must be checked by civil authority. But desire itself has no place in the political arena of discourse and lawmaking. Hobbes's egoism "is only the individuality of a creature shut up, without hope of immediate release, within the world of his own imagination. Man is, by nature, the victim of solipsism; he is an *individuae substantia* distinguished by incommunicability."[38] What communication there is takes place as a result of agreement on the definition of terms. Hence, Hobbes's nominalist method and his account of individualist egoism are fundamentally connected. Nominalism is the epistemological counterpart to an ontology of solipsistic egos.

Hobbes's rendition of the primary play of ego-bound desire is recapitulated in his account of social intercourse, described vividly by Michael Oakeshott:

> Between birth and death, the self as imagination and will is an indestructible unity, whose relations with other individu-

---

[38]Oakeshott, "Introduction" to *Leviathan*, liv.

als are purely external. Individuals may be collected together, may be added, may be substituted for one another or made to represent one another, but can never modify one another or compose a whole in which their individuality is lost. Every reason is individualized, and becomes merely the reasoning of an individual without power or authority to oblige acceptance by others: to convince a man is not to enjoy a common understanding with him, but to displace his reason by yours.[39]

This thoroughly "inviolable" ego, however, is perpetually threatened by the distinct possibility of dissolution, namely, death at the hands of a social opponent. This stark social landscape provides the essential components for Hobbes's depiction of a civil order that is either governed by the strong hand of authority (an inviolable ego in the ultimate sense) or reduced to a state of internal dissension (signifying death for civil authority as well as for particular citizens.) Clearly evident here is a thoroughgoing preoccupation with the border integrity of an ego that is strictly delineated and self-contained, and as such is a potential victim of similarly constructed egos. Natural men, along with "artificial" men (commonwealths), are similarly vulnerable to the violence of boundary skirmishes.

Norman Jacobson has suggested that "we still read *Leviathan* after three centuries . . . because we have all experienced the threat to the self implicit in the dread of personal annihilation."[40] We could further refine Jacobson's observation by asking whether this threat of personal annihilation is not also significantly tinged with a specifically masculine sense of selfhood. For what we find in Hobbes's account is a vital concern with the survival of a gendered subject conceived in modern masculine terms. The strict differentiation of self from others, identity conceived in exclusionary terms, and perceived threats to an ego thus conceived which is vulnerable to dis-

[39]Ibid., lv–lvi.
[40]Jacobson, *Pride and Solace*, 59.

placement or dissolution by an invader all recapitulate issues encountered and constructed in the process of securing a masculine identity vis-à-vis the female maternal presence. They resonate with Freud's observation: "It is only in men that I have found the fear of being eaten up."[41]

These themes receive their fullest treatment in Hobbes's state of nature, that rich imaginary zone that functions as an intermediary state of reconstruction from the rudimentary building blocks of human nature, the passions, to the completed architecture of civil society. In the state of nature, Hobbes's masculine egoism carries the day. Furthermore, the specifically gendered dimension of this egoism is underscored by a radical atomism erected on the denial of maternity.

The State of Nature: Of Men and Mushrooms

In *The Citizen*, where Hobbes elaborated in a systematic and preliminary fashion those aspects of the state of nature that would make his prescriptions for civil society in *Leviathan* so welcome and reasonable, he asks us to "consider men as if but even now sprung out of the earth, and suddenly, like mushrooms, come to full maturity, without all kind of engagement to each other."[42] Although Hobbes does not explicitly repeat this imaginative directive in *Leviathan*, it is obviously at work there in the shadows of his description of the state of nature, which recapitulates so much else from the earlier text.

The mushroom is a charming and ingenious metaphorical choice; it works in ways that "cabbages" or "maple trees" would not, conveying a host of images and associations that

---

[41]Sigmund Freud, "Female Sexuality," in *The Standard Edition of the Complete Psychological Works of Sigmund Freud*, vol. 21, trans. and ed. James Strachey (London: Hogarth Press, 1975), 237. Freud's comment continues: "This fear is referred to the father, but it is probably the product of a transformation of oral aggressivity directed at the mother. The child wants to eat up its mother from whom it has had its nourishment; in the case of the father there is no such obvious determinant for the wish."

[42]Hobbes, *The Citizen*, 205.

are worth considering. Mushrooms do seem to spring up
overnight; they grow rapidly in the wild and require no special
tending. By means of his state of nature, Hobbes wants to
eliminate factors such as socialization, education, and other
cultural means of "cultivating" human beings, removing those
"secondary" features of human behavior and motivation that
might mistakenly be attributed to "first" nature. His insistence
that "men are born unapt for society" requires a careful distinguishing of learned civility from man's innate disposition.[43]
Another feature of mushrooms is that they grow in clusters;
hence, Hobbes is able to slip in a picture of human beings in
close proximity. The image of mushrooms reminds us that
humans will inevitably confront one another as desiring machines on potentially conflicting trajectories of motion. Man
in the state of nature may be a radical individual, but, like the
mushroom, he is not solitary. Finally, mushrooms reproduce
quietly, invisibly, and asexually: spores are scattered by the
wind and land haphazardly, sprouting when temperature and
moisture conditions are just right. This feature of the metaphorical image invites the reader to accept quiescently one of
the most incredible features of Hobbes's hypothetical state of
nature. It is this: that men are not born of, much less nurtured
by, women, or anyone else for that matter.

   In the process of extracting an abstract man for rational
perusal, Hobbes has also expunged human reproduction and
early nurturance from his account of basic human nature and
primordial human relations. Such a descriptive strategy en-
sures that Hobbes can present a thoroughly atomistic subject,
one whose individual rights—sparsely conceived—clearly
precede any obligation to belong to civil society. These rights
function within Hobbesian theory as the currency of consent,
as the foundation of legitimate political authority, and as the
absolute limit beyond which political authority may not tres-

---

[43]In *The Citizen*, Hobbes devotes a lengthy footnote to the issue of the
distinction between natural and acquired behavior, apparently anticipating
popular disagreement with his unsavory formulation of an originally asocial
and egoistical human nature. It is located in the section entitled "Of the State
of Men without Civil Society," 110.

pass. With the help of the mushroom image and its associated metaphorical derivatives, Hobbes's atomism brilliantly and consistently affirms the self-sufficiency of man alone in the crowded midst of other men, even as it reveals the inherent limitations of this sufficiency in the absence of a commonly recognized political enforcer of rules.

Some readers will object that maternity is by no means denied by Hobbes, and they will cite his discussions of original mother-right in *The Citizen* and *Leviathan*. This objection, I believe, suffers from an overly literal loyalty to a few passages whose full implications, as I have already argued, were never embraced by Hobbes. Hobbes invokes the figure of the mother when she suits his purpose of developing an alternative account of legitimate power to that of the patriarchalists. He conveniently forgets her after that. The outstanding questions left in the wake of Hobbes' forgetfulness are these: How did radically equal males and females in the state of nature become so differentiated? Where in the state of nature, and how, do we account for the move from mother-right to a situation in which males are fighting over one another's possessions and "wives"? It is in this unarticulated move that the radical equality of the state of nature, used by Hobbes to undermine the legitimacy of nonconsensual forms of authority and to underscore the irresolvable anarchism of the state of nature, has become a radical equality among males, and motherless males at that.[44]

---

[44]For related discussions of the curious Hobbesian narrative of women in the state of nature, see: Seyla Benhabib, "The Generalized and the Concrete Other: The Kohlberg-Gilligan Controversy and Moral Theory," in *Women and Moral Theory*, ed. Eva Feder Kittay and Diana T. Meyers (Totowa, N.J.: Rowman and Littlefield, 1987), 154–177; Jean B. Elshtain, "Methodological Sophistication and Conceptual Confusion: A Critique of Mainstream Political Science," in *The Prism of Sex: Essays in the Sociology of Knowledge*, ed. Julia Sherman and Evelyn Torton Beck (Madison: University of Wisconsin Press, 1979), 229–249; Jane Flax, "Political Philosophy and the Patriarchal Unconscious: A Psychoanalytic Perspective on Epistemology and Metaphysics," in *Discovering Reality: Feminist Perspectives on Epistemology, Metaphysics, Methodology, and Philosophy of Science*, ed. Sandra Harding and Merrill B. Hintikka (Dordrecht: D. Reidel, 1983), 245–281. I am grateful to John Keeler for criticisms that helped me sharpen this part of the argument.

The operative point here is not whether Hobbes's state of nature is realistic. No state-of-nature construct is going to be "realistic" if what we mean is that it faithfully conforms to the contours of life as we know and cherish it. For state-of-nature devices in political theory are intended to make us more self-conscious about the unreflectively accepted particularities of our specific life forms. They could not incite this social self-scrutiny if they simply reproduced models of extant sociopolitical organization. But we do not need to ask: What is the *point* of including and excluding particular features of social life, of rearranging the available stock of "dependent" and "independent" variables? Is our understanding of the human condition enhanced or handicapped by the theoretical simplifications provided by the theorist? We are entitled to query Hobbes on his fully formed and unmothered men precisely because his individualism rests securely on this point, and also because it violates some essential features of modern social life. Just as a state of nature populated by immortal creatures would be too wide of the mark to be useful in helping us come to grips with specifically political predicaments in this life, so too does a state of nature populated by mushroomlike men throw out too much. Eliminating mothers as social actors also makes it that much easier to read "males" into "man," a train of thinking to which Hobbes (and the unwary reader), as I have argued, is already hostage.

In fairness to Hobbes, it should be pointed out that he anticipated objections to his atomistic formulation of the primordial individual and even specifically addressed the social needs of infants: "It is true indeed, that to man by nature, or as man, that is, as soon as he is born, solitude is an enemy; for infants have need of others to help them live. . . . Wherefore I deny not that men (even nature compelling) desire to come together. . . . [Yet], it is one thing to desire, another to be in capacity fit for what we desire."[45] In other words, the primordial need of infants for care should not be construed as evidence of a basic capacity for sociability within the species.

[45]Hobbes, *The Citizen*, 110.

Furthermore, Hobbes takes special pains in addressing the particular relationship between parents and their offspring.[46] Do children "owe" their parents obedience? Is parental authority legitimate; and if so, on what grounds? Hobbes's answer is most ingenious: the parent–child relationship is rendered into contract form. Children "agree" to abide by parental authority in exchange for their physical survival, just as the unfortunate inhabitants of militarily vanquished territories "agree" to abide by the conquering political authority in exchange for their lives. Parental authority, in other words, is legitimate by virtue of an implicit contract.

The mushroom imagery—in its unmistakable denial of the nurturant and intersubjective aspects of social life—makes that much more plausible a central tenet of Hobbes's theory of civil authority and obligation to that authority. As Charles Taylor has argued, the liberal doctrine of the primacy of rights relies on an atomistic conception of the individual in the sense of affirming "the self-sufficiency of man alone."[47] In this discussion, "self-sufficiency" refers not to the ability of the child to survive alone in the wilderness (as Hobbes himself admitted), but rather, to the insistent denial of the notion that characteristically "human" capacities need particular social or life forms in which to develop. In the state-of-nature scene under consideration, which we could well subtitle "The Case of the Missing Mother" (granted, mothers do make a brief appearance in Hobbes's discussion of "paternal government"), the issue concerns the ways in which early maternal and parental care provide a social, intersubjective context for the development of particular capacities in children—emotional, cognitive, and social—which are presupposed in Hobbes's state-of-nature man, who is capable of implementing compacts and contracts as well as of deducing the dictates of right reason from his natural circumstances. Hobbes's metaphor aims precisely at avoiding any discussion of the etiology

---

[46]Ibid., 211–215; Hobbes, *Leviathan*, 251–256.

[47]Charles Taylor, "Atomism," in *Power, Possessions, and Freedom: Essays in Honor of C. B. MacPherson*, ed. Alkis Kontos (Toronto: University of Toronto Press, 1979), 41.

of such capacities, and for good reason. In providing us with fully sprung men and tracing out their hypothetical social exchanges, Hobbes keeps his schedule of rights to a bare minimum: the right to life, maximum self-defined pleasure so long as it does not interfere with the pleasure or rights of others, and maximum freedom from pain. He makes social and civil obligation a purely pragmatic affair, external to the preconstituted identity of the subject; such obligation is derived from natural right and, hence, is secondary to it. Hobbes's bare-bones schedule of rights provides the theoretical justification for his carefully argued position against political rebellion. We have little to gain and much to lose by contesting political authority, unless our physical lives or the means to life are at stake. Substantive "quality of life" issues have no bearing on the formal question of legitimacy.

The Hobbesian state of nature, then, is an analytic and rhetorical device aimed at stripping bare the requirements and basic materials of civil society so that the political theorist can establish the full force of the pragmatic need for a civil order governed by virtually irrefutable authority. Such a civil order, argues Hobbes, is mandated by nature, and its role is the purely restraining one of keeping appetitive machines in check but still in motion. In civil society the atomistic individuals of the state of nature remain essentially unchanged, still mushroomlike, except for their symmetrically contracted consent to a singular civil authority brought about by the sum of their individual fears of injury, loss of property, and untimely death. Death, that most radical of equalizers in the state of nature, is transposed into the singular power of the sovereign authority to punish. And fear, which in the state of nature kept men at suspicious and preemptive odds with one another, becomes the social gluten of the civil order.

In sum, Hobbes's civil society has no transformative effect on its body politic. His grand artifice consists of a clever recombination of the given elements of the state of nature. These elements are "natural" males atomistically conceived along egoistic masculine lines. This masculine tenor may be found initially in Hobbes's conception of a self-possessed and discrete ego, one that is unassailable except in combative terms, and is socially approachable only on the terms of contracted and nominalist exchanges. It is an ego constituted in strict either-or terms of total integrity unto itself or total disintegration at the hands of a similarly constructed opposing ego. We can discern modern masculinity at work in the fantasy pattern that underlies this account: men magically sprung like mushrooms, unmothered and unfathered. While such a fantasy deals a blow to parenthood and to the organic notion of generational continuity, it strikes especially hard at the maternal contribution, whose denial is uniquely remarkable and difficult to implement since it is so biologically and socially apparent (even to Hobbes). Hobbes's omniscient and self-sprung ego owes no dues to others except those that are freely and individually contracted.[48]

Hobbes's civil order, with its contractually designated and minimally conceived obligations designed to counter the dangerous social perplexities of proximity and ambivalence, assumes distinctly modern masculine characteristics. At the heart of Hobbes's conception of the good civil order is a particular notion of the human subject. An identity that is spontaneously conceived and solipsistically self-constituted requires an all-out repudiation of interpersonal factors. Hence the denial of the maternal contribution. Within the psychoanalytic frame of reference explored in Chapter 1, modern masculinity is achieved at the cost of a denial of the maternal contribution to and in oneself. If the denial of the (m)other is elaborated and achieved at the individual level of personal identity, extending it to a generalized view of the human condition is a relatively easy step. We cannot be sure that this characterization correctly or adequately captures the original sensibility of Hobbes's thought. But I can suggest with more assurance that

---

[48]Hobbes's notion of "free" contract, of course, is stretched to accommodate situations of coercion. The child, for example, "contracts" with the parental care giver, offering obedience in exchange for physical care. This contract is "valid" even though children, according to Hobbes, are not fully rational or independent.

Hobbes's work resonated with just such a set of meanings in the minds of subsequent readers; that part of the appeal and sheer power of Hobbes's analysis may be traced to this modern psychological narrative within his theory.

Good-Bye Mother, Good-Bye Father: Postpatriarchal Authority and Obligation

Hobbes's denial of the (m)other, with its unmistakable ramifications on his portrayal of atomistic identity and contractual social intercourse, is also refracted in the political centerpiece of his theory, the account of legitimate authority and obedience due that authority. As the inaugurator of a modern liberal tradition that deliberately opposes status hierarchies in the name of the abstract individual who is equal to all other abstract individuals, Hobbes's theory attempts to break the more traditional, premodern associations between authority, persons, and their unique (often divinely ordained) attributes. As a result of this conceptual shift, authority is characterized by Hobbes as simultaneously arbitrary (that is, conventional) and absolute. It is arbitrary in the sense that the question of who might be invested with civil authority is effectively inconsequential for Hobbes. Legitimate authority and its relevant exercise has little to do with personal attributes, expertise, or status. What really matters for Hobbes is only that a strong, central, and uncontested form of authority be identifiably located in some one person or executive body and that the problem of succession be abstractly settled ahead of its required implementation. In throwing out divine right on the one hand and renewable or renegotiable majority choice on the other as legitimating foundations for political authority, Hobbes made enemies out of two key and opposed political camps of his time, traditional royalists and democratic libertarians. Small wonder that he portrayed himself as a solitary and heroic fighter in the midst of hostile opponents.[49]

This deauthorization of particular rulers and particularized

---

[49]Hobbes, *Leviathan*, 75.

citizens, pursued by Hobbes at the expense of divinely and democratically sanctioned authority, is thematically implicated in a prior deauthorization of the mother that occurs in the state of nature.[50] The connecting link lies in the depersonalization of authority. Maternal (as well as patriarchal) power embodies a view of authority and obligation to which Hobbes's modern scheme is thoroughly opposed. Not only is maternal authority indelibly personal and particular, but it also stands in a complex relation to its subjects, one that cannot be characterized in the simple, linear terms of commandments and prescriptions with merely behavioral consequences—that is, consequences that are external to the identity of the behaving agent-child. Maternal authority is at least partially introjected. (The force and content of such introjection is, of course, significantly dependent on the qualitative strength and intimacy of parent–child relations, which vary historically and culturally.) For this reason, the relation to parental authority cannot be cast in simple contractarian terms. That Hobbes went to a good deal of trouble to portray parental authority in precisely this fashion suggests that he detected some significant difficulties worth attending to. Hobbes deliberately and systematically treats the relation between parent and child, sovereign and subject, in the same way: "The preserved oweth all to the preserver." The terms of allegiance and obedience to authority are strictly external to the preconstituted identities of the participants. With this assertion Hobbes has succeeded in displacing two key parental figures: the traditional patriarch, who claimed authority on the basis of his lineage to Adam and his procreative role, and the mother, with no prior political claims within the patriarchal legacy and no subsequent chance for a "postpatriarchal" emergence as an authority figure.[51]

---

[50]For a related discussion of "deauthorization," see Zelda Bronstein, "Psychoanalysis without the Father," *Humanities in Society* 3 (Spring 1980), 199–212.

[51]*The Citizen*, 213. I use the term *postpatriarchal* with hesitation, since I agree with Carole Pateman, who argues, in *The Sexual Contract*, that the term *patriarchy* should not be limited to simple father-right but rather should be extended to include male-right. In this context, I am using *patriarchal* in the more limited sense.

The Leviathan, Hobbes's "artificial," man-made political masterpiece, is effectively composed of a body politic of social orphans who have socially acculturated themselves, whose desires are situated within the terrain and trajectory of self-generated movement. Disagreements are likely to erupt and—because there is no common or shared means for adjudicating between competing private desires—there must be a locus of authority that can definitively pronounce on such disputes. Such pronouncements must be obeyed, not because they are intrinsically correct or in our individual best interests, but simply because they are the singular voice of civil authority. The prime political directive, after all, is peace, in keeping with Hobbes's minimalist conception of the basic right to life; and justice, within the frame of Hobbes's nominalism, refers simply to a correspondence to the written law. Norman Jacobson's vivid image of the lips of Hobbes's sovereign pressed to our ears conveys this distinctive feature of Hobbesian authority.[52] We are forced to listen but "free" to obey or disobey, although we must be prepared to accept the price of disobedience. Whatever the response, however, we are essentially unchanged by the process. Our relation to sovereign authority, like our relations to fellow human beings, is purely calculating and instrumental, located within a behavioral panorama inhabited by strictly differentiated individuals whose highest civic achievement is mutual accommodation—live and let live.

Hobbes as Hero

Having explored the substance of Hobbes's political theory, I now turn to Hobbes's style and what Sheldon Wolin has termed the "informing intention" of Hobbes's work.[53] All too often in political theory, the question of theoretical substance is neatly divorced from the more aesthetic question of literary

[52]Jacobson, *Pride and Solace*, 86.
[53]Sheldon S. Wolin, *Hobbes and the Epic Tradition of Political Theory* (Los Angeles: University of California Press, 1970).

style and rhetoric, as if how a theorist communicates had little to do with what he seeks to communicate.[54] Yet substance and style, often wedded within rhetorical strategies, are not so easily separated.

In stylistic terms and in terms of the often strained relation between his "walk" and his "talk"—between his avowed philosophy of "right method" and his actual implementation of that method—Hobbes is a fascinating patchwork of contrasts, as many commentators have noted. His skeptical, deductive, and nominalist epistemology coexists with a genuine respect and eye for the empirical lessons of experience. When Hobbes insists that he would learn more about anatomy and physiology by accompanying a midwife on her rounds than from reading the Scholastic texts of physicians, or, as in the opening pages of *Leviathan*, when he entreats his readers to reflect on their experience as a test of his arguments, he is pursuing a very different tack from the one contained in his nominalist version of right knowledge:

> No Discourse whatsoever, can End in absolute knowledge of Fact, past, or to come. For, as for the knowledge of Fact, it is originally, Sense; and ever after, Memory. And for the knowledge of Consequence, which I have said before is called Science, it is not Absolute, but Conditionall. No man can know by Discourse, that this, or that, is, has been, or will be; which is to know absolutely: but onely, that if This be, That is; if This has been, That has been; if This shall be, That shall be: which is to know conditionally; and that not the consequence of one thing to another; but of one name of a thing, to another name of the same thing.[55]

[54]For some exceptions to this generalization, see Connolly, *Political Theory and Modernity*; Mary Hawkesworth, "Feminist Rhetoric: Discourses on the Male Monopoly of Thought," *Political Theory* 16 (August 1988), 444–467; Michael Shapiro, "Politicizing Ulysses: Rationalistic, Critical, and Genealogical Commentaries," *Political Theory* 17 (February 1989), 9–32.
[55]Hobbes, *Leviathan*, 131.

On the basis of this excerpt, one would feel entitled to depict Hobbes as a timid, humble, and tentative theorist.[56] Nothing could be further from the mark. Forty pages on in *Leviathan*, Hobbes invokes common experience as a measure of the soundness of his argument concerning the primordial distrust that humans harbor against one another. It is a devastating rejoinder to those who would question his account:

> It may seem strange to some man, that has not well weighed these things; that Nature should thus dissociate, and render men apt to invade, and destroy one another: and he may therefore, not trusting to this Inference, made from the Passions, desire perhaps to have the same confirmed by Experience. Let him therefore consider with himselfe, when taking a journey, he armes himselfe, and seeks to go well accompanied; when going to sleep, he locks his dores; when even in his house, he locks his chests; and this when he knows that there bee Lawes, and publike Officers, armed, to revenge all injuries shall bee done him; what opinion he has of his fellow subjects, when he rides armed; of his fellow Citizens, when he locks his dores; and of his children, and servants, when he locks his chests. Does he not there as much accuse mankind by his actions, as I do by my words?[57]

Another significant contrast may be located between Hobbes's own prescription for right method—a plodding, me-

---

[56]Hobbes was perfectly willing to portray and conduct himself as a timid man, as, for example, in his self-imposed exile to France when it looked as if he might antagonize the political authorities with his publications. His delightful autobiographical account of the circumstances of his birth also displays this avowed timidity: "I have no reason, then, to be ashamed of my birthplace, but of the evils of the time I do complain, and of all the troubles that came to birth along with me. For the rumour ran, spreading alarm through our towns, that the Armada was bringing the day of doom to our race. Thus my mother was big with such fear that she brought twins to birth, myself and fear at the same time." Thomas Hobbes, "Autobiography," trans. Benjamin Farrington, *Rationalist Annual* (1958), 23–24. Hobbes's self-professed timidity, however, contrasts sharply with his theorizing, which he executed and described in terms of warlike combat.

[57]Hobbes, *Leviathan*, 186–187.

thodical, and rational arrangement of basic definitions and propositions into the propositional form of Euclidean geometry—and the sheer power of his prose, which is characterized by an imaginative, metaphorical, and rhetorical style. Notwithstanding his protests against rhetoric and on behalf of the analytic scrutiny of language, Hobbes himself was a dazzling rhetorician and highly adept, as we have seen, at flourishing potent metaphors to convince readers of his right thinking.

Hobbes's avowed skepticism, which is rescued from a radical solipsistic stance by his faith in shared common experience, contrasts sharply with his argumentative mode, which seeks to demonstrate the airtight logic and incontestable truth of his basic premises and their consequences. One of his intellectual biographers, Miriam Reik, has this telling observation to offer on the tone of Hobbes's work: "One of the most prominent characteristics of Hobbes's philosophic impulse [is] the drive toward discovering and building on the simplest, most basic elements of reality, and reasoning about them with such force and directness that his explanations seem to become almost intellectually *coercive*."[58]

A fruitful means of exploring and accounting for this series of interesting incongruities in Hobbes's thought is provided by Wolin's thesis that Hobbes cast himself in the role of epic theorist. As we shall see, key features of this epic heroism are implicated in gendered sensibilities.

Wolin argues that Hobbes had epical intentions in writing *Leviathan*, intentions that he shared with Plato, Machiavelli, Hegel, and Marx, whose collective great works make up an epic tradition in political theory:

> The phrase "epic tradition" refers to a type of political theory which is inspired mainly by the hope of achieving a great and memorable deed through the medium of thought. Other aims that it may have, such as contributing to the existing state of knowledge, formulating a system of logically consis-

---

[58]Reik, *The Golden Lands of Thomas Hobbes*, 71.

tent propositions, or establishing a set of hypotheses for scientific investigation, are distinctly secondary.[59]

Political theories in the epic mold are intended by their authors as forms of action, where the work itself is the deed, a thought-deed that will be translated into political life. But if it is not to be actualized, the residual hope is that the thought, like the written and oral chronicles of long-dead heroes, will endure through time. Theories cast in the epic mold reveal "an attempt to compel admiration and awe for the magnitude of the achievement."[60] The epic theorist, argues Wolin, thus casts himself in the role of epic hero rather than that of scribe, bard, or poet. His aim extends beyond the relatively humble one of logical persuasion to that of astonishing his audience with a remarkable thought-deed. Like the hero of epic poetry, the heroic theorist is a single individual whose exploits surpass those of other men and whose talents and strengths are strictly secular, that is, essentially self-induced and executed rather than divinely bestowed.[61] The epic theorist, then, performs his intellectual feats through the use of his own cognitive and imaginative capacities. Finally, a point that commentators on the epic tradition have failed to note and appreciate in the absence of the insights afforded by gender theory, the hero of epic literature and the heroic theorist share another significant trait: their achievements are bound up with the gendered stuff of manhood.

It is doubtful that the gender-specific connotations we now detect in the following passage were apparent to C. M. Bowra when he first penned these lines: "Heroes are the champions of man's ambition to pass beyond the oppressive limits of human frailty to a fuller and more vivid life, to win as far as possible a self-sufficient manhood, which refuses to admit

[59]Wolin, *Hobbes and the Epic Tradition*, 4.
[60]Ibid., 5.
[61]C. M. Bowra, invoked by Wolin in his account of Hobbes as epic theorist, argues for the individualism of the hero and for the epic stress on his uniquely human capacities. See his *Heroic Poetry* (New York: St. Martin's Press, 1966), chaps. 1 and 3; and *From Virgil to Milton* (London: Macmillan, 1945), chap. 1.

that anything is too difficult for it, and is content even in failing, provided that it has made every effort of which it is capable."[62] The theme of self-sufficiency recapitulates, as I suggested in the previous chapter, one of the most distinctive psychological features of masculinity. To the extent that modern masculine identity is bound up with a repudiation of the (m)other, vigorous self-sufficiency emerges as a kind of defensive reaction formation against memories of dependence and the early symbiotic relation. Hobbes's atomistic individualism also invokes this image of self-sufficiency, which, as I have argued, is strengthened by the tacit displacement of mothers from the state of nature. We encounter it here in yet another form in the figure of the heroic theorist.

The epic hero achieves immortality by surpassing the standards of achievement set by others. Thus, competition is an essential feature of epic heroism. We should also recall that competition among presumedly equal individuals is a hallmark of the "free" market, whose ethos Hobbes articulated with uncompromising clarity.[63] It is this competitive and individualistic quality of action—competition directed at the select few who have set the highest intellectual standards of the age—which marks Hobbes's own approach. We find this competitive ethos in his "Autobiography" as well as in his depiction of man in *Leviathan*.[64] Hobbes never argued with any but the most prominent and formidable recognized intellects of

[62]Bowra, *Heroic Poetry*, 4. See Marina Warner, *Joan of Arc: The Image of Female Heroism* (New York: Random House, 1981), for helpful exploration and confirmation of the specifically masculine dimensions of heroism. Warner writes (p. 155): "Ironically, Joan's life, probably one of the most heroic a woman has ever led, is a tribute to the male principle, a homage to the male sphere of action."

[63]"The *Value*, or Worth of a man, is as of all other things, his Price." Hobbes, *Leviathan*, 151.

[64]One aspect of the intellectual opposition to Hobbes's account of human nature among his contemporaries was the ad hominem means of fomenting humorous stories about Hobbes as a fearful and paranoid man, as subsequently related by his admirer John Aubrey in *Aubrey's Brief Lives*, ed. Oliver Lawson Dick (Ann Arbor: University of Michigan Press, 1970), 156: "His work was attended by Envy, which threw several aspersions and false reports on him. For instance, one (common) was that he was afraid to lye alone at night in his Chamber; I have often heard him say that he was not afrayd of Sprights,

his time. Furthermore, these disputes were cast by Hobbes into vivid combative terminology, as this excerpt from his "Autobiography" reveals plainly:

> I brought out another little book on Principles. . . . Here my victory was acknowledged by all. In other fields my opponents were doing their best to hide their grievous wounds. Their spirits were flagging and I pressed home the assault on my flagging foes, and scaled the topmost pinnacles of geometry. . . .
> Wallis enters the fray against me, and in the eyes of the algebraists and the theologians I am worsted. And now the whole host of Wallisians, confident of victory, was led out of their camp. But when I saw them deploying on a treacherous ground, encumbered with roots thick-set, troublesome and tenacious, I resolved on fight, turned and in one moment scattered, slaughtered, routed countless foes.[65]

We also find a relevant complaint inscribed in Hobbes's criticism of the prevailing Scholastic attention to the thinkers of antiquity: "Competition of praise, enclineth to a reverence of Antiquity. For men contend with the living, not with the dead; to these ascribing more than due, that they may obscure the glory of the other."[66] Hobbes wanted to shine forth in his day, unimpeded by the ancient ghosts of the past who attracted attention to themselves and therefore detracted from the attention and glory that Hobbes and his contemporaries sought. As would-be epic theorist, Hobbes himself is in the midst of the competition for power, gain, and glory which he depicted so vividly in his political theory.

Leviathan opens with the image of Hobbes as a Ulysses figure

---

but afrayd of being knockt on the head for five or ten pounds, which rogues might think he had in his chamber; and several other tales, as untrue." Such gossip, I suspect, was at least partially aimed at Hobbes's own heroic pretensions as a theorist, and not merely at the substance of his theory.

[65]Hobbes, "Autobiography," 30.
[66]Hobbes, *Leviathan*, 161.

carefully maneuvering between the Scylla and Charybdis of liberty and authority: "For in a way beset with those that contend on the one side for too great Liberty, and on the other side for too much Authority, 'tis hard to passe between the points of both unwounded."[67] We should bear in mind that Hobbes's characterization of his enterprise here is not entirely fanciful. Many were the unfortunate victims of the political disputes of his time. Hobbes himself was lucky to have survived them. Yet, Hobbes's sense of risk here goes beyond the arena of political intrigue to that of intellectual risk as well, as he reveals so engagingly in his autobiography. Heroic honor is predicated on the willing pursuit of risk. As Bowra has argued, during historical periods of social stress and change, what seems to count in cultural estimates of heroic men "is not so much their power to destroy as their willingness to die."[68] The ultimate risk is loss of life, to which most heroes inevitably succumb, often prematurely, always bravely and gloriously, if sometimes from the view of hindsight foolishly. The casting of heroic honor in these terms, labeled by Marina Warner as "our necrophiliac culture's ideology of heroism,"[69] has tended to exclude females, who, as the anthropological record suggests, have been less willing to risk their lives in ultimate heroic confrontations.[70] This is not to say that women have been historically unwilling to risk their lives under particular circumstances. Many women have died "heroically," often in political resistance struggles and on behalf of friends and family members. But these are better understood as last-ditch efforts. The willingness to face mortal risks would seem to be

[67]Hobbes, "Dedication to Francis Godolphin," ibid., 75.
[68]Bowra, *From Vigil to Milton*, 10.
[69]Warner, *Joan of Arc*, 272.
[70]See Peggy R. Sanday, *Female Power and Male Dominance: On the Origins of Sexual Inequality* (Cambridge: Cambridge University Press, 1981), 210–211: "If there is a basic difference between the sexes, other than the differences associated with human reproductivity, it is that women as a group have not willingly faced death in violent conflict." For a discussion of the intimate relationship between masculinity and death in modern literature, see Peter Schwenger, *Phallic Critiques: Masculinity and Twentieth-Century Literature* (London: Routledge and Kegan Paul, 1984).

less of a constitutive feature or virtue of feminine identity and more an instrumental means of protecting and preserving life. The connections between heroism, masculinity, and the willingness to risk one's life are unmistakable.[71] These connections are further strengthened if we stop to ponder the gender-specific dimensions of the heroic quest for immortality. As Mary O'Brien has argued, men's alienated relationship to re-production, manifested in the uncertainties of patriarchal paternity, is carried over into their conceptions of time: "Men have always sought principles of continuity outside of natural continuity."[72] Among the many cultural forms of temporal continuity instituted by men, within which we may include patrilineal descent and the regenerative succession of political authority embodied in the state, heroic immortality is especially noteworthy. It defies the biological pronouncements of death, decay, and ultimate defeat; provides a tangible sense of generational continuity over time for the male "family" of heroes and their admirers; and, above all, assures men of an uncontested role in their reproduction through time. Like Hobbes's state-of-nature man, the immortal hero is self-made and lives in a motherless world.

Hobbes's heroism is housed, appropriately enough, within dangerous territory: the state of nature of his theoretical imagination and the political strife and upheaval of seventeenth-century England. This violent terrain serves dramatically to

[71]This suggests that female heroes, rather than being simply and deliberately hidden from history, are automatically excluded because their activities cannot be captured or framed within the existing lexicon of heroic meaning, which is distinctly masculine rather than generically humanist. Furthermore, heroism seems to require a female-occupied realm to protect, depart from, and return to. See Nancy C. M. Hartsock, "Prologue to a Feminist Critique of War and Politics," in *Women's Views of the Political World of Men*, ed. Judith H. Stiehm (Dobbs Ferry, N.Y.: Transnational Publishers, 1984), 121–150; and Warner, *Joan of Arc*, 3–10. See also the delightful and thought-provoking account of Penelope's version of her husband Ulysses's exploits by Sara Maitland, "Penelope," in *Tales I Tell My Mother: A Collection of Feminist Short Stories*, ed. Zoe Fairbairns et al. (London: Journeyman Press, 1978), 146–158.

[72]Mary O'Brien, *The Politics of Reproduction* (Boston: Routledge and Kegan Paul, 1981), 33.

enhance the heroic dimension of his own work. For as Wolin argues: "Epic heroes move in a world of dark and occult forces; they encounter great perils and horrors, sometimes at the hands of nature, sometimes by the machinations of malevolent powers; they are constantly in the midst of violent death and widespread destruction; and yet by a superhuman effort, which stretches the human will to its limits, they succeed nonetheless."[73] Hobbes's theoretical feat was to rescue his readers from an existence that would otherwise be nasty, insecure, and prone to a premature, violent ending. This salvation is made possible by the theorist's courage in exploring the dark and dangerous terrain of the state of nature, which he makes available for all to see in its full horror. Against this backdrop of miserable existence, Hobbes's creation of an artificial Leviathan out of the very components of the state of nature—namely, fear and prudence—is rendered into a remarkable achievement.

It is Hobbes's heroic agenda that helps account for the incongruity between his avowed philosophy of method and his implementation of that method. When Hobbes's political geometry is employed in a battleground environment, incongruous as well as exciting things are likely to result. This is the paradoxical stuff of Hobbes's achievement. If he had been more consistent, enacting his method to the letter of the methodological law, we would most likely not continue to read him and to be provoked by his analysis of the requirements of and possibilities for political society.

Hobbes's heroic enterprise is paradoxically aimed at eliminating future heroes by creating a civil order in which heroism would have no legitimate arena for its exercise. Citizens of his proposed Leviathan would be effectively stripped of all heroic motivation and rationale for action. Hobbes's aim, after all, is to create the risk-free society. Traditional, all too risky heroism, and with it premodern articulations of virtuous manhood, which Hobbes seeks to supplant, is sacrificed to modern

---

[73]Wolin, *Hobbes and the Epic Tradition*, 20.

peace and stability. And the choice as Hobbes presents it is overwhelmingly tempting:

> Out of this state [of civil society], every man hath such a right to all, as yet he can enjoy nothing; in it, each one securely enjoys his limited right. Out of it, any man may rightly spoil or kill another; in it, none but one. Out of it, we are protected by our forces; in it, by the power of all. Out of it, no man is sure of the fruit of his labours; in it, all men are. Lastly, out of it, there is a dominion of passions, war, fear, poverty, slovenliness, solitude, barbarism, ignorance, cruelty; in it, the dominion of reason, peace, security, riches, decency, society, elegancy, sciences, and benevolence.[74]

For obvious reasons, Hobbes argues as if he has made us an offer we can't refuse. This all-or-nothing choice between a chaotic and violent state of nature populated by solitary, motherless heroes, and a predictable and peaceful civil order which is made so by the virtually unconditional obedience of its citizens to the political sovereign, points to a solution that conveniently leaves Hobbes as the last hero. As Wolin remarks, this is another, and perhaps the crowning epic achievement of Hobbes's work.

Hobbes's political theory has been subjected to a number of critical commentaries, many of which center directly on his treatment of human nature and argue that he failed to provide a convincing account of generic humanity.[75] This failure becomes all the more evident and instructive when Hobbes is read as a modern masculine thinker. Masculinity inhabits his work across a remarkably broad range of levels, from his unself-conscious adoption of a male standpoint in his prose,

---

[74]Hobbes, *The Citizen*, 222.

[75]Alasdaire MacIntyre, *A Short History of Ethics* (New York: Macmillian, 1966), 130–140; MacPherson, *The Political Theory of Possessive Individualism;* K. R. Minogue, "Hobbes and the Just Man," in *Hobbes and Rousseau: A Collection of Critical Essays,* ed. Maurice Cranston and Richard S. Peters (Garden City, N.Y.: Doubleday, 1972), 66–84; Pateman, *The Sexual Contract;* Taylor, "Atomism."

to his depiction of a motherless state of nature, to his atomistic portrayal of the human subject in that state and in civil society, to his heroic conception of his own enterprise. The substance and style of Hobbes's work, which exemplify a particular human subject in various capacities—state-of-nature man, civil subject, and heroic intellectual—betray a specifically masculine cast, one that also ignores and debases the female contribution to social life. Hobbes's political theory is thus distinctively flawed in newly apparent ways that are both disturbing and revealing.

The most telling interpretive finding for our purposes here involves the denial of the maternal contribution to biosocial reproduction. This denial, as I have tried to show, is logically central to and required by Hobbes's atomistic account of human nature, social interaction, and civic life. In other words, the denial of the mother is not an incidental feature of Hobbes's theory; it saturates his analysis throughout. Along with the denial of the maternal contribution, the heroic dimensions of Hobbes's style also point in the direction of masculinity. Hobbes's sense of himself as a heroic intellectual actor and his depiction of the state of nature have quite a bit in common. Significantly, the persistent threat of personal annihilation in the state of nature and the promise of its elimination in Hobbes's model of civil society share with the heroic conception of risk a highly individualized and masculinized sense of selfhood. A self conceived along such lines is simultaneously vulnerable to attack and capable of heroic feats in a dangerous world. Hobbes's own feat was to cast himself as the last hero by proposing a solution to a predicament that was more masculine than human in tenor. But to the extent that heroic and narrowly calculating leaders in fact rule social and political worlds, this predicament implicates us all.[76] The solution to such a human predicament is embodied in the inviolable au-

[76]See Carol Cohn, "Sex and Death in the Rational World of Defense Intellectuals," *Signs: Journal of Women in Culture and Society* 12 (Summer 1987), 687–718; and James Der Derian and Michael J. Shapiro, eds., *International/Intertextual Relations: Postmodern Readings of World Politics* (Lexington, Mass.: D. C. Heath, 1989).

thority of the sovereign who imposes order on the otherwise unredeemable anarchy of a world populated by self-sprung men and sovereign states.

A portion of Hobbes's genius thus could be said to include the unwitting exploration of a peculiarly masculine politics, one that is premised on a distinctly gendered sense of identity. Hobbes's solution is an essentially negative, counterbalancing power that is miserly and instrumentally limited in its abilities to transform the primordial human condition. His abstract man is a creature who is self-possessed and radically solitary in a crowded and inhospitable world, whose relations with others are either contractual or unavoidably violent, whose linguistic intercourse is inevitably fraught with confusion and ambiguity, and whose freedom consists in the absence of impediments to the attainment of privately generated and rarely communicated desires. Hobbesian man thus bears the tell-tale signs of a modern masculinity in extremis: identity through opposition, denial of reciprocity, repudiation of the (m)other in oneself and in relation to oneself, a constitutional inability and/or refusal to recognize the ambivalence of identity in relation to others. Hobbes's genius and courage was to face and to articulate the momentous and uncomfortable truth of this early modern masculine revelation. His failure was the inability to recognize it as a half-truth.

CHAPTER THREE

Karl Marx:
The Poverty of Production

We set out from real, active men, and on the basis of their
real-life process we demonstrate the development of the
ideological reflexes and echoes of this life process.
—Karl Marx and Frederick Engels, *The German Ideology*

To regard society as one single subject is . . . to look at it
wrongly; speculatively.
—Karl Marx, *Grundrisse*

THE IMPULSE TO READ for modern masculinity in the political
theory of Karl Marx comes with irony. For such an attempt is
already a testament to Marx's method and critical insights,
while its findings pose an unsettling challenge to a theory
that failed to take account of its own gendered standpoint.
Proceeding from Marx and Engels's maxim that "consciousness [is determined] by life,"[1] this exploration of Marxian
theory will advance in two ways: an external feminist reading
will be brought to bear on a body of work that will also be
assessed within the frame of its own outlook, terminology,
and logic—that is to say, immanently.

In contradistinction to the work of Hegelian idealists on the

---

[1]Karl Marx and Frederick Engels, *The German Ideology*, ed. C. J. Arthur (New
York: International Publishers, 1970), 47.

one hand and bourgeois political economists on the other, Marx presented his critical theory as an account of "real individuals, their activity and the material conditions under which they live."[2] For those who believe that gender is a significant constituent of modern life experience, it is clear that Marx's individuals are by no means fully representative of humanity.[3] What is missing in Marx's theory is, of course, an explicit reckoning with gender. The criticism leveled by Marx against theoreticians of a society conceived too abstractly could similarly be applied to his theoretical and empirical accounts of class-identified men. Using Marxian terminology, we may dub this a "speculative" error, one that ignores tangible and significant sources of difference between human beings. If, as Marx argued, capitalist society is no "single subject,"[4] then neither is either of its two (or more) constituent classes.

A Question of Style

Students of Marx are well aware of the vital relationship between the substance and style of his work.[5] Marx's style may be variously characterized as arrogant, aggressive, ruthless, combative, sarcastic, sneering, relentless, and dazzling. While some find his rhetorical style distasteful and domineering, others view it as the appropriate and complementary voice for the radical critic of a brutal and dehumanizing capitalism disguised within the cool rhetoric of market relations.

[2]Ibid., 42.

[3]Marx may be similarly faulted on other grounds. For a critical reading of his account of nonindustrial cultures, see Linda Nicholson, "Feminism and Marx: Integrating Kinship with the Economic," in *Feminism as Critique*, ed. Seyla Benhabib and Drucilla Cornell (Minneapolis: University of Minnesota Press, 1987), 16–30.

[4]See Marx's discussion in *Grundrisse: Foundations of the Critique of Political Economy*, trans. Martin Nicolaus (New York: Random House, 1973), 94.

[5]There are other scholars who would prefer to keep these distinct and who focus exclusively on substance. For an example, see Jon Elster, *Making Sense of Marx* (Cambridge: Cambridge University Press, 1985).

Marx's achievement in *Capital* was to adopt theoretically the standpoint of the working class and to elaborate a description and analysis of capitalism from that vantage point.[6] What he managed to produce was a theory that was simultaneously descriptive and normative, rich in empirical detail, and radical in its incitement to revolutionary change. Classically Marxian terms such as *exploitation, surplus value, alienation, private property,* and *labor* bear witness to this powerful fusion of description and evaluation. Marx's language opens up new vistas of insights as it commits its users to a critical stance toward the reality revealed behind the bourgeois façade of fairness and formal equality.

Marx's rhetorical style, like Hobbes's, is an aggressive one, perhaps even more notably so. His typical polemical mode involves "marking out his own position by eliminating former or potential colleagues from it."[7] His approach to an issue was invariably one that proceeded over the toppled remains of existing, would-be, or fabricated opponents. It seems that he needed such "others" to get himself going. "From his student days to the time of *Capital*," writes Jerrold Seigel, "Marx's characteristic mode of defining himself was by opposition, excluding others from the personal space he occupied."[8] We may interpret this definitional mode in two nonexclusive ways. On the one hand, it bears witness to his Hegelian roots.

[6]Georg Lukács provided the first systematic elaboration of this interpretation of Marx. See *History and Class Consciousness: Studies in Marxist Dialectics,* trans. Rodney Livingstone (Cambridge, Mass.: MIT Press, 1971). For an elaboration of the notion of a feminist standpoint, see Nancy C. M. Hartsock, *Money, Sex, and Power: Toward a Feminist Historical Materialism* (New York: Longman, 1983), 115–144. See Patricia Hill Collins, "The Social Construction of Black Feminist Theory," *Signs: Journal of Women in Culture and Society* 14 (Summer 1989), 745–773, for a discussion of a standpoint with reference to African-American women.

[7]Jerrold Seigel, *Marx's Fate: The Shape of a Life* (Princeton: Princeton University Press, 1978), 182. See also Bruce Mazlish, *The Meaning of Karl Marx* (Oxford: Oxford University Press, 1984); and Saul K. Padover, *Karl Marx: An Intimate Biography,* abridged ed. (New York: New American Library, 1978). Mazlish provides the more sympathetic, if still critical, portrayal of Marx, whereas Padover's is actively hostile.

[8]Seigel, *Marx's Fate,* 182.

We could say that Marx's style takes to heart Hegel's distaste for atomistically self-defined intellectuals who deny their relational historical and social identities.[9] Furthermore, this style employs a type of Hegelian dialectical rationale whereby Marx developed and fine-tuned his concepts through confrontational exchange with other thinkers, a method that proceeds by means of immanent criticism. On the other hand, there is a disquieting familiarity in the style of a theorist who creates discursive and cognitive space for himself by invading and reappropriating the territory of threatening and therefore displaced others. Like Hobbes, Marx evinces a combative, heroic, and hence masculine style. But in the case of Marx, the overall fit between this heroic style and the larger theory is more uneven. Whereas Hobbes's heroic style is of a piece with his state of nature, Marx's style violates his ontology of social being.

In speculating on the possible sources of Marx's aggressive style, Seigel has suggested that Marx's mother may provide a clue.[10] In brief, he argues that Marx's rhetorical style may have been a reaction against Henriette Marx's intrusive and dominating maternal style. Although this interpretation contains a measure of insight, it is problematic on a few counts.

To begin with, Seigel never manages to make a convincing case for a maternal style that is in fact either intrusive or dominating. The little evidence that we do have (one letter from mother to son) shows only a mother who was solicitous of her son's well-being.[11] It is also widely known that Henriette Marx became critical of her son's inability to support himself and his family. The record further suggests that Marx showed little affection for her during his adult years and visited her infrequently, and then primarily to request money. We simply

---

[9]See section 2 of Hegel's preface to the *Phenomenology of Spirit*, trans. A. V. Miller (Oxford: Oxford University Press, 1979), 1–2.

[10]For an alternative analysis of Marx which highlights his relation with his father, and especially the significance of the father's charge of selfishness against the young Karl, see Mazlish, *The Meaning of Karl Marx*.

[11]It is reproduced in Seigel, *Marx's Fate*, 49.

do not know enough about Henriette or her relationship to Karl to characterize her as an overbearing mother.

We might well ask, however, when is maternal nurturance within the bourgeois nuclear family not intrusive and dominating? Seigel slides into the mode of "blaming the mother," whereas the real issue here, as I have argued in Chapter 1, is more a structural one. That is, the kind of family in which Karl Marx was reared is precisely that modern, intensely affective nuclear configuration in which mothers bear an inordinate amount of responsibility for and power over the lives of young children. Within such a setting, children are likely to perceive their mothers as intrusive and domineering creatures, regardless of the individual capacities for nonintrusive nurturance that specific mothers may or may not have. Furthermore, such perceptions are likely to be retained in adulthood, often in unconscious, disguised, and ambivalent forms. Such residual "memories," however, have precious little to do with actual mothers.

A second problem with Seigel's analysis of Marx's aggressive style is that it proceeds as if this style were simply an individual phenomenon, a personality quirk. In other words, Seigel fails to specify the intellectual tradition within which Marx was embedded. An adversarial, aggressive style is a notable feature of the western philosophical tradition; furthermore, it may have found in dialectics a particularly hospitable environment.[12] To characterize Marx's aggressive style simply as a feature of his personality is too exceptionalist. This is not to say that Marx the individual had nothing to do with the matter. But his intellectual style is more appropriately cast in terms that acknowledge a preexisting legacy for which he was temperamentally suited, even gifted.

Seigel's analysis may also be augmented with the argument that aggressive, adversarial discourse partakes of a masculine

---

[12]See Janice Moulton, "A Paradigm of Philosophy: The Adversary Method," in *Discovering Reality: Feminist Perspectives on Epistemology, Metaphysics, Methodology, and Philosophy of Science*, ed. Sandra Harding and Merrill B. Hintikka (Dordrecht: D. Reidel, 1983), 149–164.

cognitive ethos.[13] For Marx, as well as for Hobbes, this style may be understood, in part, to recapitulate at the level of adult intellectual practice the fantasy of struggle for a location and identity vis-à-vis the pre-Oedipal mother. This process, as described in Chapter 1, is marked by a greater sense of opposition, danger, and conflict for the boy child than for the girl. Within the experiential and symbolic frame of the modern nuclear family, differentiation from the (m)other comes to be identified with the emergence and consolidation of a specifically masculine self; modern masculine identity is cast in the form of an achieved and nonoriginary independence from the maternal sphere. The echoes of this earlier struggle for identity are discernible in Marx's polemical style, which flourishes in hostile territory and brooks no contenders. Ironically, the radical theorist of species-being and communist society, the critic of "free" market competition and of liberal individualism, embodied an intellectual stance and style that contradicted his ontology.[14]

This aggressive feature of Marx's style has also had unfortunate consequences for the political and intellectual history of Marxism, and may account in part for the fact that "the texture of Marxist thinking degenerates easily into dogma."[15] While we can also cite such factors as the subsequent positivist appropriation of Marx, the progressive teleological historical

[13]See Jessica Benjamin, "The Bonds of Love: Rational Violence and Erotic Domination," *Feminist Studies* 6 (Spring 1980), 144–174; Nancy Chodorow, *The Reproduction of Mothering: Psychoanalysis and the Sociology of Gender* (Berkeley: University of California Press, 1978); Evelyn Keller, *Reflections on Gender and Science* (New Haven: Yale University Press, 1985). For an alternative account of women's cognitive and discursive modes, see Mary Field Belenky et al., *Women's Ways of Knowing: The Development of Self, Voice, and Mind* (New York: Basic Books, 1986).

[14]For helpful discussions of Marx's social ontology, see Norman Geras, *Marx and Human Nature: Refutation of a Legend* (London: New Left Books, 1983); Carol C. Gould, *Marx's Social Ontology: Individuality and Community in Marx's Theory of Social Reality* (Cambridge, Mass.: MIT Press, 1978); Bertell Ollman, *Alienation: Marx's Concept of Man in Capitalist Society* (Cambridge: Cambridge University Press, 1971).

[15]Robert Heilbroner, *Marxism: For and Against* (New York: W. W. Norton, 1980), 143.

thrust of his theory, and the sense of privileged standpoint to account for the creeping dogmatism of the theory, the fact that Marx's own style tended to be aggressively monovocal seems relevant here.[16] Certainly it has attracted its share of similarly inclined disciples.

Seigel's analysis is vindicated, then, with the proviso that we substitute the (m)other of Marx's primary process memory for his actual mother.[17] As a projection of the modern masculine imagination, the (m)other may be said to inhabit the subtextual realm of combative, adversarial intellectual discourse.

On a final and related note to this discussion of style, let us consider one of Marx's early characterizations of his enterprise: "As philosophy finds in the proletariat its material weapons, so the proletariat finds in philosophy its intellectual weapons, and as soon as the lightning of thought has struck deep into the virgin soil of the people, the emancipation of the Germans into men will be completed."[18] What we encounter here is a language of intellectual warfare and weaponry, a violent and distinctively phallic metaphorical rendition of critical thought as a seminal lightning bolt that will turn emasculated Germans into men. The homosexual imagery also confirms a homosocial and therefore androcentric conception of political and intellectual activity. Unemancipated Germans,

---

[16]These factors, of course, are theory-bound as well as academy-bound. We need to bear in mind that political history reveals frequent instances of virulent counterrevolutionary efforts against fledgling Marxist movements and revolutions; and these are surely implicated in the political phenomenon of Marxist dogmatism.

[17]In psychoanalytic terms, primary process thinking refers to a type of thinking characteristic of the underdeveloped ego which also persists into "adult" cognition. It includes "the absence of any negatives, conditionals, or other qualifying conjunctions," and the presence of mutually contradictory ideas, representation by allusion or analogy, metonymy, and synecdoche. Finally, there is no concern with time. "Past, present and future are all one in the primary process." Charles Brenner, M.D., *An Elementary Textbook of Psychoanalysis*, rev. ed. (Garden City, N.Y.: Anchor Press, 1974), 48 and 49.

[18]"Towards a Critique of Hegel's *Philosophy of Right*: Introduction," in *Karl Marx: Selected Writings*, ed. David McClellan (Oxford: Oxford University Press, 1977), 73.

it would seem, are like sexually uninitiated boys.[19] This essay, by the way, is no obscure piece of Marx's oeuvre. It is often taught as the inspirational model for critical social theory.

Ontology and Method

These stylistic features reappear in aspects of Marx's method. The two characteristic features of his method are dialectics and materialism, which emerge in Marx's distinctive treatment of history and labor.[20] The materialistic aspect of Marx's method is the core of his "inversion" of Hegel. Displacing *Geist*, with its religious connotations, Marx relocates dialectics in the laboring activities and relationships of class-bound human beings and rereads history as a panoply of class struggle, shifting property relations, and technological innovation in economic production processes. What Marx retained after discarding Hegel's mystical shell was a belief that the social world is essentially dialectical, and that a dialectical mode of analysis is most appropriate for understanding such a world.[21] Dialectics is thus an ontology, a philosophy about the way the social world "really" is, with a corresponding

[19] I intend no indictment of male homosexual culture. What I wish to point out is the elision of women from this phallic portrayal of radical philosophy and emancipation.

[20] I have benefited from the following sources on Marx's method: Terrell Carver, ed. *Karl Marx: Texts on Method* (New York: Harper and Row, 1975); Gould, *Marx's Social Ontology*; Hartsock, *Money, Sex, and Power;* John McMurtry, *The Structure of Marx's World-View* (Princeton: Princeton University Press, 1978); John Mepham and D. H. Ruben, eds., *Issues in Marxist Philosophy*, 3 vols., vol. 1, *Dialectics and Method* (Atlantic Highlands, N.J.: Humanities Press, 1979); Mary O'Brien, *Politics of Reproduction* (Boston: Routledge and Kegan Paul, 1981); Ollman, *Alienation;* Melvin Rader, *Marx's Interpretation of History* (New York: Oxford University Press, 1979).

[21] For helpful comparisons and discussions of Marx and Hegel, see Richard Bernstein, *Praxis and Action: Contemporary Philosophies of Human Activity* (Philadelphia: University of Pennsylvania Press, 1971), 11–83; Richard Norman and Sean Sayers, *Hegel, Marx, and Dialectic: A Debate* (Atlantic Highlands, N.J.: Humanities Press, 1980).

epistemology, a philosophy about the kind of knowledge appropriate to and for such a world.

With Hegel, Marx shares an optimistic view of a progressively unfolding history which proceeds through dialectical processes of contradiction, *Aufhebung* (the creation of new unities out of the reconstituted remains of previous contradictions), and the inevitable destabilization and reconfiguration of new unities into progressively improved and expansive formations. He also retains Hegel's commitment to the notion of a teleological endpoint of history as the basis for judging how far history has come. For Marx, this endpoint consists of the self-realization of man:

> Communism [is] the positive abolition of private property and thus of human self-alienation and therefore the real reappropriation of the human essence by and for men. This is communism as the complete and conscious return of man conserving all the riches of previous development for man himself as a social, i.e. human being. Communism as completed naturalism is humanism and as completed humanism is naturalism. It is the genuine solution of the antagonism between man and nature and between man and man. . . . It is the solution to the riddle of history and knows itself to be this solution.[22]

As I understand it, the "riddle of history" is captured in the following question posed by Marx: How has man come to alienate himself?[23] That is, if man (*Homo laborans*) is the architect of his social and political world (as Marx, along with other modern theorists, insisted), how is it that he has created a social world that violates his capacities and his need for authentic self-representation? The elegance of this paradox is that it simultaneously preserves the modern ethos of self-assertion even as it criticizes a social world for frustrating this

[22]Karl Marx, *Economic and Philosophical Manuscripts*, in *Karl Marx: Selected Writings*, 89.
[23]Ibid., 80.

norm. The tragedy here is that man has done it to "himself." Like other modern theorists, Marx is caught within a problematic of distinctly modern proportions: man is made "responsible" for his own misery. Typically, however, this responsibility is too much to bear, and so it gets foisted onto other agents. These agents of human misery may be thematized as isolatable and manipulable aspects of human nature, or they may be thematized as nonhuman nature. In Marx's elaboration of the modern paradox of secular responsibility, the realm of necessity takes on the burden of this responsibility. And so freedom will bear an inverse relation to the realm of necessity. The self-realization of modern man is implicated in the steady decline and eventual elimination of necessity. This inverse relationship, as I will argue, carries gendered connotations.

As an account of the social world that involves a methodological and ontological commitment to the notion of dynamic process, dialectics describes and privileges certain types of experience. It offers a model of process that operates through the conflict of interdependent opposites and whose earliest surviving description is found in Heraclitus: "War is the father and king of all things. . . . Opposition is good; the fairest harmony comes out of differents; everything originates in strife. . . . We enter and do not enter the same rivers, we are and are not. . . . The way up and the way down are one and the same."[24] Robert Heilbroner describes dialectics as "at bottom an effort to systematize, or to translate into the realm of manageable, communicable thought, certain unconscious or preconscious modes of apprehending reality, especially social reality."[25] That is, dialectics invokes a prestructured or underdifferentiated cognitive world which bears a very close resemblance to the primary process cognitive world of infancy and early childhood. As such, dialectics is often maddeningly elusive, persistently tantalizing, and susceptible to intellectual abuse. Heraclitus provides an early example in his simultane-

[24]Trans. Richmond Lattimore, in Matthew Thomas McClure, *The Early Philosophers of Greece*, cited in Rader, *Marx's Interpretation of History*, xviii.
[25]Heilbroner, *Marxism: For and Against*, 56.

ous invocation of war and harmony. Thriving in an atmosphere of ambiguity, ambivalence, contradiction, and flux, dialectics often defies "the syntaxes of common sense and logic."[26] It would most certainly have been grossly unappealing to Hobbes in his efforts to clean up language and eliminate ambivalence and ambiguity from political and intellectual discourse. But it describes and confirms certain modes of experience that other political theorists have sought to tap rather than suppress.

Whose experience is dialectics most likely to describe? Or, to put the question a little differently, what kind of experience is most likely to generate or to resonate with a dialectical view of things?[27] An ontology of essential changefulness, flux, struggle, opposition, achieved yet vulnerable unities is, more likely than not, going to resonate with the experiences of groups of people who are alienated within a sociocultural order and therefore less likely to see themselves mirrored in that order's fixed image of itself, or whose life activities involve qualities and processes of a dialectically rendered world.

The affinity between a dialectical ontology and the life of the working class under capitalism was not lost on Marx. His description of labor is especially rich in dialectical imagery, drawing on the process of dynamic and creative interchange among laborers and between laborers and nature. Throughout *The Economic and Philosophical Manuscripts*, we see the young Marx struggling to substitute a dialectical language of things-as-relations for the predominant language of things-as-discrete-objects. Furthermore, it is precisely the dynamic, value-creating aspect of labor dialectically conceived that is simulta-

---

[26]Ibid., 38. The term *common sense* all too often functions as a disingenuous denial of the constructed and historically specific nature of knowledge. Dialectics certainly defies modern Cartesian common sense; I do not believe that it defies common sense per se, or that there is any such thing as a common "common sense" that properly serves as a normative touchstone.

[27]For an especially good discussion of the experiential underpinnings of epistemology, see Jane Flax, "Political Philosophy and the Patriarchal Unconscious: A Psychoanalytic Perspective on Epistemology and Metaphysics," in Harding and Hintikka, *Discovering Reality*, 248–250.

neously recognized and denied under capitalism, through the capitalist's appropriation of surplus value. The concept of exploitation elegantly captures this dual dimension. Marx's analysis of the commodity form in *Capital* substitutes the dialectical analysis of things-as-relations for the antidialectical repression of this knowledge within capitalism and its ideological cohort, political economy.

More recently, feminists have noticed a related set of parallels between women's experiences and dialectics. Such parallels reside in the biological and social experience of reproduction;[28] the nurture of young children;[29] "women's work";[30] and the experience of women as the objectified "other" in male-dominated society.[31] The affinities between the last-noted parallel and Hegel's rendition of developing self-consciousness on the part of the slave in the master-slave relationship have been as significant for feminists as they have been for theoreticians of working-class consciousness and liberation.

Workers and women, then, for shared and differing reasons, are both potential constituencies for dialectics. But while Marx sought to develop a dialectical theory of society, social change, and future possibility from the vantage point of the abstract laborer, he failed to incorporate successfully the sex-specific and gender-specific labor of women, which he mistakenly treated as a precapitalist relic that would necessarily be eroded by the double-edged trajectory of modern capitalist "progress": "Differences of age and sex have no longer any

[28]Chodorow, *The Reproduction of Mothering;* O'Brien, *The Politics of Reproduction.*

[29]Sara Ruddick, "Maternal Thinking," *Feminist Studies* 6 (Summer 1980), 342–367.

[30]Nancy Hartsock, "The Feminist Standpoint: Developing the Ground for a Specifically Feminist Historical Materialism," in Harding and Hintikka, *Discovering Reality,* 283–310; Ulrike Prokop, "Production and the Context of Women's Daily Life," *New German Critique* 13 (Winter 1978), 18–33; Dorothy Smith, "A Sociology for Women," in *The Prism of Sex: Essays in the Sociology of Knowledge,* ed. Julia Sherman and Evelyn Torton Beck (Madison: University of Wisconsin Press, 1979), 135–187.

[31]Benjamin, "The Bonds of Love"; Simone de Beauvoir, *The Second Sex,* trans. and ed. H. M. Parshley (New York: Random House, 1974).

distinctive social validity for the working class. All are instruments of labor, more or less expensive to use, according to their age and sex."[32] Marx has, of course, been proven wrong on the anticipated dissolution of sex-specific labor, as our own gendered labor markets and the growing feminization of poverty make clear. This empirical shortcoming of Marxian theory is bound up with a specifically gendered conception of "labor" which ignores "women's work" and privileges industrial labor.

But before we turn to a more sustained examination of Marx's analysis of labor, a final note on his method is in order. As an ontology and epistemology, dialectics partakes of a world view that is simultaneously holistic and conflictual. That is, its stress on internal relations can yield either an "everything is connected" view or an "everything is contradiction" view. Strictly speaking, these two formulations are by no means necessarily mutually exclusive. This could be expressed as "everything is connected through contradiction." A good example of this is Marx's characterization of bourgeoisie and proletariat. While each entails the other, each also opposes the other. Here we have an example of the dialectical unity of opposites. But Marx also invoked the simpler contradictory formulation of dialectical relations. This is especially evident in his view of history as class struggle. Within the frame of Marx's political utilization of dialectics, the holistic view is consigned to the arena of "after the revolution"—communist society. Marx's collapsed vision of a complementary and trouble-free relation between individuals and communist society is too seamless to admit political struggle and dialogue over society's means, ends, limits, and possibilities. That the theorist par excellence of struggle and contradiction should end up with this kind of flat vision might seem incredible. But is it? Perhaps Marx himself enacts an all-too-human limit for living with perpetual conflict. The compelling diagnosis of world history as a ceaseless play of class struggle facili-

---

[32]Marx and Engels, *The Communist Manifesto*, in *Karl Marx: Selected Writings*, 227.

tates the revolutionary, if painful and violent, cure for what ails us: explosive conflict will give way to classless peace and quiet. In this respect, Marx's ideal end state bears an uncanny resemblance to that of Hobbes.

The strength of dualistic conflict theory lies in its analytic simplicity and in its ability to see through the "civilized" and "fair" appearance of capitalist economic relations. Its weakness is manifested in its diminished ability to articulate the complex nuances of social identity.[33] As an avowed theory of revolution, Marxism has been notoriously deficient in coming to terms with the agonizingly complex features of cultural and social change, including, and especially, the constitutive place of the past in the present.[34] Perhaps this is the result of a theoretical stance that promotes a dichotomous and dualistic view of social reality, namely, theoretical oversimplification along the lines of "us" and "them." Part of the problem here may reside with the dialectical starting point. That is, while dialectics purports to be antidualistic, it is already, significantly, situated within a dualistic phenomenological horizon which is to be superceded. While dialectical opposition need not operate along the virile lines of combat,[35] it certainly takes on these contours and associations within the framework of Marx's model of class relations. Furthermore, we will also find it elaborated in his theory of labor as a "dialectic" between man and nature, which weighs more heavily on nature than on man.

Marx's dichotomous, two-player model of dialectical con-

---

[33]See William Connolly, "Personal Identity, Citizenship, and the State," and "Socialism and Freedom," in Connolly, *Appearance and Reality in Politics* (Cambridge: Cambridge University Press, 1981), 151–172 and 173–193, respectively.

[34]See Heilbroner, *Marxism: For and Against*. Sigmund Freud was also aware of this problem. See his discussion of the undertheorized relation between aggression and private property in socialist theory in *Civilization and Its Discontents*, vol. 21 of *The Standard Edition of the Complete Psychological Works of Sigmund Freud*, trans. and ed. James Strachey (London: Hogarth Press, 1975), 113–115.

[35]See, for example, O'Brien's discussion of the dialectical opposition between bodily externality and internality, in *The Politics of Reproduction*, 38–39.

flict between classes, and between humanity and nature, evokes the modern masculine cognitive stance. So too do the historically inevitable "resolutions" of these conflicts: a one-class, single-identity world; a world without threatening difference, human as well as nonhuman. On closer examination, this future world is less humanistic, less universal than Marx claimed. Certainly it is a world that has moved "beyond" the heretofore essential dialectical moment. It is a world in which "humanity" stands over nature; in which "the proletariat" stands in for humanity; and, finally, in which the embodied figure of the universal laborer comes to resemble the action of the commodity form under which he was previously oppressed. That is, "he" must deny that which he requires: female reproductive labor and its connotative relatives, nature and necessity. Marx's attempt to rethink and rewrite primordial history proves to be especially instructive on the last of these interrelated themes.

A Tale of Post-embeddedness

In *The Germany Ideology* Marx and Engels work out a specifically materialist approach to the study of history with a new set of articulated premises concerning history-making men:

> The first premise of all human existence and, therefore, of all history . . . [is] that men must be in a position to live in order to be able to "make history." But life involves before everything else eating, drinking, habitation, clothing and many other things. The first historical act is thus the production of the means to satisfy these needs, the production of material life itself.[36]

Indeed, life does involve "many other things" related to the production of material life, some of which Marx managed to

---

[36]Marx and Engels, *The German Ideology*, 48.

specify, others of which remain in the space-off of his theory.[37] Mothers are no more visible within Marx's account of fundamental human activity—labor—than they are in Hobbes's founding state of nature, or, as we shall see, in Mill's version of politics as a civilized struggle against nature. Given his theoretical stress on the laboring activities of human beings and on the material preconditions for certain forms of distinctively "human" activity, this invisibility is all the more striking in Marx in comparison to other political theorists.

Furthermore, Marx's distinctive handling of the (m)other involves not only the denial but also the appropriation of her power in the figure of two opposed "actors": self-made socialist man and a self-augmenting capitalist system. The denial of the (m)other, as I will argue, contributes to a limited and distorted account of labor, which is further implicated in Marx's treatment of nature, necessity, and freedom. Small wonder, then, that Marxist feminists have had to jump through an amazing and never quite satisfying series of theoretical hoops in order to frame women's domestic and reproductive labor within the lexicon of "surplus value."[38]

Marx and Engels discuss the general history of the division of labor and locate its first instance in the sexual division of labor in the family.[39] But they go on to categorize familial relations, including the sexual division of labor, as "natural" relations. It is difficult to come away from The German Ideology with a precise sense of what Marx and Engels actually mean by the "sexual division of labor." Sometimes the term seems to function in the simple physical sense of the heterosexual sexual act; at other times, the sexually differentiated imperatives of biological reproduction (for example, breast-feeding) seem to be connoted. Finally, the "sexual division of labor"

---

[37]I discuss the space-off in my introduction. It is a cinematic reference to the space that is inferable from, but not visible in, the film frame.

[38]See the discussions in Alison M. Jaggar, Feminist Politics and Human Nature (Totowa, N.J.: Rowman and Allanheld, 1983), 51–82, 123–167, 207–247, 303–350; Andrea Nye, Feminist Theory and the Philosophies of Man (New York: Routledge, 1989), 31–72.

[39]Marx and Engels, The German Ideology, 43–44, 52–53.

could also refer to the nurture and care of children beyond infancy, as well as to sexually differentiated labor in the arenas of household and community production. The underspecification of this term is simultaneously problematic and indicative of the relative invisibility of women within the Marxian frame of analysis. In any case, after brief mention of the sexual division of labor, Marx and Engels dismiss its historical significance by stating that a "real" division of labor emerges only with the subsequent division of manual and mental labor. Given Marx's insistence that social relations be deontologized and understood in historically specific ways, we must assume, therefore, that "sexual division of labor" functions as a natural rather than as a truly historical category in Marx's theory.

It has been argued that the Marxian focus on the historically significant division between brain and hand obscures the role of the heart in human laboring practices. As Hilary Rose writes:

> Women's work is of a particular kind—whether menial or requiring the sophisticated skills involved in child care, it always involves personal service. Perhaps to make the nature of this caring, intimate, emotionally demanding labor clear, we should use the ideologically loaded term "love." For without love, without close interpersonal relationships, human beings, and it would seem especially small human beings, cannot survive. This emotionally demanding labor requires that women give something of themselves to the child, to the man. The production of people is thus qualitatively different from the production of things. It requires caring labor—the labor of love.[40]

A plausible alternative first premise of human historical existence to Marx and Engels's limited specification of the material means to life is that we are born, that some woman has "la-

---

[40]Hilary Rose, "Hand, Brain, and Heart: A Feminist Epistemology for the Natural Sciences," *Signs: Journal of Women in Culture and Society* 9 (Autumn 1983), 83.

bored" to bring us into the world. The second premise of this alternative construction of materialist history is that we will be cared for during our early years of biological and emotional vulnerability. And this second premise calls on, but is not exhausted by, Marx and Engels's first: the production of the means to satisfy our needs for nourishment and protection from the physical elements. Still missing is a specification of the primordial need for social intercourse, a need that, within the frame of modern industrial economies, is met through the daily labor of countless women.

Reproduction enters the historical scene as the third premise of history-making men: "Men, who daily remake their own life, begin to make other men, to propagate their kind: the relation between man and woman, parents and children, the *family*."[41] Marx and Engels's sense of historical sequence here is strangely but familiarly skewed. The starting point for their analysis of the premises of history-making men is the already born and nurtured human being. Not only do mothers not make an appearance until the third act, but they are smuggled in by way of an organized family structure wherein paternity is culturally understood and socially acknowledged. Mothers and fathers enter the Marxian historical scene simultaneously. History and common sense suggest, however (as Hobbes, to his credit, understood and acknowledged), that "mothers" predated "fathers"—that is, that maternity was socially recognized prior to paternity, and that the "discovery" of paternity was a historically significant event.[42] Feminist history further suggests that fathers have gone to extensive collective lengths to eradicate this knowledge in the effort to secure their political and economic claims over women and children. In this sense, *The German Ideology* is thoroughly complicitous with patriarchal history and ideology.

The Marxian failure to acknowledge the modern figure of the laboring mother and the historical and social significance

---

[41]Marx and Engels, *The German Ideology*, 57.
[42]See O'Brien, *The Politics of Reproduction*, for a systematic appreciation and elaboration of this point.

of reproductive and caring labor directly influences the analysis of "productive" labor, artfully captured by Marx in his comparison of the architect and the bee.[43] While this comparison rightfully emphasizes the creative and self-conscious aspects of human labor, it errs in postulating an idealized and overvoluntarist image of this activity. This image issues in Marx's vision of an unalienated labor that can be so only when it has been emancipated from the realm of necessity. Hence,

> in fact, the realm of freedom actually begins *only where labour which is determined by necessity and mundane considerations ceases;* thus in the very nature of things it lies beyond the sphere of actual material production. Just as the savage must wrestle with Nature to satisfy his wants, to maintain and reproduce life, so must civilized man, and he must do so in all social formations and under all possible modes of production. With his development this realm of physical necessity expands as a result of his wants; but, at the same time, the forces of production which satisfy these wants also increases. Freedom in this field can only consist in socialized men, the associated producers, rationally regulating their interchange with Nature, *bringing it under their common control,* instead of being ruled by it as by the blind forces of Nature; and achieving this with the best expenditure of energy and under conditions most favourable to, and worthy of, their human nature. But it nonetheless remains a realm of necessity. *Beyond it begins that development of human energy which is an end in itself, the true realm of freedom,* which, however, can blossom forth only with the realm of necessity as its basis.[44]

While we should take note of the ambivalence surrounding necessity here, particularly as this involves its complex status as the transcended ground of free labor, we should also pay attention to the way in which this ambivalence is resolved

[43]Marx, *Capital,* vol. 1 (New York: International Publishers, 1967), 178.
[44]Marx, *Capital,* vol. 3 in *The Marx-Engels Reader,* ed. Robert C. Tucker (New York: W. W. Norton, 1978), 441; emphasis added.

into the form of a fixed postulate: necessity and freedom are inversely related. Necessity—that familiar and ineradicable foe—must be diminished as much as possible for a truly "human" history to flourish. Nature and humanity are thus opposed. On this level, Marx and Mill share a similar orientation with respect to nature and its mirror image, human progress as a steadily expanding control over nature. For Marx, the technological conditions for human freedom construed in this way are the conditions for such control, necessary but not sufficient guarantors of human self-realization. Marx's youthful anticipated "reconciliation" of humanity and nature, which will be explored later in this chapter, thus takes place at the dialectical expense of nature controlled.

If he had stopped to consider seriously the modern labor of mothers within industrial capitalism, Marx would have been forced in one of two directions: either to characterize such labor as less than human because it is bound to nature (that is, because it is not subject to full control and because as biological reproductive labor it is animal-like); or to rethink his account of labor to accommodate reproductive labor, which is influenced by biology and necessity, as well as by rational and voluntarist factors. In effect, the former characterization implicitly prevails. Mary O'Brien's comparison of the mother, alongside the architect and the bee, introduces some of the more stubborn and interesting features of specifically maternal labor which Marx avoided. They are worth considering in some detail:

> To comprehend a self and a world and a task to be done, to work out the way to do it, to act upon this determination, to make something and know that one has made it, to 'reproduce' oneself daily by means of the labour process; all of this is the unity of thinking and doing, the fundamental praxis of production which is embedded in socio-historical modes of production. Reproduction is quite different. . . . Biological reproduction differs in that it is not an act of rational will. . . . Female reproductive consciousness knows that a child will be born, knows what a child is, and speculates in general

terms about this child's potential. Yet mother and architect are quite different. The woman cannot realize her visions, cannot make them come true, by virtue of the reproductive labour in which she involuntarily engages, if at all. Unlike the architect, her will does not influence the shape of her product. Unlike the bee, she knows that her product, like herself, will have a history. Like the architect, she knows what she is doing; like the bee, she cannot help what she is doing.[45]

At issue here are themes of control, of the human relationship to nature, and the questionable characterization of identifiably "human" activities as nearly exclusively voluntary and rational, issuing from a self-generated agenda of action.[46] Stressing the planned, conscious, and purposive dimensions of "human" labor, Marx counterposes this labor to the realm of nature-bound necessity. As a result, he is constitutionally unable to see women's reproductive labor and its derivatives as "human" labor. The fact that "productive" labor as such would be impossible without reproductive and nurturant labor makes this blindspot all the more problematic, for Marx has failed to specify fully the preconditions for "human" labor as he defines it. (This is *not* to say that "reproductive" labor should be theorized as a mere precondition for "productive"— that is, fully "human"—labor.) At this point we may put to Marx a feminist-inspired version of the question that he put to theories that ignored the history of industry and production in their pronouncements on the psychological life of "man": "What should one think of a science whose preconceptions disregarded this large field of man's labour and which is not conscious of its incompleteness?"[47]

[45]O'Brien, *The Politics of Reproduction*, 37–38.

[46]The attempt to theorize and extrapolate from the nonvoluntarist aspects of reproductive labor is susceptible to a variety of politically divergent interpretations. Compare, for example, the very different readings of biology offered by de Beauvoir in *The Second Sex*; Carol MacMillan in *Women, Reason, and Nature: Some Philosophical Problems with Feminism* (Princeton: Princeton University Press, 1982); and O'Brien in *The Politics of Reproduction*.

[47]Marx, *Economic and Philosophical Manuscripts*, 93.

Disregarded maternal labor leaves some telling traces in
Marx's account of historical consciousness. For Marx, con-
gealed labor in the instruments and objects of production
provides the umbilical cord through time by which people
remember, identify with, and differentiate themselves from
their historical predecessors. This "dead labor" is the material
link of species continuity. O'Brien argues that women may be
privy to a different sense of historical identity: "Women do
not apprehend the reality of past ages in a meditation on the
probable history of a hammer."[48] Instead, women see it in their
children, who embody, among other things, the accumulated
reproductive labor of past generations. "Marx conflates production and reproduction, analyses productive labor only,
and thus reduces the awareness of species continuity to an
economist construction."[49]

Marx's formulation of historical continuity is, of course,
essentially forward-looking; history is interesting by virtue of
what we are becoming as a laboring species. The past carries
abbreviated teleological hints of better days to come, along
with a regressive pull that we will encounter in the political
theory of J. S. Mill in even more astounding proportions.
Hence Marx's powerful rendering of the past as a "tradition
of all the dead generations" which "weighs like a nightmare
on the brain of the living."[50] This particular sense of time, of
the relation of the present to past and future, is more likely
than not to emerge out of a position that has been forced to
construct an abstract formulation of generational continuity
as a complete substitute for that provided by nature. Nature
at least permits an anchoring with the past and future through
genetic reproductive continuity, as O'Brien argues. But given
the demoted status of nature within Marx's self-consciously

[48]O'Brien, The Politics of Reproduction, 42.
[49]Ibid., 42. Women's awareness of "species continuity" as it is defined in
Marxian terms is also potentially truncated by virtue of the fact that female
labor has often gone into perishable items rather than into obelisks, cathe-
drals, cannonballs, and the like.
[50]Marx, "The Eighteenth Brumaire of Louis Bonaparte," in Karl Marx: Selected Writings, 300.

modernist theory, such (conservative) continuity must be passed over completely in favor of a vigorous productive labor which anticipates its eventual liberation as a complete rupture with and assertion over history and nature.

Marx's accounts of labor and historical time are conceptually related in important ways. Together they presuppose and yield an ontological account of man as an essentially self-creative being: "For socialist man what is called world history is nothing but the creation of man by human labour and the development of nature for man." "Socialist man . . . has the observable and irrefutable proof of his self-creation and the process of his origin." "A being only counts itself as independent when it stands on its own feet and it stands on its own feet as long as it owes its existence to itself."[51] In this modern celebration of a self-defining and self-created humanity, Marx has effectively denied and reappropriated the labor of the mother: humanity makes itself.

What is wrong with this familiar and distinctively modern account of autonomy, freedom, creativity, and self-realization? For all of its claims to emancipation and liberation, this vision of unconstrained humanity relies on a sinister mirror image to which women, nature, and necessity are bound and against which modern men must relentlessly test their capacities and limits.

Like Mill (who also celebrates and extends the modernist dream of the self-made man), Marx relies on a plastic account of human nature. The privileged "hook" for this conventional plasticity is labor. (For Mill, rationality will be advanced as the alternative hook.) Marx provided a significant and much-needed critique of the presocial individual monad of liberal theory who is constituted as a subject prior to the society in which he resides: "The human being is . . . an animal which can individuate itself only in the midst of society. Production by an isolated individual outside society . . . is as much of an absurdity as is the development of language without individu-

---

[51]Marx, *Economic and Philosophical Manuscripts*, 95, 94.

als living *together* and talking to one another."[52] Yet, his substitute notion of the individual as "the ensemble of social relations" creates another set of problems. Furthermore, Marx's generic "man," much like Hobbes's and Mill's, is "constituted abstractly without ever being born."[53] Within Marx's account, the subject is constituted socially, particularly within the historical frame of his laboring activities, which produce him even as he produces them. But this social construction of the modern subject still presupposes the unacknowledged prior relation to an earlier laborer—the mother.

Robert Heilbroner has been especially acute in describing the hazards of a plastic conception of human nature:

> There is a severe price to be paid for a view of the human being as without any definition other than that created by its social setting. For the individual thereupon becomes the expression of social relations binding him or her together with other individuals who are likewise nothing but the creatures of *their* social existences. We then have a web of social determinations that has no points of anchorage other than in our animal bodies.[54]

And our animal bodies, within the frame of Marx's modernist analysis, cannot be trusted to reveal much about our distinctively human, as opposed to animal, selves.[55]

---

[52]Marx, *Grundrisse*, 84.

[53]O'Brien, *The Politics of Reproduction*, 184.

[54]Heilbroner, *Marxism: For and Against*, 163. This is also recognizable as one of the problems generated by the work of Michel Foucault, who treats the subject as a nearly pure social construct or effect. For a related discussion, see Dennis Wrong, "The Oversocialized Conception of Man in Modern Sociology," *American Sociology Review* 26 (1961), 183–193.

[55]Marx follows in the modern humanist tradition of defining human life as opposed to animal life: "The animal is immediately one with its vital activity. It is not distinct from it. They are identical. Man makes his vital activity into an object of his will and consciousness. He has a conscious vital activity. He is not immediately identical to any of his characterizations. Conscious vital activity differentiates man immediately from animal vital activity. It is this and this alone that makes man a species-being." *Economic and Philosophical Manuscripts*, 82.

An exaggerated emphasis on man's self-creative abilities also tends toward arrogance, for it denies our natural embeddedness and promotes resentment against a nature that has not made us godlike. It pits the active "human" essence against the sluggish "natural" backdrop of limits. This emphasis actually anticipates a state of post-embeddedness, where "the individual has ceased to become the object of uncontrolled forces and is instead *entirely self-created*, ceaselessly going beyond its own limits by means of its creativity, and continuously participating in the movement of its own becoming."[56]

"Post-embeddedness," a term coined by Jeremy Shapiro, refers to the utopian communist theme of a self-created humanity: "The dialectic of history is resolved through completion of the self-transcendence of nature that occurs when embeddedness in nature is overcome and human beings bring the historical process under control."[57] This celebrated notion of post-embeddedness is a dangerous fiction. It is also misogynist and masculinist. It is dangerous because its assertive blindness elicits the revolt of nature. It is misogynist because it perpetuates a fear of and consequent need to dominate naturalized, and hence dangerous, women. It is masculinist because it issues out of a set of perceptions and needs rooted in the acquisition of a gendered identity negatively fashioned out of opposition to the pre-Oedipal (m)otherworld.

The revolt of nature was initially theorized by Theodor Adorno and Max Horkheimer in their reassessment of the Enlightenment legacy.[58] It has subsequently been invoked and extended by feminists seeking to articulate a theory of feminist ecology.[59] What Adorno and Horkheimer detected in the his-

---

[56]Jeremy Shapiro, "The Slime of History: Embeddedness in Nature and Critical Theory," in *On Critical Theory*, ed. John O'Neill (New York: Seabury Press, 1976), 149; emphasis added.

[57]Shapiro, "The Slime of History," 149.

[58]Max Horkheimer and Theodor W. Adorno, *Dialectic of Enlightenment* (New York: Seabury Press, 1972).

[59]See Ynestra King, "Feminism and the Revolt of Nature," *Heresies* 13 (1981), 12–16.

torical trajectory of Enlightenment thought and practice was a steady "progress" in the domination of nature that was necessarily accompanied by cognitive and affective regression. Paul Connerton provides a useful encapsulated view of their argument:

> This exploitation of external nature for the purpose of freeing men from subjection to it strikes back in the repression of man's instinctual nature. Nature—his own as well as that of the external world—is 'given' to the ego as something that has to be fought and conquered. This means that, in the interest of self-preservation, the self is engaged in constant inner struggle to repress many of its own natural drives. The strain of holding the ego together in this way adheres to it in all stages; and the temptation to lose it has always been present together with the determination to maintain it. This dread of losing the self, which in its extreme form figures as the fear of death and destruction is, nonetheless, intimately associated with 'a promise of happiness, which threatened civilisation in every moment' [Horkheimer and Adorno]. That promise must therefore be suppressed. The intellect must separate itself off from sensuous experience in order to subjugate it. But this coercive separation inevitably impoverishes human potentialities.[60]

Furthermore, the modern domination of nature is a historical project that has been undertaken primarily by and on behalf of men. Women, as Adorno argued in another essay, were "not yet entirely in the grasp of society."[61] They are also implicated in this modern project in a complicated way, as

[60]Paul Connerton, *The Tragedy of Enlightenment: An Essay on the Frankfurt School* (Cambridge: Cambridge University Press, 1980), 67, citing Horkheimer and Adorno, *Dialectics of Enlightenment.*

[61]Theodor Adorno, *Prisms,* cited in Silvia Bovenschen, "The Contemporary Witch, the Historical Witch, and the Witch Myth," *New German Critique* 15 (Fall 1978), 116. For another gloss on this theme, see Adrienne Rich, "Disloyal to Civilization: Feminism, Racism, Gynephobia," in *On Lies, Secrets, and Silence: Selected Prose, 1966–1978* (New York: W. W. Norton, 1979), 275–310.

human beings who were thought to be more "natural" than men:

> [Woman] became the embodiment of the biological function, the image of nature. . . . Between her and man there was a difference she could not bridge—a difference imposed by nature, the most humiliating that can exist in a male-dominated society. Where the mastery of nature is the true goal, biological inferiority remains a glaring stigma, the weakness imprinted by nature as a key stimulus to aggression.[62]

Finally, the domination of nature also results in a longing to return to it. This return, as Silvia Bovenschen argues, is negotiated through the female: "The biological-natural moments of human existence only appear to have been fully expunged from masculine everyday life: that relationship to inner nature which has not yet been mastered is projected onto women, so that woman must pay for the dysfunctionality of man's natural drives."[63] Women "pay" for this dysfunctionality in material as well as in cultural terms. They bear the cultural brunt of the modern longing for nature by embodying and symbolizing the realm of the natural;[64] and they pay for this imposed symbolism through nonremunerated and underremunerated forms of labor which are commonly identified as "women's work." On this view, "women's work" is not really "work" at all, since it "comes naturally."

The radical pessimism of Adorno and Horkheimer's account involves their assumption that this dialectic of Enlightenment is inexorable. That is, with Hegel they take objectification as a given of human cognition and practice, but then refuse to ignore its alliance with domination. In the hands of Marx,

---

[62]Horkheimer and Adorno, *Dialectic of Enlightenment*, 248.

[63]Bovenschen, "The Contemporary Witch," 117.

[64]For closely related analyses of western racism and colonialism, see Joel Kovel, *White Racism: A Psychohistory* (1970; rpt., New York: Columbia University Press, 1984); Edward W. Said, *Orientalism* (New York: Random House, 1978).

by contrast, objectification is held up as the apex of human achievement and freedom. Various attempts to rewrite this dialectic in a less tragically inexorable fashion focus on the presumed link between objectification and domination and try to unhinge the connection. History and Marx are invoked to suggest alternative instantiations of a presumably benign form of objectification.[65]

For obvious reasons, it is difficult, if not impossible, to credit Marx with the possibility of a way out. History, however, still holds underdeveloped clues, particularly if we recall that the history of the European Enlightenment is a gender-specific history. As Sandra Harding has argued: "Once we recognize that the history of Western thought is the history of thought by members of a group with a distinctive social experience— namely, men—we are then led to a new set of questions about the social nature of that thought and about the justifiability and reliability of the interpretations of nature and social life emerging from that thought."[66]

I have argued that Marx's ontological privileging of objectification in the labor process has a specifically modern masculine component which further ignores key features of women's labor. This suggests the need for an alternative theorization of labor, one that can make better sense of the complex interface between humanity and nature.

---

[65]For an example, see Connerton, *The Tragedy of Enlightenment,* 71–79. For an example of a work that does face up to the uncomfortable links between self-assertion, objectification and domination, see de Beauvoir, *The Second Sex.* De Beauvoir's "solution" to the problem of the objectified and heretofore feminized other was to propose that the burdens of objectification be borne more equally among men and women so that women could also take their turn at "transcendence." But she had no illusions about the intractability of the dynamic itself. For a more recent attempt to delimit and thereby salvage modern objectification, see Jürgen Habermas, *The Theory of Communicative Action,* vols. 1 and 2, trans. Thomas McCarthy (Boston: Beacon Press, 1984 and 1987); and *The Philosophical Discourse of Modernity,* trans. Frederick Lawrence (Cambridge: MIT Press, 1987).

[66]Sandra Harding, "Is Gender a Variable in Conceptions of Rationality? A Survey of Issues," in *Beyond Domination: New Perspectives on Women and Philosophy,* ed. Carol C. Gould (Totowa, N.J.: Rowman and Allanheld, 1983), 44.

In spite of Marx's youthful Hegelian efforts to synthesize and transcend the dichotomized terrain of nature and culture, necessity and freedom, these efforts are resolved on behalf of a humanity that appropriates nature exclusively for its own self-defined interests. This attitude is implicated in an account of the relationship between humanity and nature that is decidedly one-sided and instrumental:

> The practical creation of an objective world, the working-over of inorganic nature, is the confirmation of man as a conscious species-being, that is, as a being that relates to the species as to himself and to himself as to the species. It is true that the animal, too, produces. . . . But it only produces what it needs immediately for itself or its offspring; it produces one-sidedly whereas man produces universally; it produces only under the pressure of immediate physical need, whereas man produces freely from physical need and only truly produces when he is thus free; it produces only itself whereas man reproduces the whole of nature. . . .
> Thus it is in the working over of the objective world that man first really affirms himself as a species-being.[67]

These themes are variously related to the psychological denial of the (m)other. An exaggerated emphasis on self-creation denies that we were born, nurtured, and originally dependent. It actively obscures the biosocial basis for species continuity and projects it exclusively into the arena of productive labor. It promotes a view of communism as severing "the *umbilical cord* of the individual's natural connection with the species,"[68] which is experienced as an unwarranted constraint. In a related fashion, it contributes to the exaggerated, if still apt, claim that under capitalism, "individuals are now ruled by *abstractions*, whereas earlier they depended on one an-

---

[67]Marx, *Economic and Philosophical Manuscripts*, 82.
[68]Marx, *Capital*, vol. 1, quoted in Jeremy Shapiro, "The Slime of History," 148; emphasis added.

other."[69] As if men and children no longer depended on women! These themes help us to ponder Mary O'Brien's suggestion that "underlying the doctrine that man makes history is the undiscussed reality of why he must."[70]

When we deny our first biosocial relationship, we deny our natural embeddedness as physical, vulnerable animal creatures. We also deny the origins and literal ground of our sociability as a species. Philosophers such as Marx who wish to articulate and promote this important aspect of human life are then forced to ground it in activities that postdate our first experiences of mutual sociability. Philosophers such as Hobbes who wish to minimize the political significance of human sociability must, however, confront this social arena and interpret it away. When we deny modern maternal labor and women's labors of caring love, which tend to arise more from a noninstrumental, cooperative, and also difficult relationship with nature,[71] we construct a skewed and deficient view of "specifically human labor" and of "species life." Without a retrospective appreciation for our longstanding biosocial origins, we are all the more likely to join Marx in viewing the past as a mere and disgusting pile of "muck." Finally, the systematic refusal to recognize the maternal arena is noteworthy precisely because this occurs within the modern cultural frame of an expanded, if not exaggerated, maternal role for women.

Second Thoughts

But Marx is a complicated and often self-contestatory theorist. In the young Marx especially, we find multiple intimations of a yearning for a more reciprocal relationship between humanity and nature. The following excerpt is particularly provocative in this regard:

[69]Marx, *Grundrisse*, 164.

[70]O'Brien, *The Politics of Reproduction*, 53.

[71]See Janet Finch and Dulcie Groves, eds., *A Labour of Love: Women, Work, and Caring* (London: Routledge and Kegan Paul, 1983); Ruddick, "Maternal Thinking"; Prokop, "Production and the Context of Women's Daily Life."

The infinite degradation in which man exists for himself is expressed in his relationship to woman as prey and servant of communal lust; for the secret of this relationship finds an unambiguous, decisive, open, and unveiled expression in the relationship of man to woman and the conception of the immediate and natural relationship of the sexes. The immediate, natural, and necessary relationship of human being to human being is the relationship of man to woman. In this natural relationship of the sexes man's relationship to nature is immediately his relationship to man, and his relationship to man is immediately his relationship to nature, his own natural function. Thus, in this relationship is sensuously revealed and reduced to an observable fact how far for man his essence has become nature or nature has become man's human essence. Thus, from this relationship the whole cultural level of man can be judged. . . . we can conclude how far man has become a species-being, a human being, and conceives of himself as such; the relationship of man to woman is the most natural relationship of human being to human being. Thus it shows how far the natural behavior of man has become human or how far . . . his human nature has become nature for him. This relationship also shows how far the need of man has become a human need, how far his fellow men as men have become a need, how far in his most individual existence he is at the same time a communal being.[72]

Certain troublesome features of this passage are worth noting at the outset, so that we can suspend our suspicion and resistance and go on to read it for its insight into the complex and instructive dimension of the nature-culture interface, for its toleration, if not celebration, of ambivalence. Let us, then, take critical note of the following: a prudish distaste for "lust"; a male standpoint ("he" is the self-referential subject, and "she" is the object of his interest and affection); the assumption

[72]Marx, *Economic and Philosophical Manuscripts*, 88.

that male-female relations are transparently "natural"; hetero-sexist assumptions about sexuality; and finally, the assumed thematic connection between females and "nature." In spite of these problems, this is a remarkable piece of writing. It is especially provocative in its intimation of the shared fate of women and nature in modern western culture. Marx also seems well aware that the sociocultural fates of men and women are intimately related; that the degradation of women results in and reflects the degradation of man. Another way of saying this is that the "woman question" is also the "man question."

Significantly, Marx invokes a nonpejorative vocabulary of nature and necessity. He further suggests that the cultural status of women and nature is an important indicator of a society's degree of well-being. And he suggests that societies may be evaluated in terms of their success or failure in integrating nature and culture—that is, that human progress requires, among other things, a bona fide accommodation with nature. Finally, he envisions a harmonious and reciprocally constitutive coexistence of individuality and community, humanity and nature. Nowhere in this account do we find nature lurking as a merely or stupendously objectified threat or limit.

Unfortunately, this visionary dialectical sensibility slides into one of a more familiar modern humanist appropriation of nature, as an older, more "mature" Marx equivocates on the meaning of "participation." The following excerpt provides a glimpse into the early stages of such a slide:

> Labour is . . . a process in which both man and Nature participate, and in which man of his own accord starts, regulates, and controls the material re-actions between himself and Nature. He opposes himself to Nature as one of her own forces, setting in motion arms and legs, head and hands, the natural forces of his body, in order to appropriate Nature's productions in a form adapted to his own wants.[73]

Here we see Marx articulating an equivalence between "human will over nature" and "human participation in nature":

[73]Marx, *Capital*, I, 177.

"Nature builds no machines, no locomotives, railways, electric telegraphs, self-acting mules, etc. These are products of human industry; natural material transformed into organs of the human will over nature, or of human participation in nature."[74]

Finally, this human will attains preeminence over a brute nature that has been permanently muted: "All production is appropriation of nature on the part of an individual within and through a specific form of society."[75] In *Capital*, Marx argues that

> the labour-process, resolved . . . into its simple elementary factors, is human action with a view to the production of use-values, appropriation of natural substances to human requirements; it is the necessary condition for effecting exchange of matter between man and Nature; it is the ever-lasting Nature-imposed condition of human existence, and therefore is independent of every social phase of that existence, or rather, is common to every such phase.[76]

But is all of labor the appropriation of nature? O'Brien, in her reassessment of women's labor of reproduction, has suggested otherwise. So too does Murray Bookchin, who argued that nature also "appropriates" us. He articulates a view of nature as something other and more than the brute, passive object of man's labors, in line with Marx's earlier argument from the *Economic and Philosophical Manuscripts:* "Not only does humanity place its imprint on the natural world and transform it, but also nature places its imprint on the human world and transforms it. . . . It is not only we who 'tame' nature but also nature that 'tames' us."[77] One way of approaching Marx, I

---

[74]Marx, *Grundrisse*, 706.
[75]Ibid., 87.
[76]Marx, *Capital*, I, 183–184.
[77]Murray Bookchin, *The Ecology of Freedom: The Emergence and Dissolution of Hierarchy* (Palo Alto: Cheshire Books, 1982), 32. For an instructive account of the western compulsion to tame "nature," including indigenous populations of the not-yet-western "new world," see Frederick Turner, *Beyond Geography: The Western Spirit against the Wilderness* (New Brunswick, N.J.: Rutgers University Press, 1983).

would suggest, is to locate him in the tension between the recognition of nature and its domination.[78]

Two distinctive and alternative interpretations of the Marxian legacy are advanced by Nancy Hartsock, who argues for the transplantation of Marx to a new gender-sensitive and avowedly feminist epistemological habitat, and by Isaac Balbus, who finds the Marxian concept of production to be the "ultimate possible expression" of "the hubris of domination," and therefore nonrecuperable for feminist purposes.[79] Hartsock and Balbus provide the two poles between which a perhaps more nuanced interpretation of Marx can be developed. I will maneuver between these by arguing, first, that the resituation of Marxism within a different and more generous (to women) epistemological terrain is quite problematic, and second, by suggesting that while Marx's theory is indeed tied up with a dialectic of domination, it is by no means the ultimate possible expression of this modernist fantasy. The argument will begin with an exploration of some of the ways in which Marx's category of productive labor contributes to the domination of nature and, by implication, to the domination of women.

Because it requires an "instrumental relationship between humans and their natural world,"[80] argues Balbus, Marx's concept of production necessarily entails the domination of nature. As the substance of necessity, nature is humanity's adversary in its quest for self-creative, self-sufficient freedom. "To conceive nature as that which must be bent or transformed by human beings is to conceptualize it as the raw material or the instrument of human labor."[81] When we approach nature

---

[78]I want to thank Sara Lennox for suggesting this to me several years ago.

[79]Hartsock, *Money, Sex, and Power*; Isaac Balbus, *Marxism and Domination: A Neo-Hegelian, Feminist, Psychoanalytic Theory of Sexual, Political, and Technological Liberation* (Princeton: Princeton University Press, 1982).

[80]Balbus, *Marxism and Domination*, 269.

[81]Ibid., 271. See how Freud inverts Marx's formulation by suggesting that our relation to nature structures our economic arrangements, in "The Question of a Weltanschauung," *New Introductory Lectures, Standard Edition*, XXII, 158–182.

on these terms, we must assume that it "has no intrinsic worth, no dignity of its own," and therefore that it makes no normative claims on humanity.[82] William Petty's analogy, quoted approvingly by Marx in *Capital*, that "labour is the father of the material world, the earth is its mother," reinforces the notion that nature provides the passive material substratum for "productive" labor, as it plays on the sexist depiction of women as "passive," "natural," and therefore less than fully human creatures. Small wonder, then, that the work of modern mothers is rendered invisible in Marx's account of labor. Like the members of nonobjectifying "primitive" cultures, who are viewed as childlike and less than fully rational, women are excluded from the Marxian account of "human" labor, unless they are working alongside men in the factories. All of this would suggest that the reaccommodation of women and nature within Marxian theory has devastating consequences for the overall structural and conceptual integrity of the theory.

As we have seen, the *Manuscripts* offer some preliminary indication that Marx's portrayal of nature is not as instrumental and objectified as Balbus argues. There we find Marx waxing eloquent on the "humanization of nature" and "naturalization of man," suggesting an eventual reciprocity between two improperly divided and opposed arenas. But Marx's subsequent vision of communism effectively renders the "humanization" of nature as its sadistic domination by humanity:

> Communism differs from all previous movements in that it overturns the basis of *all* earlier relations of production and intercourse, and for the first time consciously treats *all* natural premises as the creatures of hitherto existing men, *strips* them of their natural character and *subjugates* them to the power of the united individuals. . . . The reality, which communism is creating, is precisely the true basis for rendering it impossible that *anything should exist independently of individ-*

[82]Balbus, *Marxism and Domination*, 271.

uals, insofar as reality is *only* a product of the preceding intercourse of individuals themselves.[83]

One of the more provocative instabilities within Marx's theory lies in the ambivalent commitment to humanistic voluntarism on the one hand and sociostructural determinism on the other: "Man makes himself," and "Life is not determined by consciousness, but consciousness by life." While this tension may be artfully combined, as in Alfred Schmidt's rendition of Marx's capitalist society as a "self-made prison of uncomprehended economic determination,"[84] or as we find it in Marx's version of history in "The Eighteenth Brumaire," it also threatens to erupt in one-sided formulations. Witness the wildly divergent interpretations of Marx, from Erich Fromm's humanistic psychological appropriation to Louis Althusser's structural reading.[85] Perhaps this instability is a theoretical instance of the revolt of nature contra Marx, who, on the one hand, fears nature and, on the other, entertains extravagant expectations for its taming. Nevertheless, or precisely because of this expectation, the successful domination of nature within the arena of production promises a larger human omnipotence which is severely threatened and undermined by the constraints of existing economic organization. These threats, for Marx, take the form of humanly underdetermined or unchosen social relations. Significantly, the dynamic version of these fetters—the process of accumulation—takes on vitalistic, naturelike, and even female reproductive capacities, including dynamically regenerative ones. The banished (m)other reappears in Marx's portrayal of a fecund capitalism which reproduces and augments itself, while his own intellectual efforts

---

[83]Marx and Engels, *The German Ideology,* 86; emphasis added.

[84]Alfred Schmidt, *The Concept of Nature in Marx,* trans. Ben Fowkes (London: New Left Books, 1971), 41.

[85]Louis Althusser, *For Marx,* trans. Ben Brewster (New York: Random House, 1970); Erich Fromm, *Marx's Concept of Man* (New York: Frederick Ungar, 1972).

are cast as the contributions of a midwife helping to shorten the "birth pangs" of an incipient revolution.[86]

Is Marx's theory, then, the ultimate in Enlightenment-inspired attempts to dominate feminized nature? If we take Marx's failure to consist of "his inability to [maintain and] extend his splendid insight into the epistemological validity of sensuous experience and the sensuousness of the 'man/ nature' relationship expressed in labor,"[87] then the terms of his failure, at least, are preferable to those of others. In any event, just how do we assess who is more "ultimate" than whom? And how will this help us? What we can say is that Marx offers an instructive glimpse into the modern dynamics of masculine objectification and domination, particularly as these engage and shape the terrain of industrial civilization.[88]

Nonetheless, we had better think twice before we attempt to transplant Marx to new epistemological terrain, as Nancy Hartsock suggests. For Marx's epistemology is bound up with an ontological habitat that is detectably masculine. And the "knowledge" that issues from this framework is limited and distorting, not simply in its inability to "see" aspects of gender-differentiated experience and knowledge which call it into question, but also in its active production of a particular cognitive orientation. Marx's epistemological commitment to the arena of production is also an ontological commitment to a modern masculine sensibility. As such, this commitment lacks

---

[86]Marx, *Capital*, I, 10. On the phenomenon of the male appropriation of female reproductive powers, see Azizah al-Hibri, "Reproduction, Mothering, and the Origins of Patriarchy, in *Mothering: Essays in Feminist Theory*, ed. Joyce Trebilcot (Totowa, N.J.: Rowman and Allanheld, 1983), 81–93; Eva Feder Kittay, "Womb Envy: An Explanatory Concept," in Trebilcot, *Mothering: Essays in Feminist Theory*, 94–128; and O'Brien, *The Politics of Reproduction*.

[87]Mary O'Brien, "Between Critique and Community," review of *Money, Sex, and Power* by Nancy C. M. Hartsock, *Women's Review of Books* 1 (April 1984), 9.

[88]See Robert Heilbroner, *An Inquiry into the Human Prospect* (New York: W. W. Norton, 1980), for the argument that industrial economies, whether capitalist or socialist, share a significant number of cultural presumptions and political problems which are framed by the imperatives of "industrial civilization."

a self-conscious appreciation of its own "roots," which, within the Marxian enterprise, is the prerequisite of a genuinely critical theory. To a large extent, the "root" that Marx grasped was gender-specific proletarian man. Thus, his "real connections" were more specific and truncated than he realized.

An immanent critical assessment of Marx builds on the insights of his own sociology of knowledge, the theory of ideology, which rightfully stresses the material and social substratum of consciousness, knowledge, and historically situated political potential. While Marx defined that substratum as the arena of labor, he failed to explore the implications of the fact that modern labor is organized on the basis of sex and not simply class. Marx is not merely unaware of the possibility that the modern ontological substratum of labor might be gender differentiated; in fact, his own framework of "desirable belief"[89] is itself constituted in gender-specific terms. Hence, he has committed a version of the very "sins" with which his intellectual and political opponents were charged and found guilty: he has generalized a (gender-)specific form of practice and cognition and elaborated it into a full-blown social theory. Marx views social reality in specifically gendered ways; his critique of that reality is correspondingly gendered and genderblind.

Marx's "real connections" to his social world reflect, in part, the introjected, intrapsychic relations of the modern masculine subject. We find modern masculine identity at work in his need to clear the ground of intellectual and polemical endeavor. Like the subjects of Carol Gilligan's research on gender-differentiated psychological development, Marx joins ranks with those respondents who react to pictures of physical proximity between humans with fantasized scenarios of violence designed to widen the space between them.[90] We also find the dynamics of masculine identity acquisition echoed

[89]Harding, "Is Gender a Variable?" 48.
[90]Carol Gilligan, *In a Different Voice: Psychological Theory and Women's Development* (Cambridge, Mass.: Harvard University Press, 1982), 24–63.

in Marx's dichotomous model of antagonistic class relations. Bourgeoisie and proletariat, like (m)other and son, are intimately, but antagonistically, locked in combat. Ultimately, the survival and well-being of the latter requires the elimination of the former. Like Hobbes (to whom he is usually counterposed), Marx has had to banish the mother from his account of social reality. This permits a number of crucial and distinctive turns in his theory: a view of history as forward-moving progress, a cataclysmic theory of change, and a view of human labor that is ultravoluntarist. The first two features embody what Mary O'Brien has analyzed as the patriarchal attempt to rewrite history without the generational continuity enacted through mothers. The voluntarist account of labor is made possible and enhanced by the missing mother because it does not have to take account of her labor as activity that is not neatly voluntarist.

This account of labor is not incidental to the objectification of nature, for it requires and promotes a view of feminized nature as the passive substratum of (hu)manly active efforts. And the nature-female association, in turn, has already had a prior confirmation in the securing of masculine identity against a female (m)other-world that becomes the prototype for "nature." Marx's theory illustrates the ways in which the objectification of women and of nature are implicated in a complex spiral of self-referential and self-confirming feelings and beliefs. Modern masculine gender is also implicated in the inverse relation between freedom and necessity, which parallels the antagonistic relationship between humanity and nature. Post-embeddedness is the inevitably "utopian" endpoint of such a scheme. What it recapitulates at the level of social theory is a yearning and fantasy embedded in the deep psychology of modern masculine identity: clean and ultimate release from the (m)other.

CHAPTER FOUR

John Stuart Mill:
The Heart of Liberalism

What has been the opinion of mankind, has been the opinion of persons of all tempers and dispositions, of all partialities and prepossessions, of all varieties in position, in education, in opportunities of observation and inquiry. No one inquirer is all things: every inquirer is either young or old, rich or poor, sickly or healthy, married or unmarried, meditative or active, a poet or a logician, an ancient or a modern, a man or a woman. . . . Every circumstance which gives a character to the life of a human being carries with it its particular biases—its peculiar facilities for perceiving some things, and for missing or forgetting others. But, from points of view different from his, different things are perceptible.

—John Stuart Mill, "Bentham"

AMONG POLITICAL THEORISTS, John Stuart Mill is not one of those who heat the blood; in this respect he stands in marked contrast to Hobbes and Marx. He is neither a systems builder nor a self-styled epic hero. As a rational and soft-spoken persuader, Mill practices a style that is also markedly different from that of his immediate predecessors, Jeremy Bentham and James Mill. Urging the cultivation of "the power by which one human being enters into the mind and circumstances of another,"[1] he invokes a vision of truth made possible only by

---

[1]John Stuart Mill, "Bentham," in *The Philosophy of John Stuart Mill: Ethical,*

"combining the points of view of all the fractional truths."[2] Although Mill effectively failed to live up to this standard, we can appreciate its humbling influence on his work.

Sometimes it is tempting to condemn him for his indecisiveness, to dismiss his brand of tolerance in *On Liberty* as the comfortable intellectual stance of a member of the privileged nineteenth-century bourgeoisie, masking significant and fundamentally opposed political and economic interests.[3] In response to the Mill of "Bentham," one is tempted to praise him for his humility in the face of the multifarious complexity of social and political life. Under the different circumstances and arguments of *Considerations on Representative Government*, some of us cannot help but be flabbergasted at his arrogant presumptions of privileged access to truth. We are less inclined to forgive this intellectual child prodigy his logical and political lapses into inconsistency and myopia. Perhaps this is the fate Mill must suffer for his rationalist intellectual style and standards, for his optimistic advocacy of the powers of rational intellect.

As a defender of social tolerance and a champion of individual liberty, Mill articulated principles that make up a significant portion of the political-ideological fabric in the United States today.[4] For this reason, Mill is a less exotic thinker, more easily taken for granted, and more often taken to task for existing implementations of his principles than many other political theorists. On the one hand, then, we are the beneficiaries of his carefully worked-out principles of tolerance and liberty for the individual, most especially as these relate to freedom of expression and of life-style. On the other, we are

---

Political, and Religious, ed. Marshall Cohen (New York: Random House, 1961), 22. Subsequent references to "Bentham," "Coleridge," and "Nature," will be to this edition.

[2]Ibid., 25.

[3]For an influential essay that promotes such an interpretation, see Herbert Marcuse, "Repressive Tolerance," in *A Critique of Pure Tolerance* (Boston: Beacon Press, 1965), 81–117.

[4]The classic exposition of these ideas is presented in *On Liberty*, ed. Currin V. Shields (Indianapolis: Bobbs Merrill, 1956).

his troubled heirs, especially insofar as Mill represents "the heart of liberalism."[5] The crisis of liberalism, stretching from the revival of fundamentalist Christianity among Americans who are desperate for meaning and guidance in a secular age, to tensions within the feminist movement, to the recurring problems of the welfare state, revolves around the formulation of the relationship between the individual and society.[6] And it is this troubled and vexing relationship that lies at the heart of much of Mill's inconsistency.

One does not have to be antagonistic to Mill's enterprise to note his often troubling aberrations. Even his admirer L. T. Hobhouse described him as "the easiest person in the world to convict of inconsistency, incompleteness, and lack of rounded system."[7] Since Mill portrays himself as a man of "no system," as a practitioner of "practical eclecticism," we are neither obliged nor entitled to fault him for lack of explicit and overall systematic amplification and coherence. We are, however, entitled to query his various works and political positions singly and with reference to one another.[8]

The contradictory strands of elite rule and fully representative democracy in *Considerations on Representative Government*

---

[5]L. T. Hobhouse, *Liberalism* (London: Oxford University Press, 1942), 116–187.

[6]See Robert N. Bellah et al., *Habits of the Heart: Individualism and Commitment in American Life* (New York: Harper and Row, 1986), for an instructive account of the uneasy alliance between liberal principles of tolerance and principled ethical thinking. On the intimate if unstable relationship between liberalism and feminism, see Zillah Eisenstein, *The Radical Future of Liberal Feminism* (New York: Longman, 1981), and Alison Jaggar, *Feminist Politics and Human Nature* (Totowa, N.J.: Rowman and Allanheld, 1983). On liberalism and the welfare state, see Samuel Bowles and Herbert Gintis, *Democracy and Capitalism: Property, Community, and the Contradictions of Modern Social Thought* (New York: Basic Books, 1986), and Robert Paul Wolff, *The Poverty of Liberalism* (Boston: Beacon Press, 1968).

[7]Hobhouse, *Liberalism*, 107.

[8]I am indebted to Graeme Duncan, *Marx and Mill: Two Views of Social Conflict and Social Harmony* (Cambridge: Cambridge University Press, 1973), for this appraisal of Mill. See also Alan Ryan, *J. S. Mill* (London: Routledge and Kegan Paul, 1974), for a similar insistence on understanding Mill as a practical and eclectic thinker and writer.

are especially perplexing, although not necessarily irresolvable.[9] Mill's abstract defense of liberty, tolerance, and self-rule, which coexists with his disdain for the "ignorance," "deficiency of mental cultivations," and "degradation" of the masses, has a significant parallel in the inconsistency between Mill as an epistemological pluralist and as a monist. The latter, monistic position carries distinctive totalitarian tendencies. By totalitarian I mean that Mill envisions a future singular world of shared opinions and values that also just happen to be his. His repeated invocations of a social world inhabited by the necessary multiplicity of partial truths, explored most eloquently in the essay on Bentham, contrasts sharply with his implied vision of a future society of rational unanimity where singular Truth will prevail.[10] If we stop to consider Mill's empiricism, however, this contradiction fades to a certain extent. For Mill, truths are partial with respect to an as yet underdeciphered empirical totality, which is bound to be made eventually transparent by means of intellectual debate and exploration. Mill's truth is not a truth to be actively redeemed and created (like Marx's), nor is it the discursive effect of Hobbes's proposed nominalism; rather, Mill's truth corresponds to a prediscovered reality. Some people (the educated) are more likely than others (the uneducated) to have access to truth. Hence, Mill's fears of populist mediocrity and his defense of tolerance are both predicated on the optimistic assumption of an attainable and generalizable Truth. This assumption functions as the background guarantee for eventual social agreement on those utilities constituting the

[9]Compare Currin V. Shields's diatribe against Mill's elitism with Dennis F. Thompson's more sober appraisal of Mill's dual principles of participation and competence: Shields, "The Political Thought of John Stuart Mill," in his edition of *Considerations on Representative Government* (Indianapolis: Bobbs Merrill, 1958), vii–xl; Thompson, *John Stuart Mill and Representative Government* (Princeton: Princeton University Press, 1976).

[10]See, for example, Mill's essay "Coleridge," in *The Philosophy of John Stuart Mill*, 65, for his account of the progressive improvement in the history of thought, whereby each "oscillation" in the extremes of thought "departs rather less widely from the centre, and an ever-increasing tendency is manifested to settle finally in it."

"higher" pleasures, which Mill explores in *On Utilitarianism;* it provides the functional limit to the specter of the relativization of value, which haunts utilitarian theory as soon as utility is theorized beyond the narrow, empirically calculable terms posed by Bentham.

Such inconsistencies and implicit theoretical commitments within Mill's theory pose significant problems for the practical implementation of his political principles. Contemporary disputes over the proper extension and limitation of tolerance, concerning how a political order can simultaneously uphold tolerance and specific ethical values, are a case in point. Our perplexity in the face of the "right" of the Ku Klux Klan to hold public parades, and ongoing disputes over issues of free expression and consumer choice in the contemporary debate over pornography, attest to the unresolved difficulties inherent in many of Mill's principles. Mill's vigorous stand against relativism and unrestricted tolerance notwithstanding, he failed to provide an unambiguously principled means for the adjudication of competing claims between the liberties and rights of individuals, which is precisely what he claimed to have developed. This failure, however, ought to be understood as a larger failure of the liberal paradigm, rather than as the personal or idiosyncratic failure of Mill.[11]

Turning our attention to Mill's individualism, we observe its contrast to his ideal model of public service and public-spiritedness, which is exemplified in his own political and intellectual activities. We see in his retention of a modified utilitarianism the effort simultaneously to preserve the integrity of the self-interested and self-defined individual and to encourage the development of a creature capable of understanding his self-interest in social terms as well. Mill's pre-

---

[11]For critiques of the liberal paradigm, see the citations in note 6 and the following works: Jean Bethke Elshtain, *Public Man, Private Woman: Women in Social and Political Thought* (Princeton: Princeton University Press, 1981); Michael J. Sandel, *Liberalism and the Limits of Justice* (Cambridge: Cambridge University Press, 1982); Michael J. Sandel, ed., *Liberalism and Its Critics* (New York: New York University Press, 1984).

scriptions for civil society in *On Liberty* aim, paradoxically, at securing the greatest freedom for the individual as a self-interested creature so that he (and I do mean "he," as the subsequent analysis will suggest) will eventually evolve into a responsible, civic-minded subject. Depending on which among the various interpreters of Mill we choose to rely on, his individualism may be viewed as a logical precursor to socialism,[12] a sensible blend of diverse tendencies in a necessarily complicated subject,[13] or the ultimate defense of atomistically and solipsistically conceived subjectivity in the spirit of the Hobbesian and early capitalist legacy.[14]

The inconsistencies in Mill's thought have led, understandably enough, to a wide array of competing and diverse interpretations. To date, however, none of these accounts has engaged the gender-specific dimensions of Mill's political theory.[15]

Mill's World View

Buried among the pages of otherwise dry analysis in *Considerations on Representative Government* are some of the most telling statements Mill has to offer concerning his felt experience as social observer and participant. Here we are given a brief glimpse into Mill's sense of placement in the overall scheme

---

[12]Hobhouse, *Liberalism*.

[13]Duncan, *Marx and Mill*; Graeme Duncan and John Gray, "The Left against Mill," in *New Essays on John Stuart Mill and Utilitarianism*, ed. Wesley E. Cooper et al. (Guelph, Ontario: Canadian Association for Publishing in Philosophy, 1979), 203–229.

[14]Wolff, *The Poverty of Liberalism*.

[15]Mill's political theory has been explored, particularly by feminists, with a view to its treatment of women. For important examples of this work, see Eisenstein, *The Radical Future of Liberal Feminism*, 113–144; Elshtain, *Public Man, Private Woman*, 132–146; Richard W. Krouse, "Patriarchal Liberalism and Beyond: From John Stuart Mill to Harriet Taylor," in *The Family in Political Thought*, ed. Jean Bethke Elshtain (Amherst: University of Massachusetts Press, 1982), 145–172; Susan Moller Okin, *Women in Western Political Thought* (Princeton: Princeton University Press, 1979), 197–230.

of nature, history, and society. His Weltanschauung teems with sluggish and hostile decay incessantly threatening a vulnerable but vigorous counterforce in the form of civilization. Mill's language here is occasionally and uncharacteristically raw and vivid. Some of the key terms in these irruptions (which function as a kind of violent intrusion on the text, given the contrast to Mill's typical prose style and, especially, the fact that they are not logically required by the manifest structure of his argument) are "decay," "deterioration," "indolence," and "anarchy." Counterposed to these is a vocabulary of "activity," "energy," "courage," and "initiative." Mill effectively depicts a world order that is horizontally divided between two distinct and opposed dimensions, of life-affirming activity versus death-dealing passivity. When read in conjunction with his essay "Nature," this material provides helpful insight into Mill's "thought-world."[16] What we glean from these writings highlights the contours of an emotional substructure in which gender, cognitive orientation, and political preoccupations are intimately linked.

The key passages for our purposes occur within the frame of Mill's discussion of "order" and "progress" as two criteria of good government which are commonly conceived of as opposed or mutually exclusive. Mill goes to inordinate lengths in arguing that the two criteria are not really distinct measures of different kinds of government—that is, the stable and conservative versus the innovative—but that "order" should be defined as a subcategory of "progress," since "the agencies which tend to preserve the social good which already exists are the very same which promote the increase of it."[17] Order and progress, comprising similar qualities—"industry," "integrity," "justice," "prudence," "mental activity," "enterprise," and "courage"—and analytically differentiated only

<hr />

[16]The term "thought-world" is borrowed from Bruce Mazlish, who describes it as "involving a thinker's deepest feelings as well as ratiocinations about 'life.'" Mazlish, *James and John Stuart Mill: Father and Son in the Nineteenth Century* (New York: Basic Books, 1975), 9.

[17]*Considerations on Representative Government*, 18.

with respect to the question of their preserving or advancing the social good, are then contrasted with their genuine common antonym, the deadly specter of decay: "If there is anything certain in human affairs, it is that valuable acquisitions are only to be retained by the continuation of the same energies which gained them. Things left to take care of themselves inevitably decay." And, "the same beliefs, feelings, institutions and practices—are as much required to prevent society from retrograding as to produce a further advance."[18] From this point on, Mill has his excuse or "cue" for the remarkable passage that follows, which merits quotation in full:

We ought not to forget that there is an incessant and ever-flowing current of human affairs toward the worse, consisting of all the follies, all the vices, all the negligences, indolences, and supinenesses of mankind; which is only controlled and kept from sweeping all before it by the exertions which some persons constantly, and others by fits, put forth in the direction of good and worthy objects. It gives a very insufficient idea of the importance of the strivings which take place to improve and elevate human nature and life to suppose that their chief value consists in the amount of actual improvement realized by their means, and that the consequence of their cessation would merely be that we should remain as we are. A very small diminution of those exertions would not only put a stop to improvement, but would turn the general tendency of things toward deterioration which, once begun, would proceed with increasing rapidity and become more and more difficult to check, until it reached a state often seen in history, and in which many large portions of mankind even now grovel—when hardly anything short of superhuman power seems sufficient to turn the tide and give a fresh commencement to the upward movement.[19]

[18]Ibid., 19, 22.
[19]Ibid., 22–23.

Here lies Mill's world view. Immorality is equated with passivity, passivity with decay. Evil can be controlled only by constant exertion. All it takes is a diminution of such exertions for things to fall apart, and quickly at that. Once civilization begins to unravel, regression will proceed exponentially. Reversing the tide of indolence takes a superhuman effort; in fact, the previous level or intensity of exertion will not do. Downward movement threatens incessantly; upward movements can be maintained only through vigilant and vigorous efforts. There is a nearly unbearable sense of unrelieved striving and tension here. Life is a constant struggle against the quicksand of regression as the insistent forces of decay beckon from the sinister periphery of civilization.

Decay threatens not only from without but also from within civilization, the terrain of inner human nature, in the form of the passive personality. Mill divides human beings into two basic characters: "the active or the passive type: that which struggles against evils or that which endures them; that which bends to circumstances or that which endeavors to make circumstances bend to itself."[20] Further on, intellect is introduced as the distinguishing mark between the active and the passive character. (For obvious reasons, only the active and educated should have access to democratic political power. In the meantime, Mill advocates the education and activization of the uneducated so that they may eventually take part in the vigorous, civilized, and rational work of political decision making.)

The active character, then, is the shaper and improver of the human condition, one who "struggles with natural powers and tendencies, not that which gives way to them."[21] What, specifically, is this "nature" that the improving character struggles against? Mill's essay "Nature" provides the answer.

In that essay, Mill establishes his firm stand against the romantic notion that human beings ought to emulate nature. For Mill, such a doctrine is irrational and immoral; it is, in fact, immoral precisely because it is irrational. To the extent that

[20]Ibid., 47.
[21]Ibid., 48.

we are already natural creatures, says Mill, such a notion is tautological. But to the extent that the "natural" denotes an arena of pre- or nonhuman intervention, it avoids facing the fact that all worthy human action involves an altering of nature for the better: "If the artificial is not better than the natural, to what end are all the arts of life? To dig, to plough, to build, to wear clothes, are direct infringements of the injunction to follow nature." Our duty, says Mill, "is to co-operate with the beneficent powers . . . by perpetually striving to amend the course of nature—and bringing that part of it over which we can exercise control, more nearly into conformity with a high standard of justice and goodness."[22]

In this revealing and fascinating essay, one of Mill's last, he invokes an essentially Baconian view of a nature that must be instrumentally harnessed:

> Though we cannot emancipate ourselves from the laws of nature as a whole, we can escape from any particular law of nature, if we are able to withdraw ourselves from the circumstances in which it acts. Though we can do nothing except through laws of nature, we can use one law to counteract another. According to Bacon's maxim, we can obey nature in such a manner as to command it.[23]

And it is abundantly clear, from the subsequent description of nature that Mill offers, that "she" must be commanded. A more gruesome account would be hard to come by:

> Nature impales men, breaks them as if on the wheel, casts them to be devoured by wild beasts, burns them to death, crushes them with stones like the first christian martyr, starves them with hunger, freezes them with cold, poisons them by the quick or slow venom of her exhalations, and has hundreds of other hideous deaths in reserve.[24]

[22]J. S. Mill, "Nature," in *The Philosophy of John Stuart Mill*, 457, 488.
[23]Ibid., 455.
[24]Ibid., 463.

This characterization is extended to include animal life and the realm of human instincts as well as inanimate nature. Mill refers to "the odious scene of violence and tyranny which is exhibited by the rest of the animal kingdom," and invokes cleanliness as "a triumph over instinct," "one of the most radical of the moral distinctions between human beings and most of the lower animals." "The truth is that there is hardly a single point of excellence belonging to human character, which is not decidedly repugnant to the untutored feelings of human nature." "Nearly every respectable attribute of humanity is the result not of instinct, but of a victory over instinct."[25]

In his zealous efforts to debunk the pastoral romantic view of a benign nature worth emulating, Mill goes so far as to portray nature as the worst kind of vindictive criminal: "In sober truth, nearly all the things which men are hanged or imprisoned for doing to one another, are nature's every day performances."[26] But, of course, this is an absurd portrayal, since nature—as Mill could well appreciate—has no "motives." Mill's explicit argument that the category of the "natural" should contain no *positive* presumptions is backed up by the alternative claim that the "natural" contains a good many antivalues. At a latent level, Mill's prose communicates something altogether different from what he may have intended as part of his logical manifest argument. Nature emerges as an evil, malevolent, and destructive force, a far cry from a category having no preemptive value or claim on human aspirations. "She" stands in sharp and threatening contrast to the morality and rationality of the civilized world. And it is in large part precisely because of this dichotomous contrast that she lurks as such a threat.

Mill's depiction of nature is related, I believe, to his portrayal of politics and civilized life in *Considerations on Representative Government*; each may be considered a mirror image of the other. Civilized life as a perpetual and tension-filled striving against the forces of decay enacts the familiar modern narra-

[25]Ibid., 482, 476, 475, 474.
[26]Ibid., 462.

tive of culture versus nature. The forces of decay and destruction to which civilized life is vulnerable are the forces of nature. The "negligence," "indolence," and "supineness" of human beings is precisely what we exhibit in the absence of "artificial" discipline. These are the threatening, destabilizing features of an unfettered human nature. Discipline and self-control, which figure prominently throughout Mill's work, represent the harnessing of nature at the level of the individual.[27] Civilization can proceed only by means of constant self-control and self-discipline on the part of the human species.

Given Mill's dichotomous rendering of a world radically divided between the forces of nature and culture, an essential and unavoidable association is preserved between them as well. Hence, the work of civilization involves the deliberate undermining or harnessing of the powers of nature. Society is civilized precisely to the extent that nature is repressed. To the degree that they may be counterposed to brute nature, human activities and institutions are deemed "rational." By definition, politics as the work of culture stands opposed to nature.

A number of interpretive possibilities regarding Mill's relationship to a feminized, vindictive, and objectified nature present themselves at this point. We could speculate on the quality and conditions of his unusually bookish and emotionally starved childhood; investigate the intellectual and personal legacy of his father and rationalist utilitarianism; situate

---

[27]In the essay "Coleridge," Mill identifies the main ingredient of education, which he argues is the first condition of permanent political societies, as "restraining discipline": "to train the human being in the habit, and thence the power, of subordinating his personal impulses and aims to what were considered the ends of society; of adhering, against all temptation, to the course of conduct which those ends prescribed; of controlling in himself all the feelings which were liable to militate against those ends, and encouraging all such as tended towards them." *The Philosophy of John Stuart Mill*, 76. In "Nature" he advocates the "starving" of certain instincts by "disuse" so as to "extirpate" them. And in *On the Subjection of Women* (Greenwich, Conn: Fawcett Publications, 1971), 112, he refers to "self-respect, self-help, and self-control which are the essential conditions both of individual prosperity and of social virtue." Hobhouse, in *Liberalism*, 122, describes the liberal subject as one who can "discipline himself."

these attitudes within the framework of Victorian culture; and consider these attitudes as a cognitive and emotional accompaniment to his empiricism. A related interpretive avenue lies in a "gender-sensitive" reading of these themes.

Mill's portrayal of nature may be approached as a paradigmatic element of his overall world view, contributing to his understanding of distinctively human activity, including categories for judging the excellence or deficiency of those activities. What we have here is a world view that clearly predates Mill's life span even as it took on a particularly virulent formulation in the Victorian culture of his time. We can also appreciate the ways in which Mill's upbringing at the hands of his father must have further enhanced his sensitivity to a fearsome nature. By all accounts, James Mill was a stern father who embodied and articulated an ascetic, if hypocritical, distaste for "things of the flesh."[28]

Mill's individualism and his preoccupation with liberty and autonomy are, I suggest, intimately and systematically related to his portrayal of nature; these features of Mill's thought are also bound up with specifically modern masculine preoccupations. The primal terror of maternal reengulfment which signals the "death" of the masculine child is recapitulated in Mill's association of nature with death. This association is further strengthened in the context of Mill's discussion of sex as "the clumsy provision which she [nature] has made for that perpetual renewal of animal life, rendered necessary by the prompt termination she puts to it in every individual instance." This is not simply an example of refined bourgeois language designed to avoid the explicit description of sex; it also weds sex to death. As for the wonders of reproduction: "No human being ever comes into the world but another . . . is literally stretched on the rack for hours or days, not unfrequently issuing in death."[29] So much for nature's claim to the successive reproduction and replenishment of life.[30]

---

[28]See Mazlish, *James and John Stuart Mill.*
[29]Mill, "Nature," 463.
[30]For a very different assessment of the place of death within life, see Hans Jonas, *The Imperative of Responsibility* (Chicago: University of Chicago Press,

The equation of nature with death is, as we have already seen, evident in Mill's portrayal of nature's threatened reengulfment of civilized life in *Considerations on Representative Government*. Civilization, like the modern masculine ego, must be constantly defended in the form of vigorous efforts designed to widen the gap between nature and culture. Nature vindictively makes up the distance, and the deadly race is on. Similarly with modern masculinity, as I argued in Chapter 1, creeping intimations of feminine encroachment will not be tolerated. Mill's portrayal of nature echoes distinctive features of the process of masculine identity formation enacted within the modern, bourgeois context of child-rearing practices engaged in and supervised exclusively or primarily by females. A dehumanized nature becomes, like the dehumanized mother, the very measure of a civilized "human" (read "manly") identity to which it is negatively counterposed. What we have here, as the psychoanalytic literature suggests, is not simply a series of parallel or analogic dynamics. Rather, the themes of a feminized nature and a masculinized objective cognitive stance suggest a complex web of mutually constitutive meanings whose origins are situated in the pre-Oedipal oppositional dynamic of separation and individuation.

The trauma of early dependence on the mother takes its conscious and manifest form in the adult's compulsion to overcome the dependence on nature: "Infantile rage in the face of the independent will of the mother culminates in the 'adult' drive to annul the independence of, i.e., to dominate, nature." The domination of nature is an expression, then, of a denial of dependence on the mother. Hostility toward the (m)other is redirected toward the natural world: "The mother that does not matter reappears in the form of a nature that is reduced to mere matter."[31]

1984). I am not arguing for a beneficent view of nature as the corrective antidote to Mill's description. Mill's portrayal, however, is one-sided. One can, I think, look to nature and see destruction and death, among other things. My comment is intended to remind us of some of those other things.

[31]Isaac Balbus, *Marxism and Domination: A Neo-Hegelian, Feminist, Psychoanalytic Theory of Sexual, Political, and Technological Liberation* (Princeton: Princeton University Press), 297.

Within Mill's empiricist frame, to which we shall shortly turn, nature is reduced to mere matter: it is the objectified, mute substance of the scientist's explorations. In the essay "Nature," however, it assumes a stupendously subjective form. Each version represents the obverse of a single coin: nature objectified from a modern masculine standpoint. Mill's criminal, sadistic, and vindictive "nature" may be understood, then, as a projection of unresolved feelings toward the (m)other. These projections, in turn, serve to justify the necessary domination of objectified nature, external as well as internal. Mill's corporeal asceticism may be situated within this scheme (which, we must stress, he did not invent on his own.) His identification of sex and sexuality with death underscores the civilized western denial of the body. If, as Isaac Balbus has put it in his rephrasing of Norman O. Brown's thesis in *Life against Death*, "to embrace one's own mortality is to be able to affirm one's own flesh,"[32] Mill expresses the simultaneous and related denial and reification of sexuality and death by allying them with each other and relegating them to the foreign and distant reaches of nature.

We may also pause to consider Mill's insistence on the malleability of human nature in this context.[33] Nature is so dreadful that if human nature were not malleable, all would be lost. Our malleability is the only hope for a progressive improvement in the lot of humankind. Furthermore, our ability to manipulate nature—inner as well as outer—constitutes the modern mark of our superior humanity, to which "other" civilizations will be compared and found lacking. It is in this double sense that the malleability of human nature, a central tenet of James Mill's theory of associationism (an early version of what we now term behavioral socialization), figures so prominently in Mill's political and social theory. Mill's stress on the malleability of human nature, coupled with his fear of

[32]Ibid., 300.
[33]See the *Autobiography of John Stuart Mill*, ed. John Jacob Coss (New York: Columbia University Press, 1924), esp. 95–96 and 191–194, for Mill's discussion of his allegiance to this notion.

nature, promotes an image of the ideal human subject who is disembodied and conscience-driven, and little more. Ironically, it is this subject who simultaneously motivates and handicaps Mill's feminism.

Mill's depiction of nature and the human struggle against that nature opens the way for further analysis of the modern masculinist dimensions of his thought. Further evidence for the masculinist aspects of his theory, including the echoes of a Weltanschauung that is organized in terms of an unstable and antagonistic relation between nature and culture, reason and passion, lies in his epistemology and intellectual style, his psychology and working model of the individual, his politics, and his feminism.

Style and Method: Of Rationality and Individuals

One of the most outstanding features of Mill's intellectual style is his rationalism. His praise of Coleridge notwithstanding, all of his work is characterized by an abiding commitment to and optimism concerning the powers of reason, arrayed against the countervailing influence of passion and instinct. Careful comparison between his essays on Bentham and Coleridge suggests that Mill was capable of criticizing rationalism in its more virulent Benthamite version, but unable to apply such criticism to his own work.[34] Ironically, it is in his essay on Bentham that Mill comes closest to a passionate refutation of the limits of utilitarian rationalism:

> Knowing so little of human feelings, he [Bentham] knew still less of the influences by which those feelings are formed: all the more subtle workings both of the mind upon itself, and of external things upon the mind, escaped him; and no one, probably, who, in a highly instructed age, ever attempted to give a rule to all human conduct, set out with a more limited

[34]See Raymond Williams, "Mill on Bentham and Coleridge," in *Culture and Society, 1780–1950* (New York: Harper and Row, 1966), 49–70.

conception either of the agencies by which human conduct
is, or of those by which it *should be*, influenced.[35]

The essay on Coleridge, to which one turns expecting even
more, is disappointing. Mill gives halfhearted lip service to
Coleridge's revolt against the rationalist philosophy of the
eighteenth century. The effect of this essay, however, is to
subsume Coleridge's insights within the frame of a sensation-
alist theory of knowledge. The redeeming intellectual value
of Coleridge for Mill turns out to be his contribution to the
available stock of empirical resources for the investigation of
human nature and conduct.

Mill, then, assumes a reformist stance toward rationalism in
relation to its most excessive practitioners. From an adversarial
position, he is capable of detecting the imperfections and
limits of a method to which he is nevertheless inextricably
bound. His best effort is to soften the edges, to round out the
utilitarian description of the narrowly self-interested individual who is the calculator of a limited number of utilities.

In the essay on Bentham, Mill comes closest to articulating
the very sort of criticism that could be leveled against his own
work: "The field of man's nature and life cannot be too much
worked, or in too many directions; until very clod is turned
up, the work is imperfect: no whole truth is possible but by
combining the points of view of all the fractional truths, nor,
therefore, until it has been fully seen what each fractional
truth can do by itself."[36] Mill's description of the varying standpoints of observers whose differences relate to differences in
life circumstances comes perilously close to challenging his
presumption of a singular Truth. The Mill of "Bentham" is
the nagging but underdeveloped voice of a thinker who was
drawn to romantic intuitionism while effectively maintaining
his distance from it. Coleridge's "oscillation" in reference to
rationalism was useful to Mill precisely to the extent that it
could enrich Bentham's "slender stock of premises" concern-

[35]Mill, "Bentham," 23–24.
[36]Ibid., 25.

ing human nature. What might have been a genuine dialogue between two radically different thinkers and cognitive orientations is rendered into an accommodation that imposes much more heavily on Coleridge than on Bentham.

In spite of his avowed appreciation of Coleridge as an antidote to Bentham's single-minded pursuit of "half-truths," and even though Mill attributed his own mental breakdown in early adulthood to "the dissolving influence of analysis,"[37] Mill never divested himself of a fundamental commitment to reasoned analysis. Reason, not love, and certainly not instinct or intuition, would conquer all adversity. Michael Oakeshott's description of "the Rationalist" comes remarkably close to capturing the flavor of Mill's intellectual style:

> His mental habit is at once sceptical and optimistic: sceptical, because there is no opinion, no habit, no belief, nothing so firmly rooted or so widely held that he hesitates to question it and to judge it by what he calls his 'reason'; optimistic, because the Rationalist never doubts the power of his 'reason' (when properly applied) to determine the worth of a thing, the truth of an opinion or the propriety of an action. Moreover, he is fortified by a belief in a 'reason' common to all mankind, a common power of rational consideration, which is the ground and inspiration of argument. . . . But besides this, which gives the Rationalist a touch of intellectual equalitarianism, he is something also of an individualist, finding it difficult to believe that anyone who can think honestly and clearly will think differently from himself.[38]

Mill is indeed a skeptic, notoriously dismissive of popular opinion and "irrational" belief. Like Oakeshott's Rationalist, he is both an egalitarian and an elitist. If reason confers similar capacities on all human beings (and we need to acknowledge Mill's qualified inclusion of women here), binding them to-

---

[37] *Autobiography of John Stuart Mill*, 97.
[38] Michael Oakeshott, "Rationalism in Politics," in his *Rationalism in Politics and Other Essays* (London: Methuen, 1962), 1–2.

gether into the fellowship of humanity, it also promotes a kind of intellectual arrogance in Mill. His world is significantly divided between the intellectual haves and have-nots. As Oakeshott puts it, the Rationalist "finds it difficult to believe that anyone who can think honestly and clearly will think differently from himself." Mill's description of his young Benthamite period, when "what we principally thought of, was to alter people's opinions; to make them believe according to the evidence, and know what was their real interest,"[39] remains applicable to his later work, despite his repudiation of the arrogance of this youthful stance. It is particularly evident in *On the Subjection of Women.*

Mill shares with Oakeshott's Rationalist "an ominous interest in education." As *Considerations on Representative Government* makes abundantly clear, this emphasis on education is tied in with an emphasis on competence and technique and is closely related to the modern rationalist project of reconstructing society along lines that are deemed to be "rational" to the extent that they provide technical solutions to perceived problems. Technical, rather than practical, knowledge wins the day, setting the stage for a politics of public administration.[40] Mill advocates a structure of decision making that privileges the bureaucratic implementers, separated (and protected) from electoral politics and the democratic assembly, whose job it is to carry out the preferences of the voters as they see fit. He wants the business of government taken out of politics; popular assembly should be functionally limited to ratifying the proposals of the professionals or sending them back to the drawing board. Mill relies heavily on the twin criteria of efficiency and competence to develop his case against pure democracy.[41] The "instructed minority," having access to the knowledge of what counts as the "general" inter-

[39]*Autobiography of John Stuart Mill*, 78.

[40]Oakeshott, "Rationalism in Politics," 32. For a critique of this trend, see Jürgen Habermas, *Toward a Rational Society: Student Protest, Science, and Politics*, trans. Jeremy J. Shapiro (Boston: Beacon Press, 1970), 62–80.

[41]See Thompson, *John Stuart Mill and Representative Government*.

est, is that group which is entitled to vote. *Considerations on Representative Government* anticipates the practical separation of politics from technique that we witness in its full flowering today.

Mill's rationalism comes to bear most fully on his politics via the criterion of competence, which is an essential prerequisite of the right to vote. Competence is achieved through education, which Mill would like to see extended to as many persons as possible. It is his faith that all will eventually come to see the light already apprehended by the few—rather than his occasionally invoked vision of mutual transformation among differently constituted and situated human beings— that informs Mill's education requirement, along with his defense of tolerance. Democracy, like reason, is set in opposition to, and is therefore vulnerable to, challenges from the irrational sphere embodied in the uneducated rabble.

A distinctive feature of Mill's epistemology—methodological individualism—also warrants scrutiny as a constituent feature of his attitudes toward nature, his rationalist style, and his politics. For Mill, all scientific explanation is fundamentally of the same kind. Explanations within the physical sciences and the moral sciences (meaning the study of the laws of the mind as well as of matter, and not what we would term ethics or normative theory) are similarly patterned. Explanation in terms of motives and intentions is equivalent for Mill to the scientific explanation of physical causation. Free will, for Mill, is an antecedent or intervening cause. Hence, human behavior is causally explicable and still "free." "This . . . means," writes Alan Ryan, "that there is no ultimate difference in the causal status of persons and rocks; in both cases, things could and would have been different if, and only if, the antecedent causes had been different."[42]

Mill's empiricism in the "moral sciences" took the specific form of methodological individualism. According to Steven Lukes, the doctrine of methodological individualism involves

---

[42]Ryan, *J. S. Mill*, 86.

the notion that "facts about society and social phenomena are to be explained solely in terms of facts about individuals."[43] Mill exemplifies his commitment to methodological individualism in his repudiation of the law of the chemical mixture of effects, whereby chemical substances interact to produce qualitatively different substances. For Mill, laws governing society exemplify instead the principle of the composition of forces. The analogy, taken from physics, is that final effects can be calculated by determining the *individual* effect of each contributing force, which then adds up to the final result or product. Ryan describes Mill's view of social life as exemplifying "the mechanical interaction of individuals, not their blending into something new."[44] Mill makes his methodological commitments abundantly clear in these excerpts from his *System of Logic:*

> The laws of the phenomena of society are, and can be, nothing but the laws of the actions and passions of human beings united together in the social state. Men, however, in a state of society, are still men; their actions and passions are obedient to the laws of individual human nature. Men are not, when brought together, converted into another kind of substance with different properties.[45]

"Human beings in society have no properties but those which are derived from and may be resolved into the laws of the individual man."[46]

As an epistemological doctrine, methodological individualism rests on a number of specific assumptions concerning the human being in a social context. It presumes the integrity of an inviolable ego, one that cannot be qualitatively transformed

---

[43]Steven Lukes, "Methodological Individualism Reconsidered," in *The Philosophy of Social Explanation*, ed. Alan Ryan (London: Oxford University Press, 1973), 121.

[44]Ryan, *J. S. Mill*, 88.

[45]J. S. Mill, *Logic*, quoted in Ryan, *J. S. Mill*, 87.

[46]J. S. Mill, *Logic*, quoted in Martin Hollis, *Models of Man: Philosophical Thoughts on Social Action* (Cambridge: Cambridge University Press, 1977), 23–24.

through its transactional social relations with others: social dynamics are ultimately reducible to the behaviors and intentions of individuals qua individuals. Methodological individualism effectively denies that qualitative changes may be produced within an intersubjective context that is not quantitatively reducible to its constituent and discrete parts. The modern masculine features of this human subject at the heart of methodological individualism are not difficult to detect. There are no "field-dependent" creatures here to muck up explanations with embarrassing questions about quantity-to-quality shifts, inter- and intrasubjective nuances, the intrapsychic constitution of the self, or the ambiguous, ambivalent, and occasionally dissolving subject-object interface. All activity and its explanation is derived from "the individual" as a discrete subject of behavior and object of scientific inquiry. Methodological individualism presumes the cognitive capacity for objectivity as the central defining feature of its objects and subjects of inquiry—human beings and social scientists, respectively. The presumptive ideal at work here is that of an objective cognitive stance situated in protected relation to an external and objectifiable reality.

Evelyn Keller's inquiry into "the processes by which the capacity for scientific thought develops, and the ways in which those processes are intertwined with emotional and sexual development,"[47] has set a helpful precedent for the consideration and appraisal of the gendered features of Mill's methodological individualism. Arguing that the cognitive capacity for objectivity is acquired during the process of identity formation as a function of the child's capacity for distinguishing self from not-self, Keller explores the gendered features of that version of empiricist science modeled on the presumptive ideal of an objective cognitive stance situated in relation to an alien nature.[48] This version of science, according to Keller, "bears

---

[47]Evelyn Keller, "Gender and Science," *Psychoanalysis and Contemporary Thought* 1 (1978), 416.

[48]This version of science has also been disputed by several historians and philosophers of science. For a helpful review of the literature and disputes in contemporary philosophy of science, see Richard Bernstein, *Beyond Objectivism and Relativism: Science, Hermeneutics, and Praxis* (Philadelphia: University

the imprint of its genderization not only in the ways it is used, but in the very description of reality it offers—even in the relation of the scientist to that description."[49]

The account of self and social reality contained within methodological individualism may be traced to the earlier process of identity acquisition.[50] This hypothetical reconstruction contributes to the claim that cognitive and emotional development are vitally related to each other in mutually informative and constitutive ways. If we pause to reconsider the dynamics of separation and individuation within the modern nuclear family, we note the seeds of potential cognitive orientations that lie in the crucial interactional dynamic between mother and infant:

> In the extrication of self from mother, the mother, beginning as the first and most primitive subject, emerges, by a process of effective and affective negation, as the first object. The very processes (both cognitive and emotional) which remind us of that first bond become colored by their association with the woman who is, and forever remains, the archetypal female. Correspondingly, those of delineation and objectification are colored by their origins in the process of separation *from* mother; they become marked, as it were, as "not-mother." The mother becomes an object, and the child a subject, by a process which becomes itself an expression of opposition to and negation of "mother."[51]

This dynamic, explored in Chapter 1, holds a variety of potential consequences, ranging from various forms of reconcilia-

---

of Pennsylvania Press, 1983). For a feminist analysis of how the contemporary dissatisfaction with modern ways of knowing and logics of justification may be a dissatisfaction with specifically masculine ways of knowing, see Sandra Harding, *The Science Question in Feminism* (Ithaca: Cornell University Press, 1986).

[49]Keller, "Gender and Science," 414.

[50]Presumably, any epistemological scheme is susceptible to such analysis. The discussion of dialectics in the previous chapter is a case in point.

[51]Keller, "Gender and Science," 422–423.

tion with the primal (m)other, to extreme alienation from her. As a particular cognitive stance, methodological individualism bears the telltale signs of an undermediated struggle with the (m)other. The radical differentiation of subject and object, whose constituent failure is a disallowance of "that vital element of ambiguity at the interface between subject and object,"[52] survives in methodological individualism's strict differentiation between its objects of inquiry, on the one hand, and between and among those objects and the observers who study them, on the other.[53]

Mill's empiricism and his methodological individualism partake, along with his fearful and tension-filled account of civilization's antagonistic relationship to nature, of a cognitive orientation that may be linked to modern masculinity. That his world view and his method are thus linked should come as no surprise, particularly insofar as they share a common version of the human subject. The subject thus conceived sets the agenda for an appropriate method of observation and analysis, and vice versa. That is, like any other method, methodological individualism constitutes those objects of inquiry it claims to represent.

The object of scrutiny under methodological individualism is undeniably masculine, most notably in his strict ego boundary differentiation and in his radical separation from a nature that must be disciplined within the self and harnessed for the strenuous work of civilization. Mill's subject is also masculine by virtue of his horrific vulnerability. The revolt of nature threatens without respite, reenforcing the need for clear-cut differentiation, liberty in the service of autonomy, and unclut-

---

[52]Ibid., 420.
[53]Critics of liberalism have raised similar objections to its epistemologically constituted atomistic subject. But none of them, to my knowledge, has identified the liberal subject as a gendered, modern masculine subject. See Richard Norman, "Self and Others: The Inadequacy of Utilitarianism," in Cooper et al., *New Essays on John Stuart Mill*, 181–201; Sandel, *Liberalism and the Limits of Justice*; Charles Taylor, "Atomism," in *Power, Possessions, and Freedom: Essays in Honor of C. B. MacPherson*, ed. Alkis Kontos (Toronto: University of Toronto Press, 1979), 39–61; Wolff, *The Poverty of Liberalism*.

tered identity. Mill's political theory, to which we now turn in greater detail, is concerned with precisely these issues.

The Politics of Self-Discipline

The kind of man that liberalism requires, wrote Hobhouse, is one who can "discipline himself," whose capacities for "the development of will, of personality, of self control, or whatever we please to call that central harmonizing power which makes us capable of directing our own lives," have been developed and secured.[54] That Hobhouse, a socialist, and one of Mill's most generous interpreters, should reiterate the themes of discipline and self-control is indicative of the strength and centrality of these qualities to Mill's conception of the modern citizen. It is the capacity for discipline which, in fact, makes us moral and individual. Without the human attribute of self-control, nature would gobble us up into her chaotic and amoral (or is it immoral?) vortex. We are individuals precisely to the extent that we stand over instinct, to the degree that we set the pace and the course for the orderly progression of our lives. Individuality and morality are thus jointly and inversely related to instinct.

This scheme is reiterated in Mill's idealist version of a history that is propelled by ideas: "It is what men think that determines how they act." Those of us who would respond to Mill by suggesting that it is also how humans live that shapes how and what they think would be treated to Mill's partial and qualified agreement with this argument. The "convictions of average men are in a much greater degree determined by their personal position than by reason," but to this extent they are inferior and therefore rationally vulnerable to the ideas of others, notably those of "the united authority of the instructed."[55] Mill wants thought to be freed from its limiting material bonds. Materially situated ideas are suspect because

---

[54]Hobhouse, *Liberalism*, 122–123.
[55]Mill, *Considerations on Representative Government*, 14, 15, 16.

they invariably express partial interests. The particular is bo-gus; generalizable truth is what must be sought and defended.

Mill's concentration in *On Liberty* on freedom of thought and his correspondingly less developed focus on economic and other practical forms of freedom may be understood in relation to his ascetic conception of the individual and of intellect and his account of the causal relationship between the ideas and the material structure of the social world. Insofar as his sociology of knowledge is concerned, Mill is no material-ist. This is amply confirmed by his inability to appreciate the possibility that the ideas of "the instructed minority" might simultaneously reflect and perpetuate specific political inter-ests. (Where such interests may be found to be operative, as in the case of educated men's denying liberty to women, further instruction and legal reform are thought to provide the cure.) In *On Liberty* it is the tyranny of the majority that ought to be feared, most notably because it is an uneducated and uncultivated majority and, by extension, all too wedded to material and partial and therefore "sinister" interests.[56]

Mill's discussion of liberty ranges primarily over the terri-tory of inner consciousness and its expression. This conscious-ness inhabits and defines a singular individual who must be "sovereign" "over himself, over his own body and mind." The only warrant for intervention in the liberty of this individual is the threatened liberty of another similarly constituted indi-vidual. "The only freedom which deserves the name is that of pursuing our own good in our own way, so long as we do not attempt to deprive others of theirs." Such a conception of liberty presumes, as Mill acknowledges, that there is an arena of belief and action which is purely "self-regarding." "To indi-viduality should belong the part of life in which it is chiefly the individual that is interested; to society, the part which clearly interests society." "Each will receive its proper share if each has that which more particularly concerns it."[57] Through

<hr/>

[56]See Mill's discussion in *Considerations on Representative Government*, esp. chap. 6.

[57]Mill, *On Liberty*, 13, 16, 91.

a process of circular reasoning, which relies on deceptively self-evident principles, this formulation effectively begs the question of the public-private distinction on which it rests.[58] Furthermore, "society" may stand for the collective interests of the whole; but within the frame of Mill's methodological individualism, it can only be specific individuals and groups who decide what "society" should concern itself with.

Over and above questions involving the specific contents and borders of each delimited sphere, however, is the nagging issue of the division itself, which, on closer examination, makes remarkably little sense. As Hobhouse understood clearly enough, "there are no actions which may not directly or indirectly affect others, . . . even if there were they would not cease to be matter of concern to others."[59] The related distinctions between individual and society, private and public, also presume a division within the individual himself in terms of private identity on the one hand and social identity on the other, an equally problematic demarcation whose boundaries are easily dissolved by such "private" but politically contested activities as sexual practices, consumer habits, and child-rearing preferences. It is no small irony that many feminists continue to rely on this essentially flawed theoretical and legal framework, particularly in the area of reproductive rights.[60]

At the conclusion of *On Liberty*, Mill leaves us with two equally unhelpful principles: (1) the individual is not accountable to society for acts that concern himself only, and (2) he *is* accountable for those acts affecting others. Between the easy extremes on either side of this formulation—what color shirt I decide to wear to work on a particular day; murder—lies a massive area of gray. Most "private" decisions simply cannot

[58]See Elshtain, *Public Man, Private Woman*, 132–146.
[59]Hobhouse, *Liberalism*, 142.
[60]For a helpful exploration of the issues, see Rosalind Petchesky, "Reproductive Freedom: Beyond 'A Woman's Right to Choose,' " *Signs: Journal of Women in Culture and Society* 5 (Summer 1980): 661–685; and "Abortion Politics in the 90s: Giving Women a Real Choice," *The Nation*, May 28 1990, 732–735.

be cast in terms that have ramifications only or primarily for the acting individual. Mill's own applications of his principles to various "policy" issues of his time in the concluding chapter of *On Liberty* leave contemporary readers simultaneously gratified and perplexed. For example, his discussion of the freedom of the consumer to purchase dangerous substances which could, among other purposes, be used to murder someone is very much akin to contemporary arguments that the sale of firearms may be monitored but not absolutely restricted, thus protecting the liberty of the consumer as a rational chooser. Yet his argument in support of politically established minimal economic prerequisites for parenthood transforms the "private" right to reproductive decision making into a "public" responsibility. As far as Mill was concerned, the decision to have a child is not a private decision at all, and potential parents who lack the economic means to support their offspring have no right to reproduce. This judgment, of course, runs very much against the grain of contemporary political culture, which celebrates and protects, at least ostensibly, the private integrity of the family unit, while advancing little in the way of public support for families.

My task here is not to reformulate a viable theory of tolerance and liberty. (If it were, I would have to proceed on the basis of a much "thicker" understanding of "the individual" as a socially constituted subject.) Rather, I wish to highlight the modern masculine features of Mill's apparently abstract liberal subject. As I have argued, Mill's defense of tolerance, along with his definition of liberty, relies on a conception of a clearly demarcated, "field-independent" subject. Such a subject is effectively and affectively capable of maintaining a discrete sense of identity vis-à-vis fellow human beings and his society, to whom and to which he is cautiously related. Such an identity, as Mill understood clearly, stood to be threatened in the absence of a self/not-self demarcation and by means of incursion into its "space" by the undifferentiated mob. *On Liberty* may be understood to provide such a demarcation and consequent protection. In short, *On Liberty* is preoccupied with the liberty of a well-differentiated modern masculine subject who requires a protected zone of thought, expression, and action for his survival and well-being. Within this zone, the liberal masculine subject is constituted as a self-sufficient and sovereign entity. It is from this zone that he ventures into the social world. In the absence of specific exceptions, this individual must be protected. The burden of proof effectively falls on those who would curtail this individual, as Mill's language makes clear: "The sole end for which mankind are warranted, individually or collectively, in interfering with the liberty of action of any of their number is self-protection."[61] The social relations of Mill's individual are to be negotiated within the frame of an abstract morality of rights. At the center of this moral scheme is an individual who is not to be encroached on unless he happens to be invading the space of another individual.

Mill's individualist political morality of rights to noninterference may be usefully counterposed to a different moral scheme, one that has been identified as bearing some relation to feminine experience. As the research of Carol Gilligan suggests, women often proceed with a morality of (sometimes competing) responsibilities to others, wherein moral decisions are related to the specifics of situations and are motivated by the injunction to avoid or to minimize human hurt and to meet personal and social obligations. Furthermore, according to Gilligan, the space of moral decision making for many women (and some men) is weblike, traversed by various and occasionally competing cross-currents of affiliation. The public-private boundary makes little sense on this terrain.[62] When we place Mill's theory against this context-dependent scheme, his abstract morality of individual liberty and rights to noninterference, centering on the core presumption of an antagonistic relation between the individual, other individuals, and society at large, assumes a masculinist aura. It is precisely such an abstract morality of rights that simultaneously fuels and sabotages Mill's feminist project.

[61]Mill, *On Liberty*, 13.
[62]Carol Gilligan, *In a Different Voice: Psychological Theory and Women's Development* (Cambridge, Mass.: Harvard University Press, 1982).

Mill's feminism, to which we now turn, is inspired by a hybrid subject—female and yet masculine—who cannot help but subvert the very liberation of women that Mill so keenly fought for. Mill's paradoxical feminism recapitulates, in a new form, the tragic features of *On Liberty*, whereby his social vision of the just society was effectively bracketed by his deeply embedded theoretical and methodological assumptions concerning the individual as an essentially self-interested creature.[63] That these assumptions imbibe a distinctively masculinist orientation toward the social world could not help but problematize his feminism.

Women Subjected: Rereading *On the Subjection of Women*

Mill's standing as the only liberal thinker to have applied the tenets of modern individualism to women is often praised, and indeed it was a singular achievement among male liberal theorists.[64] How, we might well wonder, could a theoretical

[63]This sense of tragedy derives from the discrepancy between Mill's advocacy of social obligation and concern, on the one hand, and his essentially atomistic conception of the subject, on the other. For an appreciation of Mill's social sensibility, see Duncan, *Marx and Mill*. "Social feeling" for Mill is essentially prescriptive rather than descriptive. As such, it may be understood in one of two ways: (1) as an "artificial" component of denatured humanity which is added on to an originally atomistic subject, or (2) as a rational extension of original egoism, such that I am able to perceive "my" interests in the interests of others. In "Nature," 477, for example, Mill describes our innate capacity for sympathy as an extension of "sympathetic selfishness." In neither case, however, is Mill's methodologically individualist subject deeply transformed. His "social" relations and interests continue to be predicated on an essentially atomistic existence.

[64]Mill's achievement is a singular one in the context of the "male-stream" liberal tradition. One should acknowledge, however, the various historical and contemporary efforts of women to apply liberal principles across the extant borders of sexual discrimination. See Mary Wollstonecraft, *A Vindication of the Rights of Women*, ed. Carol H. Poston (New York: W. W. Norton, 1975). For discussions of several others, see Eisenstein, *The Radical Future of Liberal Feminism*; Dale Spender, *Women of Ideas (And What Men Have Done to Them)* (London: Routledge and Kegan Paul, 1983). One should also acknowledge the collaborative nature of Mill's mature writings on feminism, which were obviously influenced by Harriet Taylor. For an appreciation of this point, see, in addition to Eisenstein, *The Radical Future*, also Krouse, "Patriarchal Liberalism and Beyond"; Andrea Nye, *Feminist Theory and the Philosophies of*

discourse that attempted to secularize the ground of human dignity, made individuals the masters and architects of their destinies, and developed abstract and general principles of equality, interests, and individual rights have failed to concern itself with the sexual double standard? Usually ignored (as we have seen in the case of Hobbes), women occasionally came into view in liberal theory as subordinate exceptions rather than as equal participants. Various justifications for the differential treatment of men and women invariably invoked the marriage relation and its components: reproduction, the sexual division of labor and of authority, sexually differentiated moral and intellectual capacities, allocation of property rights.[65] To some extent, Mill also fell into aspects of this pattern, even as he tried systematically to apply the tenets of his liberalism to women. Mill *is* unique in his attempts to situate women consistently within the frame of liberal utilitarianism. Yet the previous failure of liberal political theory to incorporate women systematically on egalitarian terms with men should not be very surprising to us. This failure attests to the specifically androcentric conception of the human subject at the very heart of that theory, rather than to some irrational "blind spot" or premodern holdover of which the early liberal theorists were unaware or to which they were ideologically captive.[66] On the basis of our analysis of Hobbes,

---

Man (London: Routledge, 1989), 12–21; and Alice Rossi, "Sentiment and Intellect: The Story of John Stuart Mill and Harriet Taylor Mill," in *Essays on Sex Equality*, ed. Alice Rossi (Chicago: University of Chicago Press, 1970), 1–64.

[65]See Teresa Brennan and Carole Pateman, " 'Mere Auxiliaries to the Commonwealth': Women and the Origins of Liberalism," *Political Studies* 27 (1979), 183–200; Linda Nicholson, *Gender and History: The Limits of Social Theory in the Age of the Family* (New York: Columbia University Press, 1986); Carole Pateman, "The Shame of the Marriage Contract," in *Women's Views of the Political World of Men*, ed. Judith H. Stiehm (Dobbs Ferry, N.Y.: Transnational Publishers, 1984), 69–97; Carole Patemen, *The Sexual Contract* (Stanford: Stanford University Press, 1988); Gordon Schochet, *Patriarchalism and Political Thought* (New York: Basic Books, 1975); Mary Lyndon Shanley, "Marriage Contract and Social Contract in Seventeenth-Century English Political Thought," in Elshtain, *The Family in Political Thought*, 80–95.

[66]For evidence of the growing appreciation of this point among feminist critics of the liberal tradition, see Carole Pateman, "Women and Democratic

we are in a position to appreciate the inherited masculinist features of liberal discourse that may well have insinuated themselves into Mill's feminist enterprise.

Mill's feminist endeavor should be doubly acclaimed and scrutinized, because it is neither the simple logical fruition of previously underdeveloped possibilities in liberal theory, nor an unproblematic reformist inclusion of women as a previously excluded and ignored group. In questioning the "add women and stir" formulation, the assumption that women can be included within the liberal paradigm without significantly altering that framework, I approach Mill's feminism with a suspicion that at least one of the partners to the rapprochement, either women or liberal theory itself, will be asked to pay dearly for the new arrangement.

Mill's feminism is the tortured outcome of a system of ideas that was constitutionally unable to accommodate women as sex-specific, gendered, and nonmasculine beings. In Mill's hands, women are dealt with in the terms of exceptional and masculine individualism. As a result, his feminism is a kind of distorted compromise formation. To the extent that they can be masculinized, women are included within Mill's feminist framework. When they are not—notably in their embodied and gendered capacities as wives and mothers—Mill's liberal feminism utterly fails them. The "price" of liberal feminist liberation is transsexualism.[67] Women must be disembodied,

Citizenship," delivered at Jefferson Memorial Lectures, University of California, Berkeley, 1985; Anna Yeatman, "Despotism and Civil Society: The Limits of Patriarchal Citizenship," in Stiehm, *Women's Views of the Political World of Men*, 153–173; Iris Marion Young, "Impartiality and the Civic Public," in *Feminism as Critique*, ed. Seyla Benhabib and Drucilla Cornell (Minneapolis: University of Minnesota Press, 1987), 57–76. For an examination of historical research suggesting that women have also opposed the liberal sensibility in favor of nonindividualist moral and political schemas, see Ruth L. Smith and Deborah M. Valenze, "Mutuality and Marginality: Liberal Moral Theory and Working-Class Women in Nineteenth-Century England," *Signs: Journal of Women in Culture and Society* 13 (Winter 1988): 277–298.

[67]See Janice Raymond, *The Transsexual Empire: The Making of the She-Male* (Boston: Beacon Press, 1979). Whereas Raymond's focus is on the documented prevalence of male-to-female shifts as an instance of men's technological

desexed, degendered, and made over into the image of middle-class and upper-class men if they are to benefit from the promises of rational liberalism as Mill envisions them. They are "free" to the extent that they are enabled to emulate rational men. And Mill's feminism strategically attempts precisely such an enabling. It thus fails women just at the point where modern feminine specificity and "difference" cannot be ignored.

Mill's argument in *On the Subjection of Women* is inspired by the attempt to resolve the sociological contradiction posed by the observation that "the social subordination of women . . . stands out an isolated fact in modern social institutions." Within the specifically modern market frame of social relations, as Mill (and Marx) clearly understood, "human beings are no longer born to their place in life, and chained down by an inexorable bond to the place they are born to, but are free to employ their faculties, and such favorable chances as offer, to achieve the lot which may appear to them most desirable."[68] Sexual inequality for Mill is an antique feudal relic within a modern world where human beings act as the rational calculators of chosen utilities. Enforced perceptions of women's "nature" have legitimated their exclusion from this modern conception of the subject as an individual chooser.

Mill is perhaps at his best in his discussion of women's nature, which, he argues, "rests with women themselves—to be decided by their own experience, and by the use of their own faculties." (Unfortunately, Mill himself did not always follow his own advice here.) He understands that prevalent conceptions of women's nature are the products of a masculine imagination, and that discussion of that nature in the hands of men can serve no honest intellectual purpose. "What is now called the nature of women is an eminently artificial

---

appropriation of the female body, I detect just the opposite tendency here, that is, women being made over into men. Both tendencies, however, would seem to serve the same purpose in the end: white male definition and control of females and of the "human" standard.

[68]Mill, *On the Subjection of Women*, 36, 32.

thing."[69] Women's "nature," argues Mill, has been produced within a kind of greenhouse environment in which women have been unnaturally limited and encouraged by social conventions and rules, and their consequent behavior has been used as "proof" of this very nature. If nature prevents women from doing certain things, such limits will emerge in the course of time. In the meantime, there is no need legally to prevent women from doing what they cannot do (the forces of the market will take care of that) and no justification for barring them from what they can do: "The knowledge which men can acquire of women, even as they have been and are, without reference to what they might be, is wretchedly imperfect and superficial, and always will be so, until women themselves have told all that they have to tell."[70] What Mill did not fully anticipate is that what women had to tell might throw his entire theoretical framework into question.

Mill's politicization of the marriage relation anticipates the later slogan of Second Wave feminists: "The personal is political." Women's legal position within marriage, comparable to slavery, paves the way for bondage as a possibility within every marriage, argues Mill, although not every husband will necessarily avail himself of such despotic opportunity. Mill was also concerned that this open entitlement to the exercise of unlimited authority corrupted men as it impinged on women. Hence, he advocates legal reforms so that married persons will be equal before the law. As a substitute for patriarchal authority and feminized submission to that authority, Mill supports the equal and voluntary association of marriage partners. Nonetheless, his discussion of the politics of decision making within the marriage relation is seriously marred by two notable flaws: his failure to deal with the political implications of a sexual division of labor, especially insofar as that involves unpaid housework; and his curious discussion of the frequent age differential between husband and wife as a legitimate reason for the husband's prerogative in decision

[69]Ibid., 43, 38.
[70]Ibid., 42.

making. Mill's abstract principles of fairness and equality dissolve in the face of the specificities of household and family life.

Although he advocates "ceasing to make sex a disqualification for privileges," (as if women were the only "sex"), he impinges on the vocational and professional aspirations of women by arguing that the woman who marries has effectively chosen a "profession" as a mistress of the household:

> Like a man when he chooses a profession, so, when a woman marries, it may in general be understood that she makes choice of the management of a household, and the bringing up of a family, as the first call upon her exertions, during as many years of her life as may be required for the purpose; and that she renounces, not all other objects and occupations, but all which are not consistent with the requirements of this.[71]

The analogy that Mill draws between the housewife and "a man when he chooses a profession" is disingenuous, given the limited singularity of this "choice" for the married woman in contrast with that of her male counterpart.

While Mill acknowledges that "the *power* of earning is essential to the dignity of a woman, if she has not independent property,"[72] this essential need suddenly disappears for the woman who has committed herself to an "equal" marriage contract. Mill is unable or unwilling to question the sexual division of labor within the household, and uncritically assumes that legal equality is primary, while economic parity is its derivative.[73] He tried to preserve an arena of choice for

[71]Ibid., 68.

[72]Ibid., 67.

[73]Mill himself admitted to being totally incompetent when it came to practical everyday affairs. It is not so surprising that a man whose household affairs were handled for him by women—first his mother, then his wife, and last his stepdaughter—would be simultaneously insensitive to the ramifications of such a division of labor and threatened by the prospect of its dissolution. See Dorothy Smith, "A Sociology for Women," in *The Prism of Sex: Essays in the Sociology of Knowledge*, ed. Julia Sherman and Evelyn Torton Beck (Madison: University of Wisconsin Press, 1979), 135-188, for a relevant discussion of women's skills in making their household labor invisible. Such invisibility is a key criterion for doing such labor well.

the married woman when he wrote that "the utmost latitude ought to exist for the adaptation of general rules to individual suitabilities," but such latitude rests on "due provision" being made for her functions as "mistress of the family." Such "due provision" would, of course, fall primarily to working-class and single middle-class women. Since Mill couches this discussion in terms of the exceptionally talented woman, we are left with the distinct impression that most women would opt for the duties of housemistress. After all, how many can claim exceptional talent as the sole warrant for extrahousehold activities? We must take Mill at his word when he writes: "If there is anything vitally important to the happiness of human beings, it is that they should relish their habitual pursuit."[74] He assumes that most women will "relish" their "chosen" profession as housewives. Without such an assumption, Mill would have had to rethink radically the social relations of family life, along with the relationship between a capitalist economic order and the family on which it relies for much of the work of physical and social reproduction.

Yet Mill insists on preserving a democratic image for his family. In response to the popular argument that the family, like a society, requires a government and some ultimate ruler, Mill invokes instead the image of a business partnership. Among married "partners," argues Mill, the final decisions do not automatically rest with the male. But once again, the formulation of the principle is disingenuous, and the "partnership" begins to look suspiciously familiar:

> The real practical decision of affairs, to whichever may be given the legal authority, will greatly depend, as it even now does, upon comparative qualifications. The mere fact that he is usually the eldest, will in most cases give the preponderance to the man; at least until they both attain a time of life at which the difference in their years is of no importance. There will naturally also be a more potential voice on the side, whichever it is, that brings the means of support."[75]

[74]Mill, *On the Subjection of Women*, 68, 126.
[75]Ibid., 58-59.

Mill's lip service to the logical possibility that the wife might be the familial means of support is belied by his discussion of women's "choice" of housewifely duties. And his invocation of the presumed wisdom of age totally sidesteps any engagement with the questions of just why is it that younger women tend to marry older men, and to what extent this particular currency of desire and attraction might be embedded in power relations. In uncharacteristic fashion, Mill accepts these unexamined conventions without so much as a whimper.

In spite of his undoubtedly sincere attempts to dislodge illegitimate male authority, Mill's discussion actually strengthens it. Authority is only apparently desexed. Age and income advantages, still clearly tied to the husband, and unquestioned as sex-specific attributes, become the new modern justifications for differential power within the marriage relation. The underlying logic of this account is unmistakable: the woman who wants to reap the benefits of liberalism's egalitarian promise had better not marry.[76]

Liberal feminist theory as articulated by Mill cannot accommodate the wife and mother. When a theory of individual liberty and presumed equality (with men as the standard) is applied to women, what comes out at the other end is the corporate feminist, the career woman who can compete effectively in the world of aspiring middle-class and upper-class men.[77]

---

[76]Today, this "lesson" is understood in a related way by professional women: the aspiring professional woman can hope to achieve success only by avoiding the traditional "encumbrances" of family life, be they children, aging parents, or a husband who is unwilling to relocate. Or, like Mill's "exceptional" and financially endowed wife, she can pay other women and lower-class men unexceptional wages to provide those services for which housewives are held responsible and on which households depend.

[77]The term "corporate feminist" is Suzanne Gordon's. See her article "The New Corporate Feminism," The Nation, February 5, 1983, 143–147.

The liberal concept of equality is refined and/or contested in Zillah Eisenstein, The Female Body and the Law (Berkeley: University of California Press, 1988); Merle Thornton, "Sex Equality Is Not Enough for Feminism" in Feminist Challenges: Social and Political Theory, ed. Carole Pateman and Elizabeth Gross (Boston: Northeastern University Press, 1986), 77–98; Elizabeth Wolgast, Equality and the Rights of Women (Ithaca: Cornell University Press, 1980).

The singular failure of Mill's feminism, to which contemporary American feminism is the troubled heir, consists, in part, of the larger failure of his political theory, which effectively ignored the political dimensions of structural economic inequality and assumed that legal change would spearhead sociopolitical change. Such an approach, of course, is consistent with the notion that it is ideas that make history. Working-class women are not helped by Mill's account of an essentially bourgeois family life, although Mill does take yet another opportunity to disparage working-class men, this time for their physical abuse of women. Notably missing here is a discussion of bourgeois male exploitation of working-class women in the rampant prostitution industry of the time, a phenomenon of which Mill must have been aware.[78] In a similar vein, he was unable to appreciate and explore the possibility that political history might help explain the sexual division of labor within the household which he took for granted. Finally, it never occured to him, just as it seems to have escaped the attention of contemporary "postfeminists," that the subjection of women might be more than an outdated, premodern anachronism.

Mill's failure to identify and think through these issues could well be analyzed and forgiven as an instance of the understandable limits of human criticism. And yet, he is relentless in his critical excavation of the taken-for-granted. Over and over, he entreats his readers to rethink the unreflectively accepted conventions of their lives and times. Mill suffers from an interesting set of blind spots himself. An assessment of Mill's thought as a specifically gendered phenomenon can account for the specific failures of his feminist theory.

Simply put, Mill's feminism collapses on the terrain of "difference." It fails at precisely the point where women's activities are not directly mediated by the abstract hand of the market, and are not obviously comparable to men's activities. Mill's feminism comes up short against the messy and ambivalent terrain of the household; a halfhearted effort is made to

[78]See Stephen Marcus, *The Other Victorians: A Study of Sexuality and Pornography in Mid-Nineteenth-Century England* (New York: Basic Books, 1974).

liberalize familial relations without, however, making men bear any of the household-specific responsibilities that still accrue to women. Mill's failure to recognize the visceral realities of household life is related, I believe, to his own curiously ambivalent attitudes toward two women in his life. On the one hand, there was his mother, Harriet Mill, whom he systematically ignored and denied. On the other was his lifetime friend, colleague, and eventual wife, Harriet Taylor, whom he praised out of all proportion as the unheralded genius of the age. These attitudes, I believe, have something to do with Mill's systematic inability to understand the situation of the women of his time.

In the absence of commonly held knowledge about the biology of human reproduction, one could read Mill's *Autobiography* and assume that his father bore him: "I was born in London, on the 20th of May, 1806, and was the eldest son of James Mill, the author of the History of British India."[79] Mill refuses to acknowledge his mother's existence, much less the difficult circumstances of her life. A lingering question is whether Mill denied his mother simply because she was a mother, or because father and son regarded her as unintelligent. It seems fair to suggest that the two assessments are inextricably linked. It is in *On the Subjection of Women* rather than the *Autobiography* that Mill provides us with a brief, if unacknowledged, glimpse into his feelings about his mother:

> A man who is married to a woman his inferior in intelligence, finds her a perpetual dead weight, or, worse than a dead weight, a drag, upon every aspiration of his to be better than public opinion requires him to be. It is hardly possible for one who is in these bonds, to attain exalted virtue. If he differs in his opinion from the mass—if he sees truths which have not yet dawned on them, or if, feeling in his heart truths which they nominally recognize, he would like to act up to those truths more conscientiously than the generality

[79]*The Autobiography of John Stuart Mill*, 2.

of mankind—to all such thoughts and desires, marriage is
the heaviest of drawbacks, unless he be so fortunate as to
have a wife as much above the common level as he himself
is.[80]

Mill's (presumably) abstract description here fits perfectly
with accounts of James Mill's disparaging feelings about his
wife, which were not kept discrete.[81] Furthermore, Harriet
Mill was a living reminder of James Mill's failure to live up to
his own publicly articulated ideal of sexual asceticism. The
very same man who, according to his son, viewed the preoccupation with "the physical relation and its adjuncts" as "a
perversion of the imagination and feelings, . . . one of the
deepest seated and most pervading evils in the human
mind,"[82] managed, somehow, to father nine children. Harriet
Mill must have stood as a constant source of mortification
to her husband and eldest son, a pregnant reminder of her
husband's all-too-human desires, which had little legitimate
space within the frame of his rationalist utilitarianism. Note
that this description is meant to leave us feeling terribly sorry
for the striving husband and rather peeved with the dead-
weight wife. Note, too, the striking parallels between Mill's
rendition of nature's drag effect on rationality, progress, and
civilization (a theme explored in an earlier section of this chapter) and the wife's retardation of her husband's noble aspirations: "worse than a dead weight, a drag." Once again, we
encounter the palpable connection between a feminized nature set in opposition to a beleaguered and defensive masculine counterforce.

And then there is Harriet Taylor, who came to represent for
Mill everything that his mother was not. (No mean feat, since
Harriet Taylor was herself a mother.) She and Mill pursued
an ascetic and deep friendship for twenty years before they

[80]Mill, *On the Subjection of Women*, 114.
[81]For a sympathetic discussion of Harriet Mill, see Mazlish, *James and John
Stuart Mill*.
[82]*The Autobiography of John Stuart Mill*, 75.

finally married after the death of her first husband. Their marriage, from Mill's point of view, was a marriage of minds above all else.[83] They shared an interest in feminism which Taylor, to her credit, developed more radically and systematically than Mill did. Harriet Taylor's feminism and other intellectual accomplishments notwithstanding, it seems clear that Mill overrated her gifts. It has also been suggested that Mill found her easier to worship from afar.[84] Harriet Taylor's desexualization and overexaggerated intellectual acumen would seem to be related much in the same way that his mother's unavoidable sexuality is tied in with her reported simplemindedness.

Mill seems to have had some personal difficulties in dealing with women as creatures of flesh and blood and brain combined. Instead, he resorts to split images, denying a mother who surely existed and eulogizing a mind that probably did not. The issue here is not Mill's personal attitudes toward women. These observations are little more than icing on the cake. But they do substantiate the sense of unease with Mill's feminism as a practical and desirable model of emancipation for women. And that is because it avoids the lot of most women. Mill's denial of his mother haunts *On the Subjection of Women*, while his exaggerated portrayal of Harriet Taylor in the dedication to *On Liberty* reminds us of women's average unexceptionalness.

Mill's feminism is a feminism for the exceptional woman, as Zillah Eisenstein argues.[85] But I would add that she is exceptional in terms that go beyond those of class and educational privilege. The exceptional woman, within the rationalist terms established by Mill, is effectively regendered, for the terms of her exceptional talent and drive are modern masculine terms. To the extent that they require the conquest of inner and outer nature, an individualized and objective cognitive stance, a

---

[83]For accounts of the marriage, see Phyllis Rose, *Parallel Lives: Five Victorian Marriages* (New York: Random House, 1984), 101–140; Rossi, "Sentiment and Intellect"; and Jack Stillinger, "Introduction" to his edition of *The Early Draft of John Stuart Mill's Autobiography* (Urbana: University of Illinois Press, 1961).

[84]See Stillinger, "Introduction."

[85]Eisenstein, *The Radical Future of Liberal Feminism*, 137.

clear demarcation between self and not-self, between autonomous individuality and communitarian or familial identity, the terms of liberal individualism are indelibly masculine.

This is why Mill's feminism, along with the larger body of his liberal theory within which it is situated, fails women. The currency of modern humanist liberalism cannot but be problematic for those women who would prefer not to make the transsexual switch, for those who believe that the gendered realm of the banal—of everyday life—is at least as instructive and as ennobling as that of extraordinary effort and achievement as defined by modern masculine culture. I am reminded of the reported statement of a woman protesting the Equal Rights Amendment: "I don't care to be a person." The liberal response to such a statement would be one of incredulity. This remark however, may carry more insight than first meets the eye. For such a declaration might well be motivated by a sense of violation engendered by a liberal feminism containing an abstract Everyman as its subject.[86] Contemporary liberal feminism is in part a descendant of Mill's feminism, an assimilative feminism that preempts the critical possibilities of a feminism that would have us rethink the terms of "human" excellence and achievement even as we question and undo the gender-based allocation of differential burdens and benefits.

Mill's feminism, then, is a paradoxical theory of empowerment for women. Although his theorization of a status for women based on the utilitarian conception of individual choice enabled him to oppose the kind of thinking that legiti-

[86]The term "Everyman" comes from Wolgast, *Equality and the Rights of Women*. In this work, Wolgast develops a compelling analysis of the ways in which liberal conceptions of equality force a masculine standard of humanity on women. Unfortunately, her facile equation of liberal feminism with feminism per se promotes an analysis that tends to slide into antifeminism. For an appreciation of the complex issues involved here, see Alison Jagger, "Human Biology in Feminist Theory: Sexual Equality Reconsidered," in *Beyond Domination: New Perspectives on Women and Philosophy*, ed. Carol C. Gould (Totowa, N.J.: Rowman and Allanheld, 1983), 21–42; and *Hypatia* 2 (Winter 1987), which contains several articles on the problems of equality for feminism.

mized female inferiority in the name of women's obligations to men and in terms of their reduced or differential capacities for reason, his feminism effectively writes women out as sexed and gendered creatures. In extending his claims for the protection of liberal man to liberal woman, Mill enacts the masculine prerogative of privileged selfsame identity.[87] For the unitary disembodied subject housed by liberal theory is no abstract subject, appearances to the contrary. His motivation to separate from a dangerous nature; to observe and to inhabit a methodologically individualist terrain; to cultivate and celebrate a disembodied reason; to protect himself, and similarly constituted others, from incursion into his private space—all of this may be traced to a substratum of experiences, desires, fears, and needs that are identifiably masculine.

For all of his genuine efforts to enter into the minds and circumstances of others, for all of his discomfort with utilitarian rationalism, Mill could not get beyond the gendered terrain of his modern theoretical enterprise. What he did achieve, however, is not insignificant. He pushed the liberal enterprise as far as it might go, and perhaps a little farther. The paradoxes generated by his efforts, captured vividly in the disparity between his ethical vision of socially concerned individuals working for the improvement in social conditions of their "fellow" citizens and his protection of the isolated liberal subject, are our paradoxes still. To the extent that they might be transcended, the clues to such a project lie partially with Mill. Feminists should neither ignore him nor uncritically adopt his framework for women's emancipation. To pursue the former course would be to ignore a significant segment of the political culture; to adopt the latter would effectively preempt "womanly thinking."[88]

---

[87]For a brilliant and provocative analysis of this masculine prerogative, see Luce Irigaray, "The Power of Discourse and the Subordination of the Feminine," in This Sex Which is Not One, trans. Catherine Porter (Ithaca: Cornell University Press, 1985), 68–85.

[88]This term is Sara Ruddick's, from "Maternal Thinking," Feminist Studies 6 (Summer 1980), 342–367. It is meant to connote cognitive styles, capacities, and substantive concerns that inhere in and are generated by women's gender-specific social activities.

Rereading and Beyond

I have always thought it unfair to woman that she has never been alone in the world. Adam had a time, whether long or short, when he could wander about on a fresh and peaceful earth, among the beasts, in full possession of his soul, and most men are born with a memory of that period. But poor Eve found him there, with all his claims upon her, the moment she looked into the world. That is a grudge that woman has always had against the Creator: she feels that she is entitled to have that epoch of paradise back for herself. Only, worse luck, when chasing a time that has gone, one is bound to get hold of it by the tail, the wrong way around.

—Isak Dinesen, "The Old Chevalier," *Seven Gothic Tales*

WOMEN HAVE NEVER BEEN "alone" in the discursive world of canonical western political theory. They have never elaborated a view of political life as if men did not exist. If the temptation to do so persists it is also difficult, if not impossible, to implement. The female political theorist finds "man" fully present and inscribed with the canonical narrative of western political thought, which invariably includes sexually inegalitarian social relations and "always already" gendered norms of manhood, womanhood, and citizenship. In short, she confronts a crowded world of sensibilities and meanings within which it may be confusing and difficult to take her bearings as a reader and critic.

Various strategies for reading present themselves at this

point. The female reader may adopt a posture of *identification* with the heroic political theorist, refusing to accept her appointed place in the scheme of gender, and insisting that she be let into the theoretical "conversation" on humanist grounds of fellowship and inclusion. She will read "the tradition" for its illumination of perennial political issues. She will implicitly include "woman" in the various descriptions of and prescriptions for "man" that she scrutinizes. She will make reference to a "human condition." And she will look forward to the day, to which she sees herself as a contributor, when political theory no longer distinguishes between male and female members of the human species.

The feminist reader who feels the mark of gender more acutely may employ interpretive strategies of *reversal* whereby feminized marks of difference, oppression, and disempowerment are rendered into signs of victory and superiority. This is evocative of Nietzsche's rendition of slave morality, which initially accepts the aristocrat's account of "good" and "bad," but then reverses and transposes his scheme into the vocabulary of "good" and "evil." Subordinated women are what ruling men are not: they embody the "good," the "just," the desirable and virtuous citizen.

In a related vein, strategies of *projection* adopt the impulse of the male theorist to generalize from his own unacknowledged and situated gendered perspective to an elaboration of the "human condition." Here, an idealized "femininity" is detached from its conceptual linkages to "masculinity" and advanced as an ostensibly new ground for articulating political problems and solutions in the name of women.

Finally, strategies of *invention* turn away from the inherited and crowded world of canonical western political theory to formulate entirely new, unpolluted versions of political needs and aspirations for women as a distinct and diversified political and social constituency. At this point the impulse to reread has been transmuted into the refusal to lavish any more attention on "the tradition."

Each of these strategies, I would suggest, is implicated in a notion of paradise we would do well to scrutinize and reject.

The first and the last involve a flight from gender, a refusal to acknowledge and engage the gendered terms and terrain of political culture, past and present. The dream of a genderless world results in a failure to confront the vocabulary and machinations of an inherited, if also changing, gendered world. The two remaining strategies, by contrast, become mired in an overly literal loyalty to the terms of gender difference. "Masculinity" and "femininity" become reified; paradise, simultaneously lost and rediscovered, is feminized. These strategies and their implications are those to which feminist readers of political theory are especially, but by no means invariably, vulnerable.

The feminist reader of political theory is distinguished from other readers of political theory by her (or his)[1] interest in reading the canon for its construction and treatment of "woman," who embodies a paradox of complicated proportions: "a being that is at once captive and absent in discourse, constantly spoken of but of itself inaudible or inexpressible, displayed as spectacle and yet unrepresented; a being whose existence and specificity are simultaneously asserted and denied, negated and controlled."[2] According to Teresa de Lauretis, an important task of feminist criticism has been to disentangle this paradox so that "woman" is made visible as a discursive and historical construct, and so that women, in the full array of their diverse experiences and desires, may become the agents of their own representation. The latter goal, I believe, constitutes the core political commitment of the specifically feminist reader.

Like Dinesen's imaginary Eve, the feminist reader of canonical political theory confronts a crowded and inhospitable

---

[1]The feminist reader may, of course, be male, just as the female reader is by no means necessarily feminist. To date, however, most feminist scholarship is done by women. For engaging assessments of the complicated relationship between men and feminism, see Alice Jardine and Paul Smith, eds., *Men in Feminism* (New York: Methuen, 1987).

[2]Teresa de Lauretis, "The Essence of the Triangle or, Taking the Risk of Essentialism Seriously: Feminist Theory in Italy, the U.S., and Britain," *Differences* 1 (Summer 1989), 26.

world of meaning and sensibility which affords few reminders or illusions of unmapped territory. Within the complex and overdetermined terrain of gender, simultaneously timeless, unstable, specific, and hostile, she must find some "hook" for her efforts to reread with fresh and critical eyes. She may be tempted to situate herself within an imagined genderless paradise; but then she will have lost the incentive to reread. And so she returns to the scene of reading, looking for a point of access that is neither completely mapped in (preconstituted by gendered presumptions) nor mapped out (in an Archimedean prediscursive location of genderless innocence). We may think of this, as I have suggested, as a border space, a space between the existing terms of representation and their unthought, excluded, repressed, and required premises. In this sense, the representational figure of the (m)other offers one solution to Eve's dilemma.

The feminist reader of modern political theory may invoke the (m)other figure without adopting her as a fully articulated and singular counterexample on which to base contemporary feminist political theory. In place of the substantive feminine counterexample to modern Eurocentric "man," I have suggested the notion of the space-off as a useful location from which to reread the legacy of political theory. In this way the feminist reader need not rely on the feminine counterexample to justify or ground her critical efforts. I am by no means advocating the construction of an alternative political theory formed around a specified maternal or feminine figure. This is no "alternative," in the full sense of the term, at all.

Although the (m)other cannot promise paradise, she evokes some faint intimation of life before "man," along with reminders that this maternal era is imaginary, that it carries no independent or foundational status. More significantly, perhaps, she forces modern "man" (to whom "other" men as well as women are compared and found lacking) to abdicate something of his claims to independence and self-definition, for she carries the stubborn reminder that his self-characterization is reactive, nonoriginary, and thoroughly implicated in her mute attendance.

The modern project of autonomy, whose articulation and pursuit is chronicled in the works of Hobbes, Marx, and J. S. Mill, carries telling traces of the (m)other, who inspires, haunts, and ultimately destabilizes this project in some instructive ways. As a figure of suspicion, resistance, and memory, the (m)other inhabits the "other" side of the modern preoccupation with autonomous selfhood and agency, the modern drama of secular self-creation. In reading for the (m)other, who cannot speak for herself, the feminist reader discovers that modern man is as elusive, unstable, exotic, and impossible as his feminized other was thought to be.

A focus on the masculinist aspects of modern political theory should not be confused with the project of developing feminist alternatives, as I suggested at the start of this work. Such confusion induces the suspicion that a feminist political theory might well proceed in an analogous fashion to the masculine edifice and strategy that it seeks to displace; that is, that an articulated feminine subject would replace and stand over and against the modern Eurocentric masculine subject. Obviously this is no solution, for it replicates the hegemonic strategy that was previously criticized.[3] But it is also no solution for specifically feminist purposes, which aim for the destabilization of gender differences as well as for richer articulations of the diverse experiences of those subjects who are culturally positioned as "women." A theoretical vocabulary of "the feminine" is inadequate for each of these tasks.

Political theorizing with the goal of articulating and advancing the needs of women as a diverse political constituency, then, will not proceed on the basis of a more or less articulated

[3]This is also no solution for those who are more or less persuaded by the postmodern treatment of the subject as an effect of power rather than as the legitimating ground of liberating knowledge. I am most indebted to the work of Michel Foucault for this insight. See Kathy Ferguson, "Subject-Centredness in Feminist Discourse," in *The Political Interests of Gender*, ed. Kathleen B. Jones and Anna G. Jónasdóttir (London: Sage, 1988), 66–78; and Paul Smith, *Discerning the Subject* (Minneapolis: University of Minnesota Press, 1988).

counterexample. For it is precisely the possibility and desirability of a fully articulated and singular feminist counterexample that is problematized by feminist inquiry itself. As we are learning, the category of "women" does not signify a coherent or cohesive social subject. Furthermore, the effort to theorize such a subject invariably produces normalizing or essentialist accounts of womanhood which obscure, silence, and misrepresent a great number of women.[4]

I would argue further that feminist political theory should carefully scrutinize its relationship to the canonical literature, which may tell us quite a bit about the historical and discursive operations of western gender but very little about actual women, and some men. This issue is amplified even further when we consider the long overdue imperative to diversify and specify our accounts of women's experiences, to stop treating women as if they were invariably white, middle class, heterosexual, and stereotypically "feminine."[5] Hortense Spillers draws attention to a related liability of overinvestment in the canonical literature of western political theory in her

---

[4]Examples of recent work in feminist theory that call for the deconstruction of gender and its articulation along other dimensions of power such as race, class, and sexual or affectional preference include Judith Butler, *Gender Trouble: Feminism and the Subversion of Identity* (New York: Routledge, 1990); Denise Riley, *"Am I That Name?" Feminism and the Category of 'Women' in History* (Minneapolis: University of Minnesota Press, 1988); Joan Wallach Scott, *Gender and the Politics of History* (New York: Columbia University Press, 1988); Elizabeth V. Spelman, *Inessential Woman: Problems of Exclusion in Feminist Thought* (Boston: Beacon Press, 1988).

[5]The following works are important contributions to this literature: Gloria Anzaldúa, *Borderlands/La Frontera* (San Francisco: Aunt Lute Book Company, 1987); Ann Bookman and Sandra Morgen, eds., *Women and the Politics of Empowerment* (Philadelphia: Temple University Press, 1988); Toni Cade, ed., *The Black Woman: An Anthology* (New York: New American Library, 1970); Ann Ferguson, *Blood at the Root: Motherhood, Sexuality, and Male Dominance* (London: Pandora Press, 1989); Paula Giddings, *When and Where I Enter:The Impact of Black Women on Race and Sex in America* (New York: Bantam Books, 1984); Bell Hooks, *Feminist Theory: From Margin to Center* (Boston: South End Press, 1984); Audre Lorde, *Sister Outsider* (Trumansburg, N.Y.: Crossing Press, 1984); Cherrié Moraga and Gloria Anzaldúa, eds., *This Bridge Called My Back: Writings by Radical Women of Color* (Watertown, N.Y.: Persephone Press, 1981).

criticism of the logological dimension of contemporary feminist discourse, by which she means words that talk about
other words: "Black American women do not participate, as
a category of social and cultural agents, in the legacies of
symbolic power, they maintain no allegiances to a strategic
formation of texts." She suggests that the "process of categorical aligning with prior acts of the text [is] the subtle component
of power that bars black women, indeed, women of color, as
a proper subject of inquiry from the various topics of contemporary feminist discourse."[6]

Spillers's comments suggest that overinvestment in canonical literatures contributes to the contemporary political dynamics of racism. Those who teach the canonical literature of
western political theory should consider the potential effects
of this curriculum on their students as well as on their own
work. At the same time, however, they should avoid the
seductive notion that there is a curricular or theoretical "cure"
for the problem of racism in the academy. Political theory will
never be "good enough" until it is made by those constituencies it would serve. One small step in this process is to open
up political theory to the concerns and experiences of students
who might otherwise feel unrepresented in the literature and
who may subsequently be motivated to make their own mark
on it. This is not to say that the canonical literature of western
political theory should be dropped or ignored, but rather that
reigning assumptions about "cultural literacy" need to be expanded and enriched to take account of a much larger store
of cultural resources and historical experiences.

Gender theory itself has come under significant criticism
from readers who feel misrepresented within its account.
More specifically, the enterprise of feminist theory is involved
in a fundamental process of self-scrutiny concerning its
achievements (understood as the naming, analysis, and con-

---

[6]Hortense Spillers, "Interstices: A Small Drama of Words," in *Pleasure and
Danger: Exploring Female Sexuality*, ed. Carole Vance (New York: Routledge
and Kegan Paul, 1984), 80, 89.

testation of illicit power as it affects and constitutes "women") and failures (understood not only as the failure to analyze power adequately but also as complicity with illicit power). A key issue in this critical process of reassessment involves the category of gender.

As feminists are beginning to appreciate, thanks to the insistent prodding of many critics, the unity of the gendered "human"—that is, the "masculine" or "feminine" subject—is as much a fiction as the universal "man" divided into two. Race, class, ethnicity, and sexual or affectional orientation, among other significant dimensions of identity, social location, and relative empowerment, have been glossed over. New agents of critical insight and political need emerged to contest gender theory: lesbians, women of color, Third World women, and "postcolonial" feminists continue to be prominent in this effort. In the university, the practical counterpart to this criticism has been to stretch the established boundaries of the curriculum, of research design, of theoretical vocabularies, of student and faculty recruitment, so that determinations about "reality" will no longer be made for all by a select, relatively privileged and pale-looking few.[7] This agenda for institutional change is still very much in progress and vulnerable to counterattack.

Political issues of racism and ethnocentrism have become wedded to methodological concerns about the theoretical legitimacy of gender-based generalization and abstraction. These issues carry theoretical and epistemological implications, many of which have been articulated in the vocabulary of postmodern theory.[8] With other critics of postmodern the-

[7]For an assessment of women's studies programs in the light of this history and these imperatives, see "Women's Studies Enters the 1990s: A Special Section on Feminism in (and out of) the Classroom," a special section of *Women's Review of Books* 7 (February 1990), 17–32.

[8]For positive assessments of the postmodern turn in theory, see Nancy Fraser and Linda J. Nicholson, "Social Criticism without Philosophy: An Encounter between Feminism and Postmodernism," in *Feminism/Postmodernism*, ed. Linda J. Nicholson (New York: Routledge, 1990), 19–38; Shane Phelan, "Foucault and Feminism," *American Journal of Political Science* 34 (May 1990), 421–440; Joan W. Scott, "Deconstructing Equality-versus-Difference: Or, the Uses of Poststructuralist Theory for Feminism," *Feminist Studies* 14 (Spring

ory, I suspect that this salutary theoretical turn, carried to particular levels of extremity and application, especially within metalevel discussions about "theory," contributes to a depoliticization of stubborn political realities.[9]

Let us consider two theses that derive from Nietzsche's observations on power and knowledge. The first is that power is always epistemologically "incorrect"; that is, power invariably masks itself and its operations through illicit claims to "truth"—claims that can never actually support the empirical and epistemological burdens of proof that they endorse and require. The second Nietzschean insight is that power is ubiquitous: it is contestable, modifiable, but never completely eliminable.[10] Related to this claim is the notion that resistance is another instance of the ubiquity of power. Power begets resistance; resistance cannot be said to lie "outside of" power. The dream of the "last revolution," a struggle to end all exercises of illicit power, is a grand delusion. This is not to say that we must give in to power; on the contrary, it is to suggest that power must be continuously and vigilantly contested. These are, of course, "postmodern" observations on power, brilliantly and provocatively explored in the work of Michel Foucault.[11] And yet, I would argue, postmodern theory sometimes enacts these insights in counterproductive ways.

1988), 33–50. For negative assessments, see Frances E. Mascia-Lees, Patricia Sharpe, and Colleen Ballerino Cohen, "The Postmodernist Turn in Anthropology: Cautions from a Feminist Perspective," *Signs* 15 (Autumn 1989), 7–33; Sabina Lovibund, "Feminism and Postmodernism," *New Left Review* 178 (November-December 1989), 5–28. For an ambivalent assessment, see my essay "Dilemmas of Difference: Feminism, Modernity, and Postmodernism," in Nicholson, *Feminism/Postmodernism*, 63–82.

[9]See Barbara Christian, "The Race for Theory," in *Gender and Theory: Dialogues on Feminist Criticism*, ed. Linda Kauffman (Oxford: Basil Blackwell, 1989), 63–106; Nancy Hartsock, "Foucault on Power: A Theory for Women?" in Nicholson, *Feminism/Postmodernism*, 157–175.

[10]These insights are derived from *On The Genealogy of Morals*, trans. and ed. Walter Kaufmann (New York: Random House, 1969). See also Michel Foucault, "Nietzsche, Genealogy, History," in *The Foucault Reader*, ed. and intro. Paul Rabinow (New York: Pantheon, 1984), 76–100.

[11]See especially *The History of Sexuality*, vol. 1, *An Introduction*, trans. Robert Hurley (New York: Random House, 1980); *Discipline and Punish*, trans. Alan

Taken together, these theses on power and knowledge suggest that the search for and insistence on thoroughgoing theoretical and epistemological correctness is misplaced, if not self-refuting. In its relentless search for specificity, difference, and political tactics of constitutive exclusion in the deployment of general categories of analysis, in its principled critical opposition to general categories of analysis which bear some relation to human beings rather than to impersonal structures, postmodern theory is still hostage to the dream of grand theory, of getting it "all" and getting it "right."

To the extent that power is epistemologically incorrect and ubiquitous, epistemology and theory have a necessarily limited and circumscribed role in the activities of naming, analyzing, contesting, and combatting power relations. I suspect that this is why literature often does a far better job than theory itself of articulating the varieties of experience accruing to those who are culturally positioned as "women" and other "others." But a problem emerges when theory attempts to appropriate this aesthetic prerogative of "authenticity" for itself: theory will invariably come up short against its literary cousins. Theory, however nuanced, carefully located, and attentive to specificities, invariably does violence to the world it would represent.

The relentless (as opposed to selective) application of postmodern canons of epistemological and theoretical correctness to feminist (and other) theorizations of power will inevitably contribute to slippage between theory and the gross substance and action of power. Politics, at least as I understand it, is not about the multiple play of meaning and difference; rather, politics restricts and structures this "play."[12] The postmodern repudiation of subjects and objects, of dualisms (subject ver-

---

Sheridan (New York: Random House, 1979); and Colin Gordon, ed., *Power/Knowledge: Selected Interviews and Other Writings, 1972–1977* (New York: Pantheon, 1980).

   [12]For an example of a theoretical attempt to situate gender within the playful and aesthetic bounds of the drag performance, see Judith Butler, "Gender Trouble, Feminist Theory, and Psychoanalytic Discourse," in Nicholson, *Feminism/Postmodernism*, 324–340.

sus object, masculine versus feminine, white versus non-white), of generalizations about particular cohorts of people, fails to connect with politics as the production of determinate, rather than infinite, "difference." This is just what the terminology of gender aims to get at.[13]

Gender theory analyzes the genesis of and opposition between "masculine" subjects and "feminine" objects; it aims to invoke the feminine side of this opposition as it exposes the masculine. In other words, gender theory manipulates the forbidden material of postmodernism. Contrary to what some postmodern critics of gender theory assert, its aim is not to reify these categories but to destabilize them. The question is, how can this be achieved? From certain theoretical quarters comes the answer that we must either give up or radically refashion the category of gender so that bad dualisms are not reproduced.

Gender theory has come under critical fire for its failure to analyze issues of race and racism as central components of gender, and for its related assumption of and theoretical reliance on a white nuclear family model.[14] In one version of this critique, gender theory requires enlargement and fine-tuning to take account of experiences and symbols that are other than white. In another interpretation, dual "gender" must give way to multiple "genders" because factors of race, class, ethnicity, and sexual preference (among potential others) are not seen as qualifiers of a more "basic" gender that merits theoretical privileging. This argument is most compelling. After all, why should gender be the "main" category onto which particular qualifiers are subsequently added like afterthoughts? What kind of a mindset would be disposed to see gender as a "main"

[13]I am grateful to several exchanges with Susan Heckman which have helped me to clarify the terms of our differences and of my position. See her book *Gender and Knowledge: Elements of a Postmodern Feminism* (Boston: Northeastern University Press, 1990).

[14]See Gloria T. Hull, Patricia Bell Scott, and Barbara Smith, eds., *All the Women Are White, All the Blacks Are Men, but Some of Us Are Brave: Black Women's Studies* (Old Westbury, N.Y.: Feminist Press, 1982); Spelman, *Inessential Woman*, 80–113.

category and race as a qualifier? But consider the suggestion that dual gender must give way to multiple genders, on the presumption that in the United States today there are five major racial groups: Native American, African-American, Asian-American, Hispanic or Latino, and white.[15] All of these categories contain extremely diversified cohorts: for example, "Hispanics" come from Puerto Rico, Mexico, Cuba, and any and all Latin American countries; the cultural diversity drowned in the term *Asian-American* boggles the mind. Why has the specification stopped with this five-part scheme? Who has been left out? Now, ponder the exponential growth of these categories when we start adding categories of class and sexual or affectional preference. Which groups do and do not qualify for specified categorical status, and on what grounds? Where might the violence of theoretical generalization finally be eliminated? At what point does theoretical analysis give way to ethnographic reporting? At what point do we all become endlessly particular individuals, each with a special story to tell?

I raise these questions not because I have the answers waiting in the wings and finally ready for display. Nor do I mean to suggest that these questions warrant a return to inadequate and offensive conceptions of gender. Rather, I pose them in the hope that some alternative course, one that preserves allegiances to theoretical generalization on the one hand and thick description on the other, lies ahead, even if it is not yet discernible.

I am disinclined to give up the analytic vocabulary of "gender" for "genders." I am also disinclined to treat gender exclusively as an aesthetic "performance," for this seems to undercut the political and theoretical ability to confront specific, limited, and dualistic grids of identity, privilege, deviancy, subordination, and transgression which cross-cut and constitute particular individuals in specific but also predictable

---

[15]See, for example, Ann Ferguson, *Sexual Democracy: Women, Oppression, and Revolution* (Boulder: Westview Press, 1991), esp. the chapter titled "Racial Formations in the U.S."

ways. No single one of these grids is, of course, adequate to the theorization of social experiences and life chances for any person or group. White middle-class women in the United States, for example, are not simply gendered. They are also racialized and class-bound. But while people are rarely, if ever, adequately represented by the extant grids of categories such as race, gender, and class (even in dazzling combination), a wholesale repudiation of these categories may obscure significant patterns of illicit power and privilege. As Susan Bordo argues, "If generalization is only permitted in the *absence* of multiple inflections or interpretive possibilities, then cultural generalizations of *any* sort . . . are ruled out. What remains is a universe composed entirely of counterexamples, in which the way men and women see the world is purely as *particular* individuals, shaped by the unique configurations that form that particularity."[16]

To the extent that one is doing theory at all, it seems that one needs to use general categories of analysis that will invariably run roughshod over the multifarious textures of particular lives. While these categories should be subject to ongoing critical scrutiny, they also function as the currency of theoretical activity. In their absence, in the face of the successful deconstruction of any and all general categories of analysis, we are left with interesting stories about endlessly particular and elaborated lives. But this misses the structured texture of politics.

Generalizations, including generalizations about gender that have been formulated nearly exclusively by white western researchers and theorists, can and do obscure and perpetuate other actualities of power, particularly when these are exercised by privileged women against "other" women. At the same time, however, one cannot afford to lose sight of the ways in which women stand in some relation to "woman" just as men stand in some relation to "man." And these figures are, of course, implicated in and related through the modern

[16]Susan Bordo, "Feminism, Postmodernism, and Gender-Skepticism," in Nicholson, *Feminism/Postmodernism*, 151.

heterosexual contract. Isn't this dualism a significant part of the contemporary cultural currency of identity, place, power, and relative privilege? I do not believe that we can afford to give up the existing and potential insights of this relation, although I do believe that we must do a better job of attending to its complexities and that this job will only be done better when the "we" that is doing it is diversely and democratically constituted.

My understanding of gender provokes a sense of dissatisfaction with the methodological choice of opting between ideology critique, on the one hand, and deconstruction, on the other. (In this sense, this work should not be taken as an endorsement of an exclusive attachment to or prescription for ideology critique.) While ideology critique confronts, but also reifies, gender as a dichotomous construct, deconstruction attacks the reification but tends to lose touch with the stubborn, if dull, dichotomous polarities of power.[17] Feminist theory, I believe, should maintain allegiances to each of these approaches to gender, rather than insisting that one or the other is the only correct mode of analysis.

In any event, the future of gender theory will be decided less by contemporary debate over the "legitimacy" of gender as a category of analysis and more by its explanatory and political fruitfulness or failure in the hands of researchers, theorists, and activists.

Specifically feminist political theory is and will be a heterogeneous, collective, contested, and conflictual process in the making. It will not emerge full-blown from the heads of a few singular geniuses. Nor will it flourish within theoretical, epistemological, and methodological monocultures. To the

---

[17]In the hands of postmodern analysts, power becomes "interesting" and resistance is often rendered as "playful" transgression. I would suggest that power is also stubborn, dull, and occasionally boring, and that we should pay attention to the ways in which privileging the former version of power enhances the entertainment and prestige of the theorist and her community of readers. Hence my reminder of the "dull" polarities of power.

extent that "women are both inside and outside gender, within and without representation,"[18] the demand for the singular feminist alternative subverts the radical promise of feminist inquiry, which must simultaneously scrutinize the existing representational fare and articulate new possibilities.

In the ongoing process of articulating such new possibilities and requirements for the "good" life, which is defined, pursued, secured, and denied through political means and whose very definition is itself political, it may be helpful to know more about what to avoid, even if this cannot tell us what we should pursue. Hobbes, Marx, and Mill provide significant clues in this regard. While we cannot yet (or ever) advance a definitive or final account of alternative political theories that do representational justice to existing worlds of political struggle and to desirable worlds of political aspiration, it may be useful to know more about discursive cultural inheritances that have shaped the modern field of political thinking and sensibility. These legacies often inflect contemporary forms of political experience and, as such, provide a terrain for reflection, resistance, and reconstruction. The gendered terrain of modern political theory, with its heroic, productive, and disciplinary metaphors of modern masculine selfhood, is one such arena of contestation.

[18]Teresa de Lauretis, "The Technology of Gender," in *Technologies of Gender: Essays on Theory, Film, and Fiction* (Bloomington: Indiana University Press, 1987), 10.

Index

Library of Congress Cataloging-in-Publication Data

Di Stefano, Christine.
    Configurations of masculinity : a feminist perspective on modern
political theory / Christine Di Stefano.
        p.   cm.
    Includes bibliographical references (p.   ) and index.
    ISBN 0-8014-2534-4 (alk. paper).—ISBN 0-8014-9765-5 (pbk. :
    alk. paper)
    1. Feminist theory.   2. Political science.   I. Title.
HQ1190.D57   1991
305.42'01—dc20   90-55730